"At last we have in one volume a theoretical framework to guide network design, governance and management, combined with illuminating case studies."

— Jenny Lewis, University of Melbourne, Australia

Network Theory in the Public Sector

Networks have been described in terms of metaphors, governance arrangements, and structural or institutional arrangements. These different perspectives of networks come out of a variety of disciplines, including political science, public administration, urban affairs, social welfare, public management, and organizational/sociological research. This wealth of research, while contributing to a deeper understanding of networks, presents a dilemma that is addressed by this book. That is the question of whether there is a theory of public networks that informs networks in their various forms, and is there a need for a new theory of networks? More importantly, is network research still relevant to practice? Does network theory improve the process of governance? Are different terms and/ or approaches actually the same or different? What do these different approaches mean to theory?

This book deeply explores and integrates existing network theory and related theories from a number of perspectives, levels, and jurisdictions to develop a framework to guide network design, governance, and management. The book focuses on the important issue of network performance, looking at networks as bounded and consciously arranged; the actors who participate in them design the relationships among a bounded set of individual organizations to purse common objectives. Finally, the chapters tease out the variety of governance modes or regimes that intersect with network governance. This book offers a comprehensive, integrative, interdisciplinary approach that enables specialists, practitioners, and administrators across a wide array of interests and fields to formulate and work on problems using a common language, analytical framework, and theoretical basis.

Robyn Keast is a professor in the Southern Cross University Business School, New South Wales, Australia. Her research is focused on networked arrangements and collaborative practices within and across sectors. She recently coauthored *Negotiating the Business Environment: Theory and Practice for all Governance Styles* and is working on *Social Procurement and New Public Governance* (Routledge).

Myrna P. Mandell is professor emeritus at California State University, Northridge, and an adjunct faculty member at Southern Cross University in New South Wales, Australia. Her work includes articles and chapters on a number of different facets of networks, including how to organize and manage networks, performance measures for networks, citizen participation in networks, and leadership in networks. She is also the coauthor of a booklet specifically for practitioners in the nonprofit sector on best practices for networks. She is currently involved in research on networks in the international arena.

Robert Agranoff is professor emeritus in the School of Public and Environmental Affairs, Indiana University Bloomington, and professor in the government and public administration program at the Instituto Universitario Ortega y Gasset in Madrid. His latest book is *Collaborating to Manage: A Primer for the Public Sector* (2012). He is currently working on a book on the historical development of intergovernmental management in the United States.

Routledge Critical Studies in Public Management

Edited by Stephen Osborne

The study and practice of public management has undergone profound changes across the world. Over the past quarter century, we have seen

- Increasing criticism of public administration as the overarching framework for the provision of public services,
- The rise (and critical appraisal) of the "New Public Management" as an emergent paradigm for the provision of public services,
- The transformation of the "public sector" into the cross-sectoral provision of public services, and
- The growth of the governance of interorganizational relationships as an essential element in the provision of public services.

In reality, these trends have not so much replaced each other as elided or coexisted together—the public policy process has not gone away as a legitimate topic of study, intraorganizational management continues to be essential to the efficient provision of public services, while the governance of interorganizational and intersectoral relationships is now essential to the effective provision of these services.

Furthermore, while the study of public management has been enriched by contribution of a range of insights from the "mainstream" management literature, it has also contributed to this literature in areas such as networks and interorganizational collaboration, innovation, and stakeholder theory.

This series is dedicated to presenting and critiquing this important body of theory and empirical study. It will publish books that both explore and evaluate the emergent and developing nature of public administration, management, and governance (in theory and practice) and examine the relationship with and contribution to the overarching disciplines of management and organizational sociology.

Books in the series will be of interest to academics and researchers in this field, students undertaking advanced studies of it as part of their undergraduate or postgraduate degree, and reflective policy makers and practitioners.

Network Theory in the Public Sector

Building New Theoretical Frameworks

Edited by Robyn Keast,
Myrna Mandell,
and Robert Agranoff

Routledge
Taylor & Francis Group

LONDON AND NEW YORK

First published 2014
by Routledge

2 Park Square, Milton Park, Abingdon, Oxfordshire OX14 4RN
52 Vanderbilt Avenue, New York, NY 10017

*Routledge is an imprint of the Taylor & Francis Group,
an informa business*

First issued in paperback 2018

Library of Congress Cataloging-in-Publication Data

Network theory in the public sector: building new theoretical frameworks /
edited by Robyn Keast, Myrna Mandell and Robert Agranoff.
      pages cm. — (Routledge critical studies in public management)
   Includes bibliographical references and index.
   1. Public administration.   2. Interorganizational relations.   3. Business
networks.   I. Keast, Robyn.   II. Mandell, Myrna P.   III. Agranoff, Robert.
   JF1351.N426 2013
   351.01—dc23
   2013016390

ISBN: 978-0-415-84395-9 (hbk)
ISBN: 978-1-138-61799-5 (pbk)

Typeset in Sabon
by Apex CoVantage, LLC

Contents

Figures

Tables

Part I

Introduction to the Issues/ Current Network Theories

1 Introduction
Understanding Theory

Myrna P. Mandell

BACKGROUND

A phenomenon of the past thirty years has been the rapid rise of interest in and operation of networks, including networks and network-governance–based arrangements such as collaborations, alliances, partnerships, and "joined-up" ventures, as new and innovative ways of doing business in all sectors—government, community, and private. O'Toole (1997, 45) defines such network action as involving "structures of interdependence involving multiple organizations or parts thereof, where one unit is not merely the formal subordinate of others in some hierarchical arrangement". In this sense, the networks under analysis are goal-directed and multi-sectoral as opposed to serendipitous contacts among actors; that is, they are consciously arranged and bounded groupings, as opposed to associative clusters (Kilduff and Tsai 2003).

It has been argued across a number of research arenas that the capacity to harness the inherent benefits of networks has been, and continues to be, limited by the absence of a coherent theoretical framework informing their optimal design, governance arrangements and management, and the development of different mechanisms for evaluation (Agranoff and McGuire 2001a, b; Jones, Hesterly, and Borgatti 1997; Provan and Milward 2001; Oliver and Ebers 1998; O'Toole 1997; Provan and Milward 1995; Salancik 1995). Further complicating this understanding of networks has been a research agenda, which has been highly specialized and evolving almost independently spread across a number of areas of interest and at different levels of analysis and conceptualization (Börzel 1998; Cepiku, Meneguzzo, and Senese 2008; Cristofoli, Mandell, and Meneguzzo 2011; Oliver and Ebers 1998). In effect, the network paradigm has been restrained by "the 'Babylonian' variety of different understandings and applications of the . . . network approach" (Börzel 1998, 254), in which method, model, and theory are intermixed.

The expansion of theory in a broadened public sphere is argued to be a key and necessary step in the development of the literature on the practice and understanding of public and community sector networks. We currently rely conceptually, to a great extent, on the business literature to frame our understanding of public serving networks. However, the legally based authoritative roles of the public sector and the growing phenomenon of externalization of direct government services distinguish these types of networks from those discussed in the business literature. This book will serve to establish the study of public and public-serving governance networks as a separate and distinct field of study, working toward a distinct theoretical framework.

This book offers the potential for a comprehensive, integrative, interdisciplinary approach that enables specialists, practitioners, and administrators across a wide array of interest and fields to formulate and work on problems using a common language, analytical framework, and theoretical basis. Also of significance will be the translation of the emergent theoretical framework to inform the practical applications for which networks are meant. The practical implications highlighted or uncovered from theoretical developments center on identifying and matching the appropriate supporting managerial, cultural, and institutional arrangements necessary to sustain networks and ensure their effectiveness.

It is envisaged that in building a framework and/or theories about networks, the following outcomes would be delivered:

- Enhanced capacity for the management of different types of networks, including new and existing methods of management techniques
- Extensive knowledge on the design, operation, and evolution of networks
- Development of new performance measures that acknowledge and adequately capture the different outcomes produced through networks.

To build this framework, however, we must first understand what is meant by theory.

WHAT IS THEORY?

Theory is important because it provides a road map that clarifies our understanding (Innes and Booher 2010). It also allows researchers to see "how and why practices do or do not work in particular ways" (Innes and Booher 2010). According to *The American Heritage Dictionary*, second ed. (1982, 1260), theory is defined as including "systematically organized knowledge . . . a system of assumptions, accepted principles, and rules of procedure devised to analyze, predict, or otherwise explain the nature of behavior of a specified set of phenomenon". It can also include "abstract reasoning, speculation . . . [or] An assumption or guess based on limited information or knowledge".

Although there is much agreement as to the need for building a theoretical framework of networks, there is still disagreement as to what is appropriately considered a theory and also what is considered a good theory.

The obvious problem, based on the dictionary definition, is that theory can be about anything and have different meanings for different people. Indeed this has been debated in the academic community. For instance, Sutton and Shaw (1995, 371) indicate there is little agreement among academics as to what constitutes strong or weak theory. According to these authors there is "lack of agreement about whether a model and a theory can be distinguished, whether a typology is properly labeled a theory, or not, whether the strength of a theory depends on how interesting it is, and whether falsifiability is a prerequisite for the very existence of a theory". Sutton and Shaw go on to list five features of what a theory is not. These include references, data, lists of variables or constructs, diagrams, and hypotheses.

Weick (1995), however, takes exception with these five features as defining what is not a theory. Instead, he sees theory as a process, not necessarily a product. Weick discusses "the process of theorizing" (1995, 385). For him "most theories approximate, rather than realize the conditions necessary for a strong theory because these five features themselves [per Sutton and Shaw] have gradations of abstractedness and generality" (385). Weick cites TenHouten and Kaplan (1973) as to what is a theory. For them, theorists start with a vision for a theory and change it "from entwined ideas at the edge of words to a linear order in which the ideas are unraveled and set forth in the form of a propositional argument" (14). For Weick, theory can take many forms as indicated by the definition in the dictionary. Of course, as Weick indicates, academics will "want to underpin their theories with more empirical data . . . [and will] want a theory to incorporate more than one hypothesis" (1996, 386).

Di Maggio (1995) also has reservations as to what is a good theory. He indicates that a good theory is difficult to produce because "goodness is multidimensional" (362). For him, theory combines approaches to theorizing and results in compromise. In addition, he indicates that readers influence what is a theory. Di Maggio (1995) sees theories as hybrids that include "the best qualities of covering laws, enlightenment and process approaches" (392). In describing theory as covering laws, Di Maggio refers to "generalizations that, taken together, describe the world as we see (or measure) it" (391). Enlightenment refers to ". . . a set of categories and domain assumptions aimed at clearing away conventional notions to make room for artful and exciting insights" (391). And he describes theory as a narrative or an account of a social process and empirical tests of plausibility of the narrative.

The chapters in this book take the broader approaches to theory, as outlined above, to build a theoretical foundation of networks. The editors of this book also agree with Innes' and Booher's idea of what is a "good theory". According to them "it is a good theory if it makes sense to explain complex situations . . . it allows one to see aspects that were previously invisible, or seemingly unimportant, if those involved [in the case they are analyzing] think it is on target, and it generates new ideas, new thinking and even debate" (2010, 16).

The chapters in this book include both normative and descriptive theories. We agree with Innes' and Booher's (2010) emphasis as to why these types of theories are of value. In writing about collaborative networks, they point out that normative and descriptive types of theories are "descriptive of successful collaborative processes and normative in that [they provide] a model for the design and implementation of collaborative processes that can produce significant outcomes" (35). We see normative and descriptive theories as having great value in building a theoretical foundation for the understanding of networks. In addition, we build grounded theory based on a number of case studies. Overall, the chapters in this book are based on qualitative and quantitative analyses to better understand network constraints.

BUILDING THEORY FOR NETWORKS

The aim of this book is to establish a comprehensive, multilevel theory of networks that explains network formation and provides predictive capacity to better inform the design, operation, and management of networks to meet effectiveness and sustainability requirements and capitalize on the inherent collaborative advantage and synergistic benefits of these new organizational forms.

With their focus on trust, reciprocity, and mutual gains, networks require a shift from conventional hierarchical authority to processes and operational arrangements that are more horizontal, equalitarian, and relational in their orientation (Ansell 2000; Chisholm 1996; Rhodes 1996). As a consequence of this differential orientation, networks are more than 'business as usual' and require different design principles, management, and governance arrangements and performance measures (Agranoff and McGuire 2001a; Keast et al. 2004; Mandell and Keast 2008; Mandell and Steelman 2003; Provan and Milward 2001).

Some early research and theoretical development on networks in both the public and private sectors has provided some speculative insights on the structural properties and governance arrangements of networks (Laumann and Knoke 1987; Provan and Milward 2001). For example, during the 1990s several initial conceptualizations and theoretical considerations of network operation and governance were established. In the human services arena, Provan and Milward (1995) developed a preliminary theory of network effectiveness, while in the business sector Jones, Hesterly, and Borgatti (1997) proposed a general theory of networks. While these network theories made a noteworthy contribution to thinking about network operation, they were largely descriptive and tended to overemphasize governance and structural considerations at the expense of establishing a predictive capacity for network formation, operation, and effectiveness. This has led Salancik

(1995) and others (Oliver and Ebers 1998) to call for a comprehensive theory of networks.

It is contended that a comprehensive theory of networks has been constrained by three main factors: the fragmentation of the research field, a tendency to rely on prior management literature based on interorganizational theory as the basis for all network research, and a propensity to treat networks as undifferentiated.

The first factor has emerged from a research and practice history that has proceeded from disparate perspectives and sectors as well as taking place at multiple levels of theorizing and operation (Oliver and Ebers 1998). For instance, Börzell (1998) has demonstrated that network research and conceptualization have occurred through two main conceptual strands—the networks as disparate policy instruments focus preferred by the U.K. and the networks as governance model of Europe. Further complicating this duality of the network concept, as Oliver and Ebers (1998) have shown in their analysis of interorganizational relationships, there has been rapid expansion of research in this area resulting in a lack of conceptual consolidation (549). This view is supported by a number of other researchers examining interorganizational and network arrangements including Nohria (1992) and Alter and Hage (1993). In addition a study by Cristofoli, Mandell, and Meneguzzo (2011) highlights the varied and conflicting perspectives that are part of the literature based on analyses by researchers from the U.S., Australia, and Europe. The overall effect of this divergence of interests, locales, perspectives, and levels of analysis has been a fragmentation of thinking and theorizing about networks and an associated need for the development of a more coherent or comprehensive understanding of networks.

A further constraining factor to a theory of networks has been the failure to adequately define networks (Jones, Hesterly, and Borgatti 1997). At a minimal level, networks are defined as two or more organizations working together (O'Toole 1997). Such a broad conceptualization, while providing an overarching description of networks and indicating their orientation, fails to acknowledge the diversity of networks and their formation, governance, and management requirements (Keast, Mandell, and Brown 2006.

A more detailed review of the literature identified two main conceptualizations of networks. First, are the interorganizational networks, which are the coming together of still relatively independent organizations for the mostly instrumental purposes of advancing their own profit base (Gulati 1998; Powell and Smith-Doerr 1994; Ring and Van de Ven 1992). The goal of stabilization of resource flows lead to improved, but nonetheless independent relations such as preferential provider arrangements leading to the formation of alliances, partnerships, and joint venture arrangements (Alter and Hage 1993; Jones, Hesterly, and Borgatti 1997; Powell 1990; Powell and Smith-Doerr 1994). These arrangements, while underpinned by some relationships, retain a mostly contractual and profit focus (Sagawa and Segal 2000). As a consequence of this 'self-interested' focus, these arrangements are mostly about cooperative and coordinating arrangements and in this context collaboration is difficult to achieve and sustain. Because the emphasis remains on interorganizational relations, such network models are informed by theories based in this domain such as Resource Dependency Theory, Contingency Theory, and Transactional Cost Analysis (Börzell 1998; Kickert, Klijn, and Koppenjan 1997; Oliver and Ebers 1998) as well as intergovernmental relations (Gage and Mandell 1990). In the policy network context, which is similar to interorganizational networks, the focus is on the coming together of different/independent policy actors. Pluralist and Elitist theories are used to explain the formation of these bodies.

In comparison, there are also networks that are based on the notion of network governance in which bonds of interpersonal relationship, trust, mutuality, and reciprocity are the defining 'collaborative outcome' (Sagawa and Segal 2000; Huxham 2000; Innes and Booher 2010; O'Leary and Bingham 2009; O'Leary, Gerard, and Bingham 2006), and are therefore moving beyond interorganizational arrangements to more transformational networks in which new systems are created (Mandell and Steelman 2003; Keast et al. 2004). Governance Theory was introduced to explain the shift from hierarchical and interorganizational interactions to models that have a strong 'bottom-up' aspect and are horizontal in their orientation (Kickert, Klijn, and Koppenjan 1997; Rhodes 1996; Sørensen and Torfing 2007).

Despite these differences, to date much of the development of network theory has relied on the inter-organizational relations perspective as a basis for theory development and is therefore contingent on broader theories of organization (Börzell 1998; Oliver and Ebers 1998; Provan and Milward 1995), rather than developing a separate theoretical basis for the study of networks. While these theories such as Transactional Cost Analysis and Resource Dependency Theory may offer insights into the formation of inter-organizational arrangements they are not relevant to more transformational network arrangements underpinned by network governance principles (Keast and Waterhouse 2004; Kickert, Klijn, and Koppenjan 1997; Sørensen and Torfing 2007).

There have been some attempts to correct this misrepresentation (Innes and Booher 2010; Keast, Mandell, and Brown 2006; Mandell and Steelman 2003), but by and large most researchers do not make the distinctions between interorganizational and transformational networks and their underpinning differences in formation, operation, and theories clear in their work, thus limiting the ability to prescribe outcomes. A key focus of this book will be the expansion of this area of theoretical development.

A third contributing factor and closely linked to the above is the lack of distinction, by most researchers in the field, of the different types of networks and how these differences can and do affect their effectiveness (Brown and Keast 2003; Keast and Waterhouse 2004; Keast et al. 2004; Mandell and Steelman 2003; O'Leary, Gerard, and Bingham 2006). Some of the literature has moved toward differentiating between networks but this has not happened in a consolidated way. Noted exceptions include Rhodes (1996) and Rhodes and Marsh (1992), who classified policy networks along seven dimensions; Innes and Booher (2010), who develop a theory of collaborative networks; and others such as Alter and Hage (1993), Alexander (1995), and Mandell and Steelman (2003), who provided typologies of various forms that networks might take.

The case study by Keast and Waterhouse (2004) and publications emerging from this (Brown and Keast 2003) have extended these conceptualizations and developed a differentiated network framework indicating which network for what purpose, structural requirements, outcome orientation, related risks and rewards, and institutional arrangements. The basis of this thesis and an emerging area of network research and practical consideration is that treating networks as one dimensional and undifferentiated hinders their optimal application and restricts the power and benefits that working differently through networked arrangements can offer (Brown and Keast 2003; Keast, Mandell, and Brown 2006). That is, networks need to be built 'fit for purpose'.

By not distinguishing among the different types of networks, researchers and practitioners continually fail to recognize the richness of networks. This failure also leads to a lack of understanding of why some networks can be effective while others are not. In addition this lack of distinctions also limits understanding of their subsequent impact on public policy and their potential for the development of innovations in government.

Taken together, these deficits provide a strong argument for a research initiative that pulls together the various threads of theoretical development, highlights the differential nature of networks, and their various operating, governance, and management aspects. Doing so will advance the usefulness of networks as a concept that has great potential for the future of public policy and other arenas. It is intended that the theoretical foundations developed throughout this book will address this broad theoretical gap and the related subtheme issues.

Together, the chapters in this book provide a coherent theoretical basis informing the optimal design, governance, and management of networks. The focus of the chapters is on enlightening the readers (both academics and practitioners) with insights about the conditions under which networks emerge, operate effectively, and are sustained. In doing so, it is hoped that this book will enable the inherent benefits of networks to be capitalized on and leveraged to meet their full potential.

OUTLINE OF CHAPTERS

Part I of this book provides an introduction to the issues and current theories of networks.

This first chapter provides the background for the need to build a theoretical framework and/or different theories about networks. In doing so, it addresses the basic question of "What is theory?" and provides the foundation for the inclusion of the chapters in this book

Chapter 2, "Network Theory Tracks and Trajectories: Where From, Where To?" by Dr. Robyn Keast, clarifies the concept of network and its characteristic elements to provide a basis against which the theoretic propositions and contributions can be assessed. The material is then reorganized, highlighting theoretical divisions, overlaps, limitations, and directions. The chapter concludes restating the findings and how this positions network theory for the future, as well as pointing to the shifts in research practice required to facilitate new theoretic thinking.

Part II presents the basis for developing new theoretical frameworks.

In Chapter 3, "A Composite Theory of Leadership and Management: Process Catalyst and Strategic Leveraging: Deliberative Action in Collaborative Networks", by Drs. Robyn Keast and Myrna Mandell, the authors develop a new theoretical model of leadership and management that specifically applies to the unique characteristics of collaborative networks. The idea of a process catalyst is used to highlight the way relationships in collaborative networks become network assets that must be managed to achieve broader public goals. In addition, the concept of strategic leveraging is introduced to highlight the need for deliberative network action in collaborative networks to leverage the relationships needed to produce the synergies that can result from them.

In Chapter 4, "Building and Using the Theory of Collaborative Advantage", by Drs. Siv Vangen and Chris Huxham, the authors update their theory of collaborative advantage by providing two new and two recent conceptualizations and frameworks relating to goals, trust, culture, and leadership. They introduce different ways of conceptualizing the issues, tensions, and challenges that underpin collaboration in practice and identify issues that need to be managed if collaboration is to yield advantage rather than inertia. They also indicate how these four "themes" integrate with others that have not been included in this chapter to provide an overall sense of the theory and practice of collaborative advantage.

In Chapter 5, "The Democratic Potentials of Governance Networks in Intergovernmental Decision-Making", by Dr. Eva Sørensen, the author provides a new theoretical framework that brings together network theory and social network analysis to show how governance networks could contribute to developing intergovernmental democracy. This framework addresses the void that now exists around the question of how to democratically regulate intergovernmental policy-making and shows how meta-governance in governance networks becomes a positive contribution rather than a threat to the development of an intergovernmental democracy.

In Chapter 6 "Governance Network Performance: A Complex Adaptive Systems Approach" by Dr. Chris Koliba, the author draws on a governance network analysis lens to situate network performance management as a necessary condition of network learning and knowledge transfer that takes into account network performance outcomes and processes. Contemporary theories of performance management and organizational learning are blended with complexity and network science to advance a theory of network learning that may be applied to theory development, empirical analysis, and network management practice.

In Chapter 7, "Governing Through Networks: A Systemic Approach", by Debra Rice, the author bridges the two prevailing conceptualizations of networks: on one hand from a structuralist and functional strand, and on the other, an institutional strand by outlining theoretically how governance networks, as a specific type of organization, can affect large-scale societal structures. In the second part of the chapter, this systemic view is then applied to network governance, seeking to answer the question as to whether cross-sector cooperation among state actors, business actors, and civil-society organizations has the potential to change the state as we know it.

In Chapter 8, "Developing Network Management Theory Through Channels and Roles" by Dr. Joris Voets addresses two major research questions regarding how network managers try to make network strategies and activities effective and which different management roles are required to make network management effective. To answer these questions, he introduces the concept of management channels and defines a set of network management roles.

In Part III, theoretical perspectives are linked to practical approaches to theory. A number of case studies illustrating a variety of issues based on a number of theoretical frameworks are presented.

Chapter 9, "Network Management Behaviors: Closing the Theoretical Gap", by Drs. Michael McGuire and Robert Agranoff, analyzes a multi-method project to provide an in-depth look at fundamental management within the formation and operation of one networked high school. Using a grounded theory approach to cast light on a specific network management framework, the paper seeks to add to the theory of network management by taking a deep look into the formation and operation of an action type network that is actively engaged in developing operating policies and programs as well as carrying out its agreements and decisions

In Chapter 10, "What Can Governance Network Theory Learn from Complexity Theory: Mirroring Two Perspectives on Complexity", by Drs. Joop Koppenjan and Erik-Hans Klijn, the authors examine the concept of governance network theory and complexity and apply it to a major project in Rotterdam. Their analysis highlights the gaps in each theory and presents the challenge with regard to theory building to incorporate the critical ideas from each to provide a more coherent framework for the study of networks.

In Chapter 11, "Network Performance: Towards a Dynamic Multidimensional Model", by Dr. Denita Cepiku, the author engages in a theory-building endeavor aimed at developing an interpretative model on network performance by systematizing and enhancing the existing literature and by analyzing a longitudinal case study. The case study covers five years in the Northern Ethiopian region of Tigray. The chapter contributes to improving our understanding on how to evaluate general interest networks for their performance, especially when these are community-based and composed of both public and private actors.

In Part IV, the concluding chapter, Dr. Robert Agranoff draws out the implications and conclusions that result from the chapters in this book. This volume aspires to contribute to the theoretical base of public networks and in the long run to the theory of networks. In approaching this task the volume incorporates both the qualitative and quantitative research cultures, bridging research questions, data analysis modes, and methods of inference. This final chapter presents the issues that the papers in this volume have advanced; identifies one set of the unanswered issues in network theory, that of their limitations; and raises the even broader question of the status/role of the public sphere.

REFERENCES

Agranoff, R., and M. McGuire. 2001a. "After the Network is Formed: Processes, Power and Performance." In *Getting Results Through Collaboration: Networks and Network Structures for Public Policy and Management*, edited by M. P. Mandell, 11–29. Westport CT: Quorum Books.

———. 2001b. "Big Questions in Public Network Management Research." *Journal of Public Administration Research and Theory* 11:295–326.

Alexander, E. 1995. *How Organizations Act Together: Interorganizational Coordination in Theory and Practice*. London: Gordon and Breach Publishers.

Alter, C., and J. Hage. 1993. *Organizations Working Together*. Newbury Park, CA: Sage Publications.

Ansell, C. 2000. "The Network Policy: Regional Development in Western Europe." *Governance* 13:303–33.

Börzel, T. 1998. "Organizing Babylon—On the Different Conceptions of Policy Networks." *Public Administration* 76:253–73.

Brown, K., and R. Keast. 2003. "Citizen-Government Engagement: Community Connection through Networked Arrangements." *Asian Journal of Public Administration* 25:107–31.

Cepiku, D., M. Meneguzzo, and M. Senese. 2008. *Innovations in Public Management and Governance in Italy*. Rome: Aracne Editrice.

Chisholm, R. 1996. "On the Meaning of Networks." *Group and Organization Management* 21:216–26.

Cristofoli, D., M. Mandell, and M. Meneguzzo. 2011. "Public Networks Say Americans, Public Networks Reply Europeans, But Are They Talking About the Same Thing?" Paper presented at the International Research Symposium for Public Management Conference. Dublin, Ireland.

Di Maggio, P. J. 1995. "Comments on What Is Not Theory." *Administrative Science Quarterly* 40:391–97.

Gage, R., and M. P. Mandell, eds. 1990. *Strategies for Managing Intergovernmental Policies and Networks*. New York: Praeger Books.

Gulati, R. 1998. "Alliances and Networks." *Strategic Management Journal* 19: 293–317.

Huxham, C. 2000. "The Challenge of Collaborative Advantage." *Public Management* 2:337–57.

Innes, J., and D. Booher. 2010. *Planning With Complexity*. London and New York: Routledge, Taylor and Francis Group.

Jones, C, W. S. Hesterly, and S. P. Borgatti. 1997. "A General Theory of Network Governance: Exchange Conditions and Social Mechanisms." *Academy of Management Review* 22:911–945.

Keast, R., and J. Waterhouse. 2004. "Participatory Evaluation: A Missing Component in the Social Change Equation for Public Services." *Strategic Change* 15:23–35.

Keast, R., M. P. Mandell, and K. Brown. 2006. "Mixing State, Market and Governance Modes: The Role of Governments in 'Crowded' Policy Domains." *International Journal of Organization Theory and Behavior* 9:27–50.

Keast, R., M. Mandell, K. Brown, and G. Woolcock. 2004. "Network Structures: Working Differently and Changing Expectations." *Public Administration Review* 64:363–71.

Kickert, W. J. M., E.-H. Klijn, and J. F. M. Koppenjan. (1997). "Managing Networks in the Public Sector: Findings and Reflections." In *Managing Complex Networks: Strategies for the Public Sector,* edited by W. J. M. Kickert, E.-H. Klijn, and J. F. M Koppenjan, 166–188. London: Sage Publications.

Kilduff, M., and W. Tsai. 2003. *Networks and Organizations*. Newbury Park, CA: Sage Publications.

Laumann, E. O., and D. Knoke. 1987. *The Organizational State*. Madison: University of Wisconsin Press.

Mandell, M. P., and R. Keast. 2008. Special Issue: "Collaborative Networks: New Performance Challenges." *Public Management Review* 10:687–98.

Mandell M. P., and T. Steelman. 2003. "Understanding What Can Be Accomplished Through Interorganizational Innovations: Importance of Typologies, Context and Management Strategies." *Public Management Review* 5:197–224.

Nohria, N. 1992. "Is a Network Perspective a Useful Way of Studying Organizations?" In *Networks and Organizations: Structure, Form and Action,* edited by N. Nohria and R. G. Eccles, 1–22. Boston: Harvard Business School.

O'Leary, R., and L. B. Bingham. 2009. *The Collaborative Manager.* Washington, D.C.: Georgetown University Press.

O'Leary, R., C. Gerard, and L. B. Bingham. 2006. "Introduction to the Symposium on Collaborative Public Management" *Public Administration Review* 66:6–9.

Oliver, A. L., and M. Ebers. 1998. "Networking Network Studies: An Analysis of Conceptual Configurations in the Study of Inter-organizational Relationships." *Organization Studies* 19:549–583.

O'Toole, L. J. 1997. "Treating Networks Seriously: Practical Research-Based Agendas in Public Administration." *Public Administration Review* 57:45–52.

Powell, W. W. 1990. "Neither Market nor Hierarchy: Network Forms of Organization." *Research in Organizational Behavior* 12:295–336.

Powell, W. W., and L. Smith-Doerr. 1994. "Networks and Economic Life." In *The Handbook of Economic Sociology,* edited by N. J. Smelser and R. Swedberg, 368–402. Princeton, NJ: Princeton University Press.

Provan, K. G., and H. B. Milward. 2001. "Do Networks Really Work? A Framework for Evaluating Public Sector Organizational Networks." *Public Administration Review* 61:414–23.

———. 1995. "A Preliminary Theory of Network Effectiveness: A Comparative Study of Four Community Mental Health Systems." *Administrative Science Quarterly* 25:200–25.

Rhodes, R. A. W. 1996. "The New Governance: Governing Without Government." *Political Studies* XLIV:652–67.

Rhodes, R. A. W., and D. Marsh. 1992. "New Directions in the Study of Policy Networks." *European Journal of Political Research* 21:181–205.

Ring, P. S., and A. H. Van de Ven. (1992). "Structuring Cooperative Relations Between Organizations." *Strategic Management Journal* 13:483–98.

Sagawa, S., and E. Segal. 2000. "Common Interest, Common Good: Creating Value Through Business and Social Sector Partnerships." *California Management Review* 42:105–22.

Salancik, G. R. 1995. "WANTED: A Good Network Theory of Organization." *Administrative Science Quarterly* 40:345–349.

Sutton, R. I., and B. M. Shaw. 1995. "What Theory Is Not." *Administrative Science Quarterly* 40:371–381.

Sørensen, E. and J. Torfing, eds. 2007. *Theories of Democratic Network Governance*. London: Palgrave-McMillon.

TenHouten, W. D., and C. D. Kaplan. 1973. *Science and Its Mirror Image*. New York: Harper and Row.

The American Heritage Dictionary, second edition (1982). Boston: Houghton Mifflin Co.

Weick, K. E. 1995. "What Theory Is Not, Theorizing Is." *Administrative Science Quarterly* 40:385–390.

2 Network Theory Tracks and Trajectories
Where from, Where to?

Robyn Keast

INTRODUCTION

Networks are a cornerstone of contemporary public sector institutional architecture (Castells 1996). As networks and network research have expanded, questions related to network theorizing have re-emerged. Earlier positions that networks were a-theoretical; that is, exhibiting descriptive rather than explanatory insights (Salancik 1995, 348) and containing no theory of their own (Oliver and Ebers 1998; Börzel 1998), have been challenged. It is now acknowledged that a broad array of network theories abounds across many areas of scholarship (Börzel 2011; Borgatti and Foster 2003; Kilduff and Tsai 2003), resulting in as Oliver and Ebers (1998, 549) described as a ". . . cacophony of approaches and theories".

The objective of this chapter is to examine key strands of network theorizing relevant to public sector administration. It is envisaged that by articulating the various streams, their overlaps and departures, it may be possible to go beyond the current network theory confusion to provide a more solid foundation on which new combinations can be formed or enable creation of new generation network theories.

This chapter commences by clarifying the concept of a network and its characteristic elements to provide a basis against which theoretic propositions and contributions may be assessed. Following this is a section in which the material is re-organized, highlighting theoretical divisions, overlaps, limitations, and directions.

The chapter concludes by restating the findings and how this positions network theory for the future, as well as pointing to the shifts in research practice required to facilitate new theoretic thinking.

NETWORKS DEFINED

At its most basic or abstract level, a network consists of a relatively stable set of actors or nodes (people, organizations, or sectors) linked by a set of ties (such as friendship or exchanges) (Mitchell 1969; Fombrun 1982).

This all-encompassing view runs the risk of assigning all social entities as networks. Accordingly, a more defined and somewhat instrumental perspective has been assigned. In this regard, a network is defined as a set of goal-oriented interdependent actors that come together to produce a collective output (tangible or intangible) that no one actor could produce on his or her own (Alter and Hage 1993).

From a distinctly public sector perspective, O'Toole (1997, 45) defined a network as "structures of interdependence involving multiple organizations, or part thereof, where one is not merely the subordinate of others in some hierarchical arrangement". Although the definition of a network can vary considerably within and between sectors and disciplines (Börzel 1998; Considine 2002), all share as a common denominator an agreed notion that networks are about different types of relationships, whether these are the objectively measurable resource or economic ties or subjective emotional links (Wasserman and Faust 1994). There is an element of differentiation between different groups of network proponents as to the most defining relational element within networks, with some following the depiction for generic ties as outlined above by Wasserman and Faust (1994), others—particularly business network proponents, for example Jones, Hesterly, and Borgatti (1997) and Grandori and Soda (1995) stressing the transactional connecting function, and others still, positioning interpersonal relationships as the core dimension of these exchanges (Church et al. 2002; Freeman 2004). On this latter position, Powell (1990, 300) succinctly noted: "certain forms of exchange are more social that is, more dependent on relationships, mutual interests, and reputation . . . as the glue that binds".

Networks as Metaphors

This notion of connections through ties brings into play the image of 'webs of affiliation or nets of links'. Such metaphors are a powerful way of conceptualizing, presenting, and discussing networks. As Auster (1990, 65) noted, the benefit of the vision of a network is that it changes the imagery from a focus on the individual to one of "constellations, wheels and systems of relationships". Similarly, Kenis and Schneider (1991, 25) considered a network to be a metaphor to capture the "architecture of complexity" increasingly evident in contemporary society. Despite the benefits that the network metaphor evokes, its abstractness or highly descriptive level has been criticized as being too broad for practical application. Dowding (1995), for example, argued that the network descriptor was often applied to any type of grouping and therefore not explicit in relation to the characteristics under examination, the boundary of analysis, or the specification of expectations. Accordingly, the network concept has been described as "imagery without technique" (Schrum and Mullins 1988, cited in Conway, Jones, and Steward 2001, 3) and more detailed frameworks and theories to organize network concepts around have been sought (Salancik 1995; Dowding 1995).

KEY THEORETIC THEMES

As highlighted above, the network paradigm is wide reaching, covering many different practice and research arenas. Focusing on the public sector, this chapter necessarily presents only a partial account of this diversity and does not claim to be an exhaustive account of the available literature. Specifically, it examines three broad research strands and related disciplines: network theory, interorganizational relations and policy, governance, and public management networks (Berry et al. 2004; Klijn 2008; Isett et al. 2011; McGuire and Agranoff 2011).

Network Theory

Network Theory represents the first attempt to rise above the metaphoric depictions of networks as threads and nets. It is grounded in the work of the sociologist Moreno (1934), who introduced the socio-gram to depict individuals as a set of nodes connected by lines, to diagrammatically isolate relations among people and guide interventions. In late 1950s, Cartwright and Harary (1956) connected social network theory with graph theory and mathematics, giving rise to structuralist traditions that remain current today. The emphasis on the relationships between actors rather than their individual characteristics is a key point of differentiation between network and other theories (Scott 2000). Social network theory therefore posits that the position of the actors, and the type and nature of their relationship with the other actors in the network, determines the outcomes (Borgatti and Foster 2003; Kilduff and Tsai 2003).

In a recent review Borgatti and Halgin (2011) distilled two main theory categories informing this perspective: flow and bond, both of which have relevance to public sector networks. Seminal social structure theories such as Granovetter's (1973) strength of weak ties (SWT) and Burt's Structural Holes theory (SH) (Burt 1992) fit within this model because they present social systems as flows or pipelines of, for example, information or resources. The flow model has also generated a number of important theoretical propositions, including the link between position, flow speed, and structure and performance outcomes, such as getting a job (Granovetter 1983) and creating innovation (Burt 2004).

The bond model draws also on notions of relational strength to generate theories centered on cohesion, such as network coordination (Provan and Milward 1995), small world networks or hubs (Milgram 1967), and network organizations (Jones, Hesterly, and Borgatti et al. 1997). Here the network tie serves as a bond that aligns and integrates action (Borgatti and Halgain 2011). Social capital theory is a prominent example of the bonding perspective, because it argues that the social connections between people and communities make collective action possible (Putnam 1993; Stone 2000; Lin 2001). The bonding model also allows for mathematically derived theories such as cliques (Luce and Perry 1949) and structural equivalence (Lorrain and White 1971), which have been operationalized through, for example, the work of Provan and Sebastain (1998) and their study of service sector cliques.

As evidenced above, the network approach has generated considerable theoretical development explicating this relationship between network structure and behavior, largely within the organizational arena (Borgatti and Foster 2003; Borgatti and Haglin 2011). Attention has also been directed to the ability of network actors to occupy more central or powerful positions within the network structure (Freeman 1979) and the management of the network (Cross and Thomas 2009; Balkundi and Kilduff 2006). Thus with the help of network theory and network analysis, public sector networks can not only be measured, but also better managed. Yet, with the exception of some exemplar work, for example by Provan and Milward (1995) and program evaluations, network theory and analysis have yet to be widely embedded within the public sector arena.

Interorganizational Networks

The study of interorganizational relations (IOR) as networked forms commenced in the 1960s with the growing realization that organizations are not isolated entities but part of a larger environmental system (Dill 1958). The starting point for IOR is that external environment conditions such as the availability of resources, economic factors, or changing governmental policies affected organizations and led to changes in their behavior. To secure a level of control or certainty over their environment, organizations entered into exchanges and arrangements such as joint ventures, consortia, and networks that varied from weak to tight relationships (Barringer and Harrison 2000). Theoretical attention has been directed to the nature of the links between organizations, the buffering strategies used and structures adopted to influence the exchange processes (Cook 1977; Benson 1975). Such arrangements were not confined to the business sector, with public and community sector agencies also adopting exchange relations and longer-term arrangements to secure necessary resources and ensure longevity and prosperity (Hasenfeld 1983).

A number of theories inform the IOR network strand (Oliver and Ebers 1998). One of the more central, the Resource Dependency Theory (RDT) proposes that, lacking essential resources, organizations seek to establish relationships with those organizations possessing the necessary properties. Within this perspective, organizations are viewed as coalitions altering their patterns of behavior and structure to acquire and maintain needed external resources and secure a level of certainty in an uncertain environment. Within this framework, power is a resource that when exercised enables an actor or groups of actors the ability to exert some degree of control over an uncertain environment (Benson 1975). In this way, RDT is aligned with institutional and ecological theories, where the former is focused on explaining why organizations move toward networks and the latter are concerned with the environmental context of organizations.

Exchange Theory (e.g. Levine and White 1961) also begins with the assumption that as their operating domains become more populated and problems more complex, organizations become more interdependent on each other for resources and shared solutions. Therefore, a central task is to reduce the uncertainties encountered through the development of networked forms and collaborative practices. However, there is a sharp contrast between social/relational (exchange theory) and RDT. Under RDT, organizations are largely self-interested and enter into arrangements to achieve their own objectives, while from the social exchange perspective the new connected relationship is the result of organizations recognizing the interdependence of problems and the benefits of developing reciprocal relationships aimed at solving them.

Also related to the IOR strand is Institutional Theory (IT), which proposes that the "institutional climate" can pressure organizations to acquire legitimacy and obey socially dominant practices, including the development of networks (Oliver 1990; Clegg 1990). Furthermore, it considers the processes by which structures, including rules, norms, and routines become embedded as behavioral guidelines (Scott 2001). Different components of IT explain how these elements are created, adopted, and diffused within and across organizations. For example, agencies can improve their status or funding opportunities by partnering themselves with agencies that are perceived to be successful and progressive or be compelled to link up via the mandates of more powerful organizations. The norms of these new practices are imitated, willingly or not, via isomorphic approaches and processes referred to as mimetic isomorphism (DiMaggio and Powell 1983) to further align with the dominant bodies, including funding bodies and government.

The diversity of the IOR perspective provides a suite of theories with which to explain interorganizational networks. For example, the resource dependency frame, focuses on resource acquisition, exchanges, and power; the social exchange perspective directs attention to the level of interdependency between agencies and the adoption of joint efforts; the institutional approach is dedicated to unpacking the legitimacy drivers; and (not discussed here) the transaction analysis approach looks for an economic explanation. Collectively the IOR set of theories directs attention to the development of strategies and processes to better manage the external environment, including boundary spanning (Boardman 2012), stakeholder engagement (Friedman 1984), and strategic management theories (Gulati 2007).

Policy, Governance, and Public Management Networks

This network perspective emerged during 1960 to the 1970s, arising initially from a move away from the 'rational actor' to more pluralistic, process models of public policy decision-making and implementation. Two dominant schools of network thought shaped this body of work: One that views networks as interest-mediation processes and the other as an alternative form of governance structure. Developed across a number of jurisdictions, the former tracked the movement from the narrow and closed functioning of iron triangle policy development to structures and processes that facilitate more expansive state/society participation, such as issue networks (Heclo and Wildavsky 1974), politikverflechung (political entanglement) (Scharpf 1978), and subsequently policy networks or communities (Richardson and Jordan 1979; Jordan and Richardson 1983; Rhodes 1997) and implementation structures (Herjn and Porter 1981; Pressman and Wildavsky 1983).

Researchers from this tradition drew upon predominantly qualitative material to develop typologies of policy network types, related network structures to resource dependencies, and explored links between network structures, policy outcomes, and policy continuity. Marsh and Rhodes (1992) for example, emphasized the structure of the network, showing how the structure of the network affects policy outcomes and, in so doing, identified a continuum of types of policy networks ranging from 'policy communities' at one end to 'issue networks' at the other. These authors postulated that tight policy communities involving powerful interests controlling key resources tend to produce policy continuity. In contrast, looser issue networks, characterized by more limited control over resources, are often faced with open contests with interest groups outside the network, and this tends to produce policy discontinuity.

The policy network school and its various typologies therefore focused on understanding how power is exercised in policy decision-making and the way in which power relationships are structured, negotiated, and subverted in the operation of these networks (Rhodes 1986; Waarden 1992). Critics of this structural approach, such as Dowding (1994) argued that greater weight should be directed instead to understanding the interactions between agents, such as bargaining and resource exchanges. Another limitation of the policy network approach is that it has not been able to develop a systematic explanation of the relationship between different structural arrangements of policy networks and policy outcomes (Skelcher and Sullivan 2008). As yet, no theory has been developed to systematically link a particular type of policy network with a specific character or outcomes of the policy process (Börzel 2011).

Implementation Structures and Service Networks

Implementation structures (Hjern and Porter 1981) are a core element of this strand and have their origin in IOR and related intergovernmental management, research, and theorizing (Gage and Mandell 1990). From this perspective, policies and programs are implemented by complex clusters of public and private organizations, in which local implementation actors can participate alongside central actors and play a key influential role. Thus conventional top-down implementation arrangements were supplemented and often replaced by bottom-up approaches, and subsequently mixes of both. This expansion and blending of participation called for different structures and processes and the development of new cross-organizational management strategies to facilitate the accomplishment of joint tasks. Theorists from this perspective therefore focused their analysis on the characteristics and functions of the implementation structure rather than at the organizational level (Hanf and Scharpf 1978).

Changing society-government relations, reflected in less dominant hierarchical orientation and greater reciprocity and a sense of interdependency, led to a shift in research emphasis to service networks. As Provan and Milward (1991) indicated, networks have a primary function of linking; coordinating and facilitating joint work for improved social outcomes (see also Church et al. 2002). From this perspective, the theoretical focus was not only restricted to explaining complex interdependent relationships and their management, but also developing structures of coordination (Klijn 2005) and as a consequence a wide array of service delivery typologies emerged. Some focused on governance structures (Provan and Kenis 2007), while others aligned relationship strength with degree of connection (Konrad 1996) or with purpose (Keast, Brown, and Mandell 2007; Keast 2011), or distinguished networks based on the extent to which partners cooperate to accomplish tasks (Agranoff 2007; Ferlie and Pettigrew 1996). Another set, as exemplified by the Mandell and Steelman model (2003) coupled linkage strengths with context, problem orientation, and breadth of action. Together, these typologies for public sector networks point to a growing appreciation of network differentiation, and therefore must be built, governed, and managed accordingly (Keast et al. 2007). Despite the contribution of service delivery frameworks and typologies, their largely descriptive focus means it is argued they fall short of what is considered to be a 'full explanatory' theory (Sutton and Staw 1995).

The strong practice orientation of service delivery directed theoretical attention toward network management and performance. During this time several theorists, notably Agranoff and McGuire (2001), McGuire (2002), Mandell (1994), and Meier and O'Toole (2001; 2005) made significant advancements elucidating the difference between conventional management and network management. Adopting an empirical approach, Meier and O'Toole (2002) modeled the impact of network management on performance, while earlier work by O'Toole (1996) identified the different management skills and competencies required for intergovernmental work. Specifically, Agranoff and McGuire set out a four-phase process: activating, framing, mobilizing, and synthesizing as the alternative to POSDCORB (Agranoff and McGuire 2001). Their subsequent developments drew on grounded theory to distil the actual practices of network managers and provide practitioners with rational direction (Agranoff and McGuire 2003; Agranoff 2007; McGuire 2002).

In 1995, Provan and Milward presented a preliminary theory of network effectiveness, which proposed that "networks will be effective under structural conditions of centralized integration and direct, non-fragmented external control, but that effectiveness would be highest when the system is also stable and environmental resources are relatively munificent" (1995, 23). This theory allowed for variance among networks, including differentiation across networks. Later, Provan and Milward (2001) argued that highly dense and centralized networks work well in public service delivery if environmental and institutional norms support cooperation. Extending this work, a configuration theory of network performance has emerged, which combines several sets of factors (goals/strategy, governance mode, structure, people, and management) and argues that overall network effectiveness is contingent on the internal alignment of these factors as well as the fit between overall configuration and the network context (Raab and Suijkerbuijk 2009). Turrini et al.'s (2010) meta-analysis also has made clear the link between network management (steering) and performance.

Governance Network Theory

Alongside the service delivery network model came a reconceptualization of governance (Rhodes 1997). Networks were equated with a new form of governance arising in situations where there are high levels of interdependence between organizations and where hierarchical forms of command and control are no longer the most effective methods for policy development or implementation (Kooiman 1993; Kickert, Klijn, and Koppenjan 1997). In this context, governance is seen as signifying a change from top-down government to governance via self-organizing interorganizational networks (Rhodes 1997, 35). More specifically, Kickert, Klijn, and Koppenjan (1997, 6) defined governance networks as "more or less stable patterns of social relations between interdependent actors, which take shape around policy problems and/or policy programmes". Accordingly, theorists operating from this perspective focus on a wider set of actors than just those overtly engaged in policy-making to include multiple agencies, private firms and organizations (for profit and not-for-profit) (Goldsmith and Eggers 2004; Koppenjan and Klijn 2004; Sørensen and Torfing (2007). Considine (2005) noted that the governance networks paradigm as a breakthrough in public administration and organizational theory because it provided a means by which to tackle problems in a multidimensional and locally flexible way.

In the absence of centralized authority, governance networks were to be enacted to efficiently and effectively deliver outcomes (Kickert, Klijn, and Koppenjan 1997; Koppenjan and Klijn 2004). In this context, policy-making and action are equated with game-playing, albeit from a more qualitative and interactive perspective than economic game theory. Accordingly, attention is paid to the role of network actors in shaping the context and conditions for effective network performance. Specifically Klijn and Koppenjan (2000) identified two roles for network managers: process management (generating improved interactions between existing members) and network constitution (making changes to existing networks in terms of members rules). Policy performance is thus explained by the ability of network members to identify which role to play and to play that role effectively. On their theoretical contribution, Koppenjan and Klijn (2004, 12) noted that they aimed to: "link network theory to the cognitive aspects of problem solving and policy processes".

The two theoretical approaches present different foci for the analysis and measurement of network operation and performance. Policy network theories emphasize the structured interaction of actors, ignoring the agency of actors in the interactions, while the network governance approach focuses on the role of network managers as active agents in enacting outcomes. On this point, Skelcher and Sullivan (2008) in their review of potential approaches to network effectiveness, suggested that there was an opportunity for transference across the approaches, strengthening both.

TAKING STOCK AND MOVING FORWARD

This stock take has traced the development of networks and network theories and shows it to continue as a growing enterprise. Development has occurred in two ways. The first transpired through the focused attention of individual strands or disciplines of network research that produced theories particular to their context or tradition. Granovetter's (1973) strength of weak ties and Burt's (1992) structural holes are seminal examples of such particularized network theory development. While highly instructive, the often specific nature of these theories can overlook the alternative explanations. The second way arises from overlap and synthesis across various related and increasingly disparate traditions. Researchers, including public sector researchers, have long borrowed from and adapted theories from other disciplines to explain networks and network functioning. Although a stand-alone explanation for networks, resource dependency theory is also presented as an underpinning or foundation to network theory (Oliver and Ebers 1998; Börzel 1998; Hibbert, Huxham, and Ring, 2008). While the expansion of old and new developments serves to alert public management research and theory to new phenomena and ways of analyzing and explaining networks, the resulting diversity and overlay of the theories has been argued to undermine the coherence of the overall research tradition. However, along with divergence there is also ample evidence of core areas of cohesion, particularly around notions of network management and performance that provides a solid foundation for ongoing work and theory development!

Remaining Gaps

Arising from the interplay and exportation of theoretical elements and constructs is a somewhat terminological quagmire, with some terms retaining their meaning and others being co-opted and applied to different yet related constructs. Such inconsistencies, although contributing to the richness of the field, can create barriers among scholars and may come at the cost of overall programmatic coherence. Many authors (Dowding 1994; Isett et al. 2011) have called for greater specification and agreement on the term network, arguing that this is a necessary step to overcome the enduring abstractness of network theorizing. Furthermore, an extended array of different research approaches and methodologies has been identified as applied within and across strands, ranging from the ubiquitous in-depth, single case study to mid-range *n* cases, as well as quantitatively derived studies. A defining point of difference seems to be the units of analysis generally applied within each of the strands: IOR (single/dyads), SNA (multiple dyads to networks), policy and governance networks (dyads/multiple), and service delivery networks (multiple dyads/networks). It is argued that the propensity to mix theory, method and models continues to restrain the potential to develop network thinking and theory (Börzel 1998, 254). Berry et al. (2004, 549) stress that our tendency to focus on the instrumental implication of networks should be tempered by a commitment to get an empirically accurate picture of networks.

Also evident from the review is a preference toward the development of typologies and conceptual frameworks, most notably in the policy and service delivery strands. The usefulness of typologies is widely contested, with some arguing that they fall short of making clear, conceptual distinctions between elements (McKelvey 1982) and thus occupy intermediatory theory status (Sutton and Staw 1995). For theoretical advancement to occur, it is argued that the typologies require greater expansion of the number of entities under examination (Kickert and Koppenjan 1997, 45), increased use of medium and large *n* study approaches to isolate key variables, and a strong emphasis on enhancing their current explanatory powers (Klijn 1997).

It is clear from this review that much has been learned about network characteristics, antecedents, and functioning processes from the application of existing theories. However, there are still gaps in knowledge and, as attention to networks and how they operate continues, there is a growing need to address existing and emergent issues including extending typologies, network performance and effectiveness measures, distillation of the microelements of network functioning, and expanded understandings of governance structures, especially under conditions of complexity and change. To address this situation several approaches to network theory development may be required: (a) a continuation of single or narrowly focused theories that drill down into the microelements of network functioning, (b) more pluralistic approaches that mix various theoretical positions to capture the complexity and multiplicity of factors that are networks, leading to what Möller and Wilson (1995) describe as 'fuzzy theorization', and (c) the development of breakthrough and innovative theoretical approaches that can be applied to address nascent phenomena and, perhaps, intractable network problems. This book is intended as a vehicle to facilitate this development.

REFERENCES

Agranoff, R. 2007. *Managing within Networks: Adding Value to Public Organizations.* Washington, DC: Georgetown University Press.

Agranoff, R., and M. McGuire. 2001. "Big Questions in Public Network Management Research." *Journal of Public Administration, Research and Theory* 11 (3): 295–326.

———. 2003. *Collaborative Public Management: New Strategies for Local Governments.* Washington, DC: Georgetown University Press.

Alter, K., and J. Hage. 1993. *Organizations Working Together.* Newbury Park, CA: Sage Publications.

Auster, E. 1990. "The interorganizational environment: Network theory, tools and applications." In *Technology Transfer: A Communication Perspective,* edited by F. Williams and D. Gibson, 63–89. Newbury Park, CA: Sage Publications.

Balkundi, P., and M. Kilduff. 2006. "The Ties That Lead: A Social Network Approach to Leadership." *The Leadership Quarterly* 17 (4): 419–39.

Barringer, B., and J. Harrison. 2000. "Walking a Tightrope: Creating Value Through Interorganizational Relationships." *Journal of Management* 26 (3): 367–403.

Benson, J. K. 1975. "The Interorganizational Network as a Political Economy." *Administrative Science Quarterly* 20: 229–40

Berry, F., R. Brower, S. Choic, W. Goas, H. Jan, M. Kwon, and J. Ward. 2004. "Three Traditions of Network Research: What the Public Management Research Agenda Can Learn from other Research Communities." *Public Administration Review* 64 (5): 539–52.

Boardman, C. 2012. "Organizational Capability in Boundary Spanning Collaborations: Internal and External Approaches to Organizational Strategy and Personnel Activity." *Journal of Public Administration Research and Theory* 22 (3): 497–526.

Borgatti, S., and P. Foster. 2003. "The Network Paradigm in Organizational Research: A Review and Typology." *Journal of Management* 29 (6): 991–1013.

Borgatti, S. and D. Halgin. 2011. "On Network Theory." *Organization Science* 22 (5): 1168–81.

Börzel, T. 1998. "Organising Babylon. On the Different Conceptions of Policy Networks." *Public Administration* 76 (2): 253–73.

———. 2011. "Networks: Reified Metaphor or Governance Panacea?" *Public Administration* 89 (1): 49–63.

Burt, R. 1992. *Structural Holes: The Social Structure of Competition.* Cambridge, MA: Harvard University Press.

Burt, R. S. 2004. "Structural Holes and Good Ideas." *American Journal of Sociology* 110: 349–99.

Cartright, D., and F. Harary. 1956. "Structural Balance: A Generalization of Heider's Theory." *Psychological Review* 63: 277–93.

Castells, M. 1996. *The Information Age: Economy, Society and Culture Vol. 1: The Rise of the Network Society.* Oxford: Blackwell Publishing.

Church, M., M. Bitel, K. Armstrong, P. Fernando, H. Gould, S. Joss, A. de la Torre, and C. Vouhé. 2002. *Participation, Relationships and Dynamic Change: New Thinking on Evaluating the Work of International Networks.* London: No 121 Development Planning Unit.

Clegg, S. 1990. *Modern Organizations: Organizational Studies in the Modern World.* London: Sage Publications.

Considine, M. 2002. Joined at the Lip? What Does Network Research Tell Us about Governance? *Knowledge Networks and Joined-up Government: Conference Proceedings*, University of Melbourne, Centre for Public Policy.

———. Conway, S., O. Jones, and F. Steward. 2001. "Realising the potential of the network perspective in innovation studies." In *Social Action and Organisational Change: Aston Perspectives on Innovation Networks*, edited by O. Jones, S. Conway, and F. Steward, London: Imperial College Press.

Cook, K. S. 1977. "Exchange and Power in Networks of Interorganizational Relations." *Sociological Quarterly* 18: 62–82.

Cross, R., and R. Thomas. 2009. *Driving Results Through Social Networks: How Top Organizations Leverage Networks for Performance and Growth.* San Francisco, CA: Jossey-Bass.

Dill, W. 1958. "Environment as an Influence on Managerial Autonomy." *Administrative Science Quarterly* 2: 409–43.

DiMaggio, P., and W. Powell. 1983. "The Iron Cage Revisited: Institutional Isomorphism and Collective Rationality in Organizational Fields." *American Sociological Review* 48: 147–60.

Dowding, K. 1994. "Policy Networks: Don't Stretch a Good Idea too Far." In *Contempory Political Studies,* edited by P. Dunleavy and J. Stanyer, 59–78. Belfast: Political Science Association.

———. 1995. "Model or Metaphor? A Critical Review of the Policy Network Approach." *Political Studies* 43 (1): 136–58.

Ferlie, E. and A. Pettigrew. 1996. "Managing Through Networks: Some Issues and Implications for the NHS." *British Journal of Management* 7 (March): 81–99.

Fombrun, C. J. 1982. "Strategies for Network Research in Organizations." *Academy of Management Review* 7(2): 280–91.

Freeman, L. C. 1979. "Centrality in Networks: Conceptual Clarification." *Social Networks* 1: 215–39.

Freeman, L. 2004. *The Development of Social Network Analysis: A Study in the Sociology of Society.* Vancouver, BC: Empirical Press

Friedman, R. 1984. *Strategic Management: A Stakeholder Approach.* Boston: Pitman Press.

Gage, R., and M. Mandell, eds. 1990. *Strategies for Managing Intergovernmental Policies and Networks.* Praeger: New York.

Goldsmith, S., and W. Eggers. 2004. *Governing by Network: The New Shape of the Public Sector.* Washington DC: The Brookings Institution.

Grandori, A., and G. Soda. 1995. "Inter-firm Networks: Antecedents, Mechanisms and Forms." *Organization Studies* 16 (2): 183–214.

Granovetter, M. 1973. "The Strength of Weak Ties." *American Journal of Sociology* 78: 1360–80.

———. 1983. "The Strength of Weak Ties: A Network Theory Revisited." *Sociological Theory* 201–33.

Gulati, R. 2007. *Managing Network Resources: Alliances, Affiliations and other Relational Assets.* New York: Oxford University Press.

Hanf, K. and L. J. O'Toole. 1992. "Revisiting Old Friends: Networks, Implementation Structures and the Management of Inter-Organizational Relations." *European Journal of Political Research,* 21 (1): 163–80.

Hanf, K. and F. W. Scharpf, eds. 1978. *Interorganizational Policy Making: Limits to Coordination and Central Control.* London: Sage Publications.

Hasenfeld, Y. 1983. *Human Services Organizations.* Englewood Cliffs, NJ: Prentice-Hall.

Heclo, H. and A. Widavsky. 1974. *The Private Government of Public Money.* London: Macmillan.

Hibbert, P., C. Huxham, and P. Ring. 2008. "Managing Collaborative Inter-Organizational Relations." In *The Oxford Handbook of Inter-Organizational Relations* edited by S. Cropper, Mark Ebers, C. Huxham, and P. Smith Ring, 390–416. Oxford: Oxford University Press.

Hjern, B., and D. Porter. 1981. "Implementation Structures: A New Unit for Administrative Analysis." *Organizational Studies* 3: 211–37.

Isett, K. R., I. A. Mergel, K. LeRoux, P. A. Mischen, and R. K. Rethemeyer. 2011. "Networks in Public Administration Scholarship: Understanding Where We Are and Where We Need To Go." *Journal of Public Administration Research and Theory* 21 (1): 167.

Jordan, G., and J. J. Richardson. 1983. "Policy Communities: The British and European Style." *Policy Studies Journal* 11 (4): 603–15.

Jones, C., W. Hesterly, and S. P. Borgatti. 1997. "A General Theory of Network Governance: Exchange Conditions and Social Mechanisms." *Academy of Management Review* 22 (4): 911–45.

Keast, R. 2011. "Joined-up Governance in Australia: How the Past Can Inform the Future." *International Journal of Public Administration* 34 (4): 221–31.

Keast, R., K. Brown, and M. P. Mandell. 2007. "Getting the Right Mix: Unpacking Integration Meanings and Strategies." *International Public Management Journal* 10 (1): 9–33.

Kenis, P., and V. Schneider. 1991. "Policy Networks and Policy Analysis: Scrutinizing a New Analytical Toolbox." In *Policy Networks. Empirical Evidence and Theoretical Considerations,* edited by B. Marin and R. Mayntz, 25–59. Frankfurt: Campus.

Kickert, W. J. M., and J. Koppenjan. 1997. "Public Management and Network Management: An Overview." In *Managing Complex Networks: Strategies for the Public Sector,* edited by W. Kickert, E-H. Klijn, and J. Koppenjan, 35–61. London: Sage Publications.

Klijn, E-H. 1997. "Policy Networks and Network Management: A State of the Art." In *Managing Complex Networks: Strategies for the Public Sector,* edited by W. Kickert, E-H. Klijn, and J. Koppenjan, 14–34. London: Sage Publications.

———. 2005. "Networks and Inter-organisational Management, Challenging Steering, Evaluation and the Role of Public Actors in Public Management." In *The Oxford Handbook of Public Management Oxford,* edited by E. Ferlie, L. Lynn, and C. Pollitt, 257–81.

———. 2008. "Policy and Implementation Networks: Managing Complex Interactions." In *The Oxford Handbook of Inter-Organizational Relations,* edited by S. Cropper, M. Ebers, C. Huxhan, and P. Smith-Ring, 118–46. London: Routledge.

Klijn, E-H., and J. Koppenjan. 2000. "Public Management and Policy Networks: Foundations of a Network Approach to Governance." *Public Management Review* 2 (2): 135–58.

Kickert, W. J. M., E. Klijn, and J. Koppenjan, eds. 1997. *Managing Complex Networks: Strategies for the Public Sector.* London: Sage Publications.

Kilduff, M., and W. Tsai. 2003. *Social Networks and Organizations.* London: Sage Publications.

Konrad, E. 1996. "A Multidimensional Framework for Conceptualising Human Services Integration Initiatives." In *Evaluating Initiatives to Integrate Human Services: A Publication of the American Evaluation Association Number 69,* edited by J. M. Marquart and E. Konrad. San Francisco: Jossey-Bass.

Koppenjan, J., and E-H. Klijn. 2004. *Managing Uncertainties in Networks.* London: Routledge.

Kooiman, J. 1993. *Modern Governance: New Government-Society Interactions.* London: Sage Publications.

Levine, S., and P. White. 1961. "Exchange as a Conceptual Framework for the Study of Interorganizational Relationships." *Administrative Sciences Quarterly* 6 (4): 395–420.

Lin, N. 2001. *Social Capital: A Theory of Social Structure and Action.* London: Cambridge University Press.

Lorrain, F., and H. White. 1971. "Structural Equivalence of Individuals in Social Networks." *Journal of Mathematical Society* 7: 49–80.

Luce, R., and A. Perry. 1949. "A Method of Matrix Analysis of Group Structure." *Psychometrika* 14 (2): 95–116.

McKelvey, B. 1982. *Organizational Systematics: Taxonomy, Evolution, Classification.* Berkeley: University of California Press.

McGuire, M. 2002. "Managing Networks: Propositions on What Managers Do and Why They Do It." *Public Administration Review* 62 (5): 599–609.

McGuire, M., and R. Agranoff. 2011. "The Limitations of Public Management Networks." *Public Administration* 89 (2): 265–84.

Mandell, M. P. 1994. "Managing Interdependencies through Program Structures: A Revised Paradigm." *American Review of Public Administration* 24(1): 99–121.

Mandell, M. P., and T. Steelman. 2003. "Understanding What Can Be Accomplished Through Interorganizational Innovations: The Importance of Typologies, Context and Management." *Public Management Review* 5(2): 197–224.

Marsh, David, and R.A.W. Rhodes, eds. 1992. *Policy Networks in British Government.* Oxford: Clarendon Press.

Meier, Kenneth J., and Laurence J. O'Toole. 2002. "Public Management and Organizational Performance: The Impact of Managerial Quality." *Journal of Policy Analysis and Management* 21 (4): 629–43.

———. 2001. "Managerial Strategies and Behavior in Networks: A Model with Evidence from U.S. Public Education." *Journal of Public Administration Research and Theory* 11(3): 271–93.

Meier, K. J. and L. J. O'Toole. 2005. "Managerial Networking: Issues of Management and Research Design." *Administration and Society* 37 (5): 523–41.

———. Milgram, S. 1967. "The Small-World Problem." *Psychology Today* 1 (1): 61–7.

Mitchell, J.C., ed. 1969. *Social Networks in Urban Situations.* Manchester: Manchester University Press.

Möller, K., and D. T. Wilson. 1995. "Interaction and Network Approach to Business Marketing: A Review and Evaluation." In *Business Marketing: An Interaction and Network Perspective*, edited by K. Möller and D. Wilson, 587–613. Boston, Kluwer.

Moreno, J. L. 1934. *Who Shall Survive?* Washington, DC: Mental Diseases Publishing Company.

Oliver, A., and M. Ebers. 1998. Networking Network Studies: An Analysis of Conceptual Configurations in the Study of Inter-Organizational Relationships. *Organization Studies* 19 (4): 549–83.

Oliver, C. 1990. "Determinants of Interorganizational Relationships: Integration And Future Directions." *Academy of Management Review* 15: 241–65.

O'Toole, L. J. 1996. "Hollowing the Infrastructure: Revolving Loan Programs and the Network Dynamics in the American States." *Journal of Public Administration Research and Theory* 6: 225–42.

O'Toole, Jr., L. J. 1997. "Treating Networks Seriously: Practical and Research Based Agendas in Public Administration." *Public Administration Review* 57, 45–52.

Powell, W. W. 1990. "Neither Market nor Hierarchy: Network Forms of Organization." *Research in Organization Behavior* 12: 295–336.

Pressman, J., and A. Wildavsky. 1983. *Implementation: How Great Expectations in Washington are Dashed in Oakland*. Berkeley: University of California Press.

Provan, K.G., and H. B. Milward, 1991. "Institutional Level Norms and Organizational Involvement in a Service Implementation Network." *Journal of Public Administration Research and Theory* 1(4): 391–417.

———. 1995. "A Preliminary Theory of Inter-organizational Network Effectiveness: A Comparative Study of Four Mental Health Systems." *Administrative Science Quarterly* 40 (1): 1–33.

———. 2001. "Do Networks Really work? A Framework for Evaluating Public-Sector Organizational Networks." *Public Administration Review* 61 (4): 414–23.

Provan, K. G. and J. Sebastain. 1998. "Networks Within Networks: Service Link Overlap. Organizational Cliques and Network Effectiveness." *Academy of Management Journal* 41 (4): 453–63.

Provan, K.G. and P. Kenis. 2007. "Models of Network Governance: Structure, Management and Effectiveness." *Journal of Public Administration Research and Theory* 18: 229–252.

Putnam, R.D. (1993). *Making Democracy Work: Civic Traditions in Modern Italy*. Princeton, NJ: Princeton University Press.

Raab, J., and S. Suijkerbuijk. 2009. "Heading Towards a Network Theory of Effectiveness: A Replication with Set-Theoretic Extension of Provan and Milward (1995)." Paper presented at the XXIX Sunbelt Conference, San Diego, CA: March 10–15.

Rhodes, R. A. W. 1986. *European Policy Making, Implementation and Sub-central Governments: A Survey*. Maastricht: European Institute of Public Administration.

Rhodes, R. (1997). *Understanding Governance: Policy Networks, Governance, Reflexivity and Accountability*. Buckingham: Open University Press.

Richardson, J. J., and A. G. Jordan. 1979. *Governing Under Pressure*. Oxford: Martin Robertson.

Salancik, G. R. 1995. "WANTED: A Good Network Theory of Organization." *Administrative Science Quarterly* 40 (2): 345–54.

Scharpf, F. F. W. 1978. "Interorganizational Policy Studies: Issues, Concepts and Perspectives." In *Games Real Actors Play: Actor Centered Institutionalism in Policy Research,* edited by K. Hannf and F. Scharpf. Boulder, CO: Westview Press.

Scott, J. 2000. *Social Network Analysis: A Handbook,* second edition. London: Sage Publications.

Scott, W. Richard. 2001. *Institutions and Organizations,* 2nd ed. Thousand Oaks, CA: Sage Publications.

Shrum, W. and N. Mullins. 1988. "Network Analysis in the Study of Science and Technology." In *Handbook of Quantitative Studies of Science and Technology,* edited by A. van Ran, 107–33. Amsterdam, Elsevier.

Skelcher, C., and H. Sullivan. 2008. "Theory Driven Approaches to Analyzing Collaborative Performance." *Public Management Review* 10 (6): 751–71.

Sørensen, E., and J. Torfing. 2007. *Theories of Democratic Network Governance.* Baskingstoke, Hampshire: Palgrave Macmillan.

Stone, W. 2000. *Measuring Social Capital, Research Paper No. 2.* Melbourne: Australian Institute for Family Studies.

Sutton, R., and B. Staw. 1995. "What Theory Is Not." *Administrative Science Quarterly* 40 (3): 371–84.

Turrini, A., D. Christofoli, F. Frosini, and G. Nasi. 2010. "Networking Literature About Determinants of Network Effectiveness." *Public Administration* 88 (2): 528–50.

Waarden, F. 1992. "Dimensions and Types of Policy Networks." *European Journal of Political Research* 21 (1) Special Issue: 29–52.

Wasserman, S., and K. Faust. 1994. *Social Network Analysis: Methods and Applications.* Cambridge: Cambridge University Press.

New Theoretical Frameworks

Informing Design, Governance
Arrangements, and Management

3 A Composite Theory of Leadership and Management

Process Catalyst and Strategic Leveraging—Theory of Deliberate Action in Collaborative Networks

Robyn Keast and Myrna P. Mandell

INTRODUCTION

Networks have become such an accepted part of our understanding of how public policies and programs can be achieved that they are almost taken for granted. Unfortunately this general acceptance has often turned into an idealistic complacency, one in which the focus is more on the promise of networks, rather than their realities. The end result of this has often been failures that could have been avoided, learning opportunities missed and, increasingly, a "bad name" for networks. Collaborative networks are a particular case in point. These structures can deliver on high expectations, but the unique properties that make them viable can also render them vulnerable. Of major importance is a focus on achieving systemic changes, the existence of reciprocal interdependence between actors as well as deeper/denser relationships and a focus on relationships not tasks, and therefore different ways of working and behaving.

All networks are focused on accomplishing tasks by working with others. However, in collaborative networks this aspect, while important, is not the critical emphasis. Instead, collaborative networks are centered on changing the way people are accustomed to working in their individual organizations. This shift requires participants to first recognize their reliance on each other and then to agree to behave differently, both in terms of their relationships and dealings with each other, and within their own organizations. The focus is therefore not primarily about how to work more efficiently with others, but is instead about how to build new types of relationships among the participants to change their behavior. Because there are no "followers" or superior-subordinate relationships in collaborative networks, it is argued that traditional "leadership" approaches do not always apply. The process catalyst function has been presented as a viable alternative (Mandell and Keast 2009).

Several network management approaches have been developed that clearly distinguish between management in a single organization and management of a network of organizations (Klijn and Koppenjan 2000; Agranoff and McGuire 2001; Agranoff 2007; McGuire 2002). While important foundations, these management models generally underestimate the need to strategically connect and leverage relationships for collaborative advantage (Mandell and Keast 2009). This is critical in collaborative networks where participants must also strategically leverage their relationships to "reinvent" themselves and build a new collective whole (Innes and Booher 2010) necessary for systems change. It therefore becomes important for collaborative network leaders to not only conceptualize and facilitate the relationships that connect people; they must also actively manage these social resources to be converted to public value.

Given the current proliferation of collaborative networks and the fact that they are likely to continue for some time, concerns with the leadership and management of such arrangements for optimal outcomes are increasingly relevant. It is hypothesized that the achievement of collaborative advantage via collaborative networks is a product of leadership action that conceptualizes and builds relational connections and a management approach that makes connections and leverages these to produce the synergies necessary for change. The goal of this chapter therefore is to test a synthesis model of network leadership and management based on the concepts of process catalyst and strategic leveraging and investigate the implications of this new, composite direction in network theory.

The chapter first highlights the unique characteristics of collaborative networks. This is followed by a description and explanation of the concepts of process catalyst and strategic leveraging, culminating in a proposed composite theoretical model. This theoretical model is then tested on a set of public sector case studies. The chapter concludes with theoretical implications for the future.

COLLABORATIVE NETWORKS DEFINED

In the literature, networks have often been loosely referred to as collaborations (see for example Huxham and Vangen 1996, 2005; Isett et al. 2011) indicting any type of arrangement in which individuals from different organizations and/or groups work together on a project(s) or problem(s). A number of authors have developed typologies providing clear points of differentiation for various network types, including collaborative networks (Agranoff 2007; Konrad 1996; Keast, Brown, and Mandell 2007). Collaborative networks are used in this chapter, not in the general sense of collaborating, but rather as a distinct and unique type of network. Collaborative networks go beyond networks that operate with stridently autonomous and independent organizations and loose, even competitive, relationships, to more complex *reciprocal interdependencies* and closer, denser relationships in which participants are engaging in *system changes* (Keast et al. 2004; Keast, Brown, and Mandell 2007).

Collaborative networks are formed to deal with very complex problems that no one organization or group is able to deal with on their own.

The participants recognize that the way they currently operate is no longer working and new and innovative solutions that go beyond just cooperating and sharing information or coordinating their present operations are needed (Keast, Brown, and Mandell 2007). As Innes and Booher (1999, 12) note "rather than a solution to a known problem [collaboration produces] a new way of framing the situation and developing unanticipated combinations of action that are qualitatively different from the options on the table at the outset". According to these authors, negotiations in collaborative networks occur not in the sense of finding compromises or quid pro quo arrangements, but rather in creating "new collective value" (Innes and Booher 1999, 15). This means that the members are engaged in activities that go beyond making changes at the margins in how they operate. Instead they are involved in actions requiring major changes in their operations. By focusing primarily on relationships, rather than just achieving tasks, the emphasis in collaborative networks is on building the kind of trust that will allow participants to find new ways of working together.

A further characteristic of a collaborative network is that the purpose is not to develop strategies to solve problems related to the tasks of any one organization per se (although this does take place), but rather to *leverage relationship assets* to meet future/intended outcomes through developing more innovative solutions (Innes and Booher 2010; Mandell 1994, 2001; Steelman and Carmin 2002; Kilduff and Krackhardt 2008).

Although all networks are assumed to be made up of interdependent members (O'Toole 1997); in collaborative networks the type of interdependence involved is more expansive. In a collaborative network, members know they are dependent on each other in such a way that for the actions of one to be effective they must rely on the actions of another. There is an understanding that "they cannot meet their interests working alone and that they share with others a common problem" (Innes and Booher 2000, 7). This goes beyond just resource dependence, data needs, common clients, or geographic issues, although these may be involved. It involves a need to make a collective commitment to change the way in which they are currently operating (Mandell 1994, 107). We refer to this type of interdependence as *reciprocal interdependence*.

In the next sections, the effect of the unique characteristics of collaborative networks on leadership and network management are highlighted and the concepts of process catalyst and strategic leveraging are developed.

SYNTHESIZING LEADERSHIP AND MANAGEMENT: PROCESS CATALYST AND STRATEGIC LEVERAGING

Increasingly there has been a shift away from the conventional "single leader and multi-follower concept and to organizational leadership in a pluralistic sense" (Barnes and Kriger 1986, 15) and a growing network leadership theoretic (Bass 1990; Kilduff and Tsai 2003). An increasing awareness of the importance of social relations in the leadership contract (Bolden, 2004) has led to more recent studies concerning themselves with the notion of leadership as a more relational process. Referred to as informal, emergent, or dispersed and distributed, these new models present leadership as an emergent property of a group or network of interacting individuals, rather than a phenomenon that arises from the individual or the context. Furthermore, because leadership within this perspective is centered on performing acts that assist the network/group to meet goals and maintain itself, varieties of expertise are distributed across many members.

Many of the new leadership aspects, with their emphasis on facilitation rather than direction and a focus on interactions not individuals, have strong resonance with networks and network leadership characteristics (Huxham and Vangen 1996, 2005). This chapter argues that while these newer theories and understandings of leadership apply quite well to most networks, they are not sufficient to fully explain leadership in collaborative networks. Because collaborative networks rely on reciprocal relationships, the leadership focus is directed to the interactions and dynamic processes required to build the requisite relational strengths capable of breaking through existing mindsets and operating mechanisms and creating new relationships and support systems. The term "process catalyst" developed by Mandell and Keast (2009) describes this new type of leadership. The process catalyst leadership role places greater value and emphasis on establishing an environment for building strong relationships, and securing commitment to common goals rather than on just achieving tasks.

The key in collaborative networks is not on reaching agreement among members, per se, but rather recognizing the overriding need to be committed to the change process as a whole. Thus as Edwards and Stern (1998, 13) note: "partners need to fully explore alternatives and avoid agreeing simply to maintain harmony". To do this requires a high level of trust among participants and takes much time and effort to develop. The process catalyst type of leadership therefore calls for a leadership style that is able to make connections, to bridge diverse cultures, and that can get participants to be comfortable sharing ideas, resources, and power.

Innes and Booher (1999, 14) discuss the focus of collaborative networks as being "on inventing strategy to change a broad array of interlinked activities" and to create "new collective value" (1999, 15). It is argued that creating new collective value arises from the combinations and recombinations of the various perspectives, resources, skills, and commitment of diverse actors; a process referred to as synergy (Fried and Rundall 1994). Lasker, Weiss, and Millier (2001, 184) asserted that synergy is the core goal of collaboration because it is through this combination of resources that "something new and valuable" is created that moves beyond making changes at the margins of operations to generating major changes. These major changes may range from deleting or changing the rules and regulations within the participants' organizations or agreeing to give up or take on new responsibilities in carrying out their operations, or even forming entirely new entities. In this way relationships are more than the integrating mechanism, they become network assets that must be managed to achieve broader public goods (Gulati 2007). The need to leverage relationships and capitalize on the synergies generated is a different kind of management tool than those in the existing literature. It is a tool that is strategic to the effectiveness of collaborative networks. We refer to this as *strategic leveraging*.

Strategic Leveraging

Strategic leveraging recognizes the worth of each participant and the importance of the interactions among them. More importantly, relationships must also be "mobilized, managed and leveraged to secure value" (Keast 2011, 227–228) Successful integrative arrangements require a careful assessment of the nature and strength of relationships and a strategic approach to their formation and management (Gage and Mandell 1990; Keast, Brown, and Mandell 2007).

Managers need to leverage the particular mix of properties inherent in collaborative networks that allow the synergies to be created. The focus is on the interactions and processes that are required to build strong and ongoing relationships, capable of breaking through existing mechanisms and creating new systems and innovative responses.

Attention is still paid to accomplishing tasks, but managers and persuasive individuals in networks need to change the norms by which people operate in their individual organizations. As a first step, this means participants need to practice and grow accustomed to behaving differently, both with one another in the network setting and within their own organizations.

Strategic relationship building in collaborative networks involves establishing new terms of engagement by getting participants to listen to each other and to recognize each other's worth. This goes beyond just building trust among participants. The key is not only to begin to understand and respect each other, but also to be able to *capitalize on these relationships for further efforts*.

In collaborative networks, managers must possess an adaptive capacity that enables them to understand how to strategically manage relationships. This includes attracting and engaging the right people, including people that might be considered "unlikely" or different, and facilitating their capacity to build a new whole and mobilize needed resources sufficient to making the effort work. Simply put, this kind of network practice must produce innovative outcomes (Keast 2011, 227). Strategic leveraging provides managers the framework through which to make this happen.

Doing this successfully involves *carefully curating* who needs to be involved in the network, gauging and evaluating the strengths of various relationships among participants, understanding how and when to facilitate relationships, and recognizing opportunities to help network members see and seize strategic leverage for synergistic outcomes. Respectful and complex relationships among members are necessary in collaborative networks, but capitalizing on those relationships is critical for success. As Mandell (1994, 107) noted, the "techniques that make use of the network are utilized rather than the techniques that just try to manipulate, coordinate, and otherwise maneuver through individual organizations".

In the next section, a set of case studies of collaborative networks are presented to show how the application of both process catalyst and strategic leveraging activities made a difference in their ability to deliver effective outcomes.

RESEARCH DESIGN

Four cases were drawn from multiple levels of government and community operation, including The Kimberly Process (KP), the Tropical North Queensland Tourism Development Program (TNQTDP), The Water Forum (WF), and the Service Integration Project (SIP). A multiple case study approach was applied to overcome the limitations of single-case analysis and add to the rigor of the findings (Stewart 2012; Isett et al. 2011).

Semi-structured interviews were undertaken to build the cases. Interview respondents included network members as well as identified key informants in the external environment. The use of a semi-structured interview approach allowed respondents to describe their understandings and experiences of the network—in particular the impact of leadership and management approaches—in their own words (Denzin 1984). In addition, in the Australian cases focus groups were used to gain additional information from participants on their experience in shaping and operating within networks. In all cases a review of relevant written documentation, such as project reports and internal correspondence as well as background data secured from the Internet, was used to supplement the interview information. This array of data sources and data-gathering mechanisms has allowed for results to be "triangulated", with the findings of one research tool testing and confirming the results of others.

CASE OVERVIEW AND ANALYSIS

The Kimberly Project and Tropical North Queensland Tourism Development Project

The KP is an international network formed to stem the flow of "conflict" or "blood diamonds" throughout the world. It represented a major undertaking, involving countries from around the world, nonprofit agencies/

nongovernment organizations (NGOs) and major commercial interests in the diamond industry (Beffert and Benner 2007a). As a result of the network's efforts, the United Nations (UN) passed Resolution 1306 in 2000 prohibiting the direct or indirect import of rough diamonds from Sierra Leone. The network also established a Certification Scheme to ensure that conflict diamonds would not be traded in member countries, nor would member countries import diamonds from or export diamonds to nonmember countries (Beffert and Benner 2007b, 240).

The emphasis in the beginning stages of the KP centered on bringing the right players on board, building relationships and connections between them, and securing commitment to common goals. Initially Global Witness (an NGO committed to bringing attention to the problem of blood diamonds) was responsible for bringing key actors on board and building commitment using processes from previously successful collaborative initiates, including informal meetings allowing members to better know one another, gain clarity about one another's positions, and build areas of trust and mutual confidence. This allowed the focus to be kept on reaching consensus during subsequent meetings and led to the initial agreement on the Kimberley Process Certification System. Other members, for example Great Britain and the United States, acted as mediators between potentially problematic relationships and used their "power" to sponsor the project. This helped make the early stages of the KP fast-moving and highly productive.

Over time, the NGOs stepped back from the process and let the international body proceed with developing working groups to carry out the tasks that needed to be accomplished. Specific network leadership was provided by the group chair. This individual, an acknowledged expert on conflict diamonds, brought legitimacy and critical skills to the process. More importantly, he kept participants focused on the big picture and helped them to stay "on track" and avoid becoming bogged down in minor issues (acting as a process catalyst leader).

The emphasis in the beginning stages of the KP was on ensuring that it was built on solid ground. Global Witness and the other NGOs involved were less concerned with how tasks would be accomplished than they were with how to maintain the eventual process that resulted.

Global Witness also understood the need to deal with both the political and economic factors that had an impact on the process. In this instance, they understood the need to put pressure on both the UN and the diamond industry to support the KP. This provided the leverage needed to not only form the network, but also to ensure that all key stakeholders would be part of the process. The network's representatives from Great Britain also engaged in strategic leveraging when they brought together additional representatives from key importing countries to secure their commitment. Many of the members were part of the G8 Summit and their involvement resulted in the continued support of the KP in crafting political solutions to the problem.

The TNQTDP was formed to find innovative ways to boost the regional tourism industry in Tropical North Queensland (TNQ), Australia. Initial project scoping reports by a team of consultants from Southern Cross University (SCU) identified that there were opportunities to develop farm-food- and nature-based tourism experiences. To support the establishment of this new tourism enterprise, participants such as local farming, hospitality, and natural resource management stakeholders; government bodies (including economic development and land use planning); and local councils formed a Project Management Committee (PMC) and a Stakeholder Reference Group (SRG). These groups, coupled with associated structures and processes, provided the framework for collaborative action under the overall guidance of the consultants.

The work of the PMC and the SRG went beyond just briefing participants about the region and its tourism potential. They also laid the groundwork for an understanding of the importance and benefit of building on existing strategies through working together. This action resulted in all the relevant agencies in government and industry working collaboratively in new ways and contributing to a "big picture approach" to regional food and tourism development. There was also recognition from the outset by the SCU team of the need to educate and train participants in how to build new types of relationships. This occurred through meetings, ostensibly focused on the sharing of food, which enabled participants to relate to each other on a different level. The goodwill generated was then capitalized upon when they were involved in discussions around agriculture and tourism.

Work undertaken through the SRG enabled new thinking around these issues and has resulted in amendments to the state government legislative planning frameworks for the TNQ region. This development has opened the way for new, more accommodative policies to be included in local government land use and economic development plans.

It was understood that just getting the right people together was not enough when working through a collaborative network. Instead, the emphasis was on strategic relationship leveraging. This was achieved in this case in a number of ways. First and foremost, from the outset the consultants recognized the need to identify the most influential local people to involve in the program and the need to bring them on board. This action set the stage for a two-pronged approach. On the one hand, the SRG provided the leverage for key decision-makers to influence and ensure support from key policy-makers. In addition, the workshops conducted by the consultants not only provided education and training for all the participants of the collaborative network, but fostered new understanding among organizations that previously did not relate to each other. This has led to the diversification of both the agricultural and tourism industries in the TNQ region and has resulted in strengthening the region's economic base.

By leveraging the synergy created by those involved in the TNQTDP, there was a positive effect on the policy environment in areas such as land use planning and economic development within the region. Further funding and commitment of resources by stakeholders in the regional SRG has enabled implementation of the recommendations arising from the TNQ Food Tourism Strategy. The collaborative process has had a positive effect as evidenced by the growing number of projects that are being modeled on the TNQTDP approach.

Service Integration Project and the Water Forum

Both the SIP and WF were established by government agencies to overcome a major crisis. In SIP it was the death of an elderly citizen clearly linked to fragmented policies and services (Keast et al. 2004; Boorman and Woolcock 2002). In the WF, it was due to the growing problems of water supply for the Sacramento region of California (Connick 2006). The initial idea in both cases was that all that was needed was for the various agencies and organizations involved to better coordinate their efforts through joint planning and programming. From the outset, however, both sets of network members recognized that they needed to fundamentally change the way that they interacted and worked together. Central to this was the realization that they had to build better relationships to be able to achieve the collaborative outcomes deemed necessary. In both cases it was imperative to change the way programs were usually run. The focus was on building new types of relationships. In the WF case, the city and county actors acknowledged that that new relationships needed to be established and that their role was not being "in charge", but rather allowing participants to develop new ways of working with each other. As a result, all representatives were treated equally and allowed to develop the process as necessary to reach new agreements. Similarly, SIP members practiced new ways of working together and developed a set of mutually agreed upon terms of engagement to guide their interactions and activities.

To further facilitate these improved relationships, both networks drew on specialist programs—with SIP members undertaking a graduate certificate in interprofessional development and the WF engaging in interest-based negotiation. For both SIP and the WF, there was evidence of an awareness that different people brought specific skills, attributes, and linkages to the network and there were times when these people would "come to the fore and share the leadership roles" (Keast 2004, 143). However, both projects also relied heavily, at least initially, on outside consultants who helped repair previously strained relations between members and to build sufficient levels of connection to achieve change. Such a function was important in both cases, but particularly in the WF where most of the participants had not only been adversaries, but also litigants in a number of court cases. In the SIP case, although the facilitator remained involved in a peripheral manner, two internal leaders gradually emerged to take on the "group-ware" or "process minding" role. By way of their overall view of the network these leaders also refined and sustained the vision, identified points of synergy, and began to make relational connections.

Simultaneous to the new leadership roles, within the two cases the role of a network "driver" was constantly mentioned as a necessary function to keep network members on track and working toward directed action and collective outcomes. SIP respondents indicated a realization that building better relationships, while necessary, had to be used to deliver outcomes. One respondent expanded the concept: "she is the driver; she sticks the pins in and keeps us on track" (Keast 2004, 146). Within the WF, the driver function was provided by an outside consultant who monitored the process and ensured participants focused on the big picture.

As a result of a highly deliberate approach to relationship building, strategic connection, and leveraging of relational/social capital, both the SIP and WF were able to meet their goals. For SIP, this was the provision of integrated, locally specific services and programs, a new governance regime, and improved infrastructure and facilities (Boorman and Woolcock 2002; Keast et al. 2004). For the WF, it was the establishment of a memorandum of understanding, which commits the signatories to work together in new ways over the next 30 years.

Table 3.1 provides a summary of each of the cases, highlighting their change foci, various leadership functions, and achievements against their goals.

Each of these cases demonstrates that while distributed leadership is a feature of collaborative networks, the existence of a process catalyst type of leader—focused on building and minding relationships, identifying points of connection and cleavage, and making synergistic connections—coupled with the strategic leveraging or "driving" of these relationships are also crucial to secure value-added network outcomes. Participants recognized the importance of acting strategically to build the relationship strength necessary for collaboration, creating connections with potential synergies, and then leveraging from this value-added relational capital to affect change.

Moreover, it is evident that this mix is the result of deliberate action based on a solid cognition of the network relationships and engineering these to the network purpose. In all cases there was evidence of the importance of the catalyst or driver role. What is interesting to note is that this role was not necessarily confined to the participants in the collaborative networks. In the TNQTDP, SIP, and WF, for instance, this role was played (at least initially) by an outside consultant.

Table 3.1 *Case summary*

Case	Description, Change Foci	Process Catalyst	Strategic Leveraging	Outcomes
Kimberly Process (KP)	International network formed to try to stem the flow of "conflict diamonds" or "blood diamonds".	Initial Efforts: NGO group brought the key players on board and ensured their commitment. Ongoing Efforts: Core group and key leaders sustained big picture focus for participants; relationship-building events, common purpose and commitment established and checked; ongoing negotiation and resolution.	Initial Efforts: To elevate awareness internationally about the prospects and problems of buying conflict diamonds. Inclusion of all relevant stakeholders to gain their ongoing commitment. Ongoing Efforts: Britain's involvement with representatives of all the governments involved resulted in the leaders of the G8 countries acknowledging the problems associated with conflict diamonds. Initiating core countries built on earlier work and processes to maintain the focus on the big picture and deliver outcomes.	KP Certification Scheme UN Resolution condemning blood diamonds and supporting the continued work of the KP. Agreement by diamond import/export countries and diamond industry to monitor diamond trade.

(Continued)

Table 3.1 *(Continued)*

Case	Description, Change Foci	Process Catalyst	Strategic Leveraging	Outcomes
Tropical North Queensland Tourism Development Project (TNQTDP)	To find innovative means to boost the regional tourism industry in North Queensland, Australia.	Initial Efforts: Consultants to educate and train participants in building new types of relationships. Ongoing Efforts: PMC and SRG focused on a big picture approach Workshop leaders encouraged and relationships developed among all participants, and emphasized the benefits of networking and the value of leveraging strategic relationships.	Initial Efforts: Coordinators recognized the need to identify the most influential local people to involve in the program and bring them on board. Ongoing Efforts: Consultants focused on relationships within the network and ensured support from members' parent organizations via broader engagement strategies and application of pressure on core bodies. Regional stakeholders provided knowledge and a support network for participants; acted as advocates for change and collaboration.	Diversification of both the agricultural and tourism industries in the TNQ region and has resulted in strengthening the region's economic base. All the relevant agencies in government and industry working collaboratively in new ways and contributing to a "big picture approach" to regional food and tourism development. Regional Food Network steering committee established and the TNQ Regional Food Network has been incorporated and is now actively recruiting members with a key objective to begin developing local groups to feed into the Regional Food Network and enterprise. Strengthening of the region's economic base

SIP	Integrated social services and regional governance	Initially undertaken by facilitator Grad Cert set "agreed process check" for membership	Use of new language and a set of mutually agreed terms of engagement to guide actions Undertaken by a core leader/ management duo within the network; described as driving relationships through the development of new relationship-building skills	Integrated, locally specific services and programs, a new governance regime, and improved infrastructure and facilities
WF	Management of regional water supply in Northern California	The use of interest-based negotiations initially by an outside consultant and later used by the subcommittees to keep the focus on the importance of maintaining new relationships. Consultant continued to monitor the interactions and relationships and provide feedback against collaborative principles Subcommittees used interest-based negotiations to keep the focus on the importance of maintaining new relationships	All key stakeholders in the region are included in the process. All participants brought all potential agreements to their parent organizations for approval before the network reached agreement.	Memorandum of Understanding (MOU) committing all members to work together and to be committed to implementing changes for the next 30 years. Numerous other contracts and agreements among participants to work together in new ways

THEORETICAL IMPLICATIONS AND CONCLUSIONS

This chapter confirms the theoretical proposition that to match and achieve their potential collaborative networks require leadership and management approaches over and above those used in other types of networks. Furthermore, it has shown that it is the combination of the process catalyst and strategic leveraging functions that enable network actors to establish and use their relationships to secure outcomes. A number of theoretical considerations therefore arise.

First, network leaders/managers require an ability to accurately identify and conceptualize the nature and patterns of connections and/or cleavage between members, as well as potential synergies and develop strategies that forge effective change coalitions. The capacity to read the network and act as a "connector" involves both high-level social intelligence capability (Goldman 2006; Koch and Lockwood 2010) as well as an appreciation of network structure and positions as influence mechanisms (Balkundi and Kilduff 2006). As Evans and Wolf (2009, 36–37) note, collaborative leaders "connect people by being very well connected themselves". These are skills that are generally not appreciated or supported in conventional practice and will need to be developed and fostered for collaborative networks to prosper (Keast and Mandell 2012). Associated with this is the development of social tools and mechanisms that facilitate and explicate the higher relational capital needed for collaborative networks. A number of authors have provided useful exemplars of such tools and artifacts, including training and education programs and narrative story-telling in relation to the former (Keast 2004; Keast et al. 2004; Huxham and Vangen 1996) and, for the latter, social network analysis, mental mind maps, and argumentative mapping (Kilduff and Tsai 2003; Church et al. 2003; Dragicevic and Balram 2004).

The second consideration relates to a combination of process catalyst and strategic leveraging functions. While often depicted as separate functions, the overlap apparent across the cases indicates a level of integration between leadership and management in collaborative networks. Gratton and Erikson (2009) refer to this relationship and task mix as ambidextrous leadership and indicate that this ought to be a core development goal for network workers. As collaborative network managers/leaders consider their role, they will need to know and perform as both. Finally, collaborative networks demand more than ad hoc or opportunistic linking. To deliver on their potential they require very deliberate, purposeful action, directed at strategically building and using connections to meet current problems or provide future opportunities. This purposeful position shares some similarities with Van de Ven and Poole (1995) findings, but differs in that it has a less interventionist perspective, assuming that common mission alone drives outcomes. Figure 3.1 graphically illustrates the synthesis of these elements, providing the basis for a composite theory of Process Catalyst (collaborative leadership) and Strategic Leveraging (collaborative management).

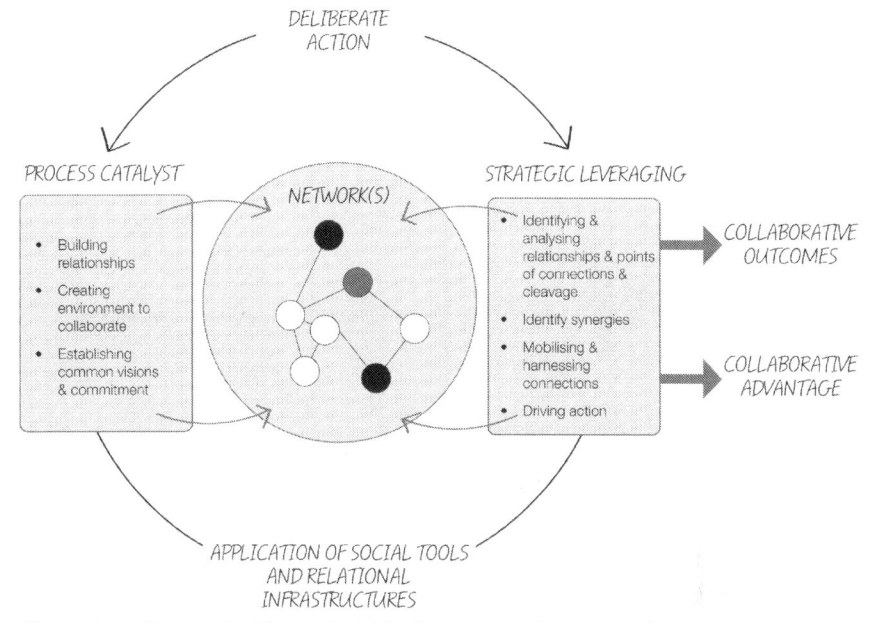

Figure 3.1   Composite Theoretical Model: Process Catalyst and Strategic Leveraging

It is apparent that collaborative networks are not "business as usual". They are based on a set of unique social relational elements. Accordingly this chapter has presented an alternative theoretical proposition which, while acknowledging the unique potential of the relational properties of collaborative networks, proposes that these social resources must be strategically harnessed, leveraged, and managed to achieve change goals. Establishing that collaborative networks draw upon different types of leadership and management, process catalyst and strategic leveraging that work together to create effective outcomes also helps to synthesize the disconnect between leadership and management theories and activities. Furthermore, it pushes new directions in network theory by clearly articulating a more deliberate, calculated approach to network relations and connections in collaborative networks that is often not present in lower-level network types.

REFERENCES

Agranoff, R. 2007. *Managing Within Networks*. Washington, DC: Georgetown University Press.

Agranoff, R., and M. McGuire. 2001. "Big Questions in Public Network Management Research." *Journal of Public Administration Research and Theory* 11 (3): 295–326.

Balkundi, P., and M. Kilduff. 2006. "The Ties that Lead: A Social Network Approach to Leadership." *The Leadership Quarterly* 17: 419–39.

Barnes, L. B., and M. P. Kriger. 1986. "The Hidden Side of Organizational Leadership." *Sloan Management Review* 28(1): 15–25.

Bass, B. (1990). "From Transactional to Transformational Leadership: Learning to Share the Vision." *Organizational Dynamics* 18(3): 19–31.

Beffert, D., and T. Benner. 2007a. "Stemming The Tide Of Conflict Diamonds—The Kimberley Process (Part A). Hertie School of Governance Case Program." Accessed December 14, 2011. www.globalpublicpolicy.net.

———. 2007b. "Stemming The Tide Of Conflict Diamonds—The Kimberley Process (Part B). Hertie School of Governance Case Program." Accessed December 14, 2011. www.globalpublicpolicy.net.

Bolden, R. 2004. *What is Leadership?* Exeter: Leadership South West, Centre for Leadership Studies. University of Exeter, UK.

Boorman, C., and G. Woolcock. 2002. "The Goodna Service Integration Project: Government and community working together for community well-being." In *Governing Local Communities: Building State and Community Capacity,* edited by T. Reddel. Brisbane, Australia: University of Queensland.

Church, M., M. Bitel, K. Armstrong, P. Fernando, H. Gould, S. Joss, M. Marwaha-Dierdrich, A. Laura de la Torre, and C. Vouhé. 2003. *Participation, Relationships and Dynamic Change: New Ways of Evaluating International Networks.* Working Paper 121. Development and Planning Unit, University College London.

Connick, S. 2006. *The Sacramento Area Water Forum: A Case Study.* Posted at the eScholarship Repository, University of California. http//repositories.edlib.org/iurd/wps/WP-2006–06.

Denzin, N. J. 1984. *The Research Act: A Theoretical Introduction to Sociological Methodology.* Englewood Cliffs, NJ: Prentice Hall.

Dragicevic, S., and S. Balram. 2004. "A Web GIS Collaborative Framework to Structure and Manage Distributed Planning Processes." *Journal of Geographical Systems* 6 (2) 133–53.

Edwards, S. L., and R. F. Stern. 1998. *Building and Sustaining Community Partnerships for Teen Pregnancy Programs.* Working paper. Cornerstone Consulting Group, Washington, DC. http://aspe.hhs.gov/hsp/teenp/teenpreg/teenpreg.htm.

Evans, P., and B. Wolf. 2009. "Collaboration Rules." *Harvard Business Review* (July–August): 96–104.

Fried, B., and T. Rundall. 1994. "Managing Groups and Teams." In *Health Care Management: Organizational Design and Behavior,* edited by S.M. Shortell and A.D. Kaluzny, 137–163. Albany, NY: Delmar.

Gage, R., and M. P. Mandell, eds. 1990. *Strategies for Managing Intergovernmental Policies and Networks.* New York: Praeger Books.

Goldman, D. 2006. *Emotional Intelligence.* London: Bantam Books Inc.

Gratton, L., and T. Erikson. 2009. "Eight Ways to Build Collaborative Teams." *Harvard Business Review on Collaborating Across Silos* (1–26). Boston, MA: Harvard Business School Publishing Corporation.

Gulati, R. 2007. *Managing Network Resources: Alliances, Affiliations and Other Relational Assets.* Oxford: Oxford University Press.

Huxham C., and S. Vangen. 1996. "Working Together: Key Themes in the Management of Relationships Between Public and Non-Profit Organisations." *International Journal of Public Sector Management* 9 (7): 5–17.

———. 2005. *Managing to Collaborate.* London: Routledge.

Innes, J. E., and D. E. Booher. 2010. *Planning With Complexity.* London: Routledge.

———. 1999. "Consensus Building as Role Playing and Bricolage." *Journal of the American Planning Association* 65 (1): 9–24.

———. 2000. *Collaborative Dialogue as a Policy Making Strategy.* Working Paper, University of California Berkeley: Institute of Urban and Regional Development.

Isett, K. R., I. A. Mergel, K. LeRoux, P. A. Mischen, and R. K. Rethemeyer. 2011. "Networks in Public Administration Scholarship: Understanding Where We Are and Where We Need To Go." *Journal of Public Administration Research and Theory,* 21 (1): 167–73.

Keast, R. 2004. *Integrated Public Services: The Role of Networked Arrangements.* Unpublished dissertation. School of Management, Queensland University of Technology.

———. 2011. "Joined-Up Governance in Australia: How the Past Can Inform the Future." *International Journal of Public Administration,* 34 (2): 221–31.

Keast, R., and M. Mandell. 2012. "The Collaborative Push: Moving Beyond Rhetoric and Gaining Evidence." *Journal of Management and Governance* (online publication 9 October).

Keast, R., K. Brown, and M. Mandell. 2007. "Getting the Right Mix: Unpacking Integration, Meanings and Strategies." *International Public Management Journal* 10 (1): 9–34.

Keast, R., M. Mandell, K. Brown, and G. Woolcock. 2004. "Network Structures: Working Differently and Changing Expectations." *Public Administration Review,* 64 (3): 363–72.

Kilduff, M., and D. Krackhardt. 2008. *Interpersonal Networks in Organizations.* Cambridge: Cambridge University Press.

Kilduff, M., and W. Tsai. 2003. *Social Networks and Organizations.* London: Sage Publications.

———. 2000. "Public Management and Policy Networks." *Public Management Review* 2(2): 135–58.

Koch, R., and G. Lockwood. 2010. *Superconnect: The Power of Networks and the Strength of Weak Links.* London: Little Brown.

Konrad, E. 1996. "A Multidimensional Framework for Conceptualising Human Services Integration Initiatives." In *Evaluating Initiatives to Integrate Human Services,* edited by J. Marquart and E. Konrad. San Francisco: Jossey Bass.

Klijn, E-H. and Koppenjan, J. 2000. "Public Management and Policy Networks." *Public Management* 2 (2):135–158.

Lasker, R. D., E. S. Weiss, and R. Millier. (2001). "Partnership Synergy: A Practical Framework for Studying and Strengthening the Collaborative Advantage." *The Milbank Quarterly* 79 (2): 179–205.

McGuire, M. 2002. "Managing Networks: Propositions on What Managers Do and Why They Do It." *Public Administration Review* 62 (5): 426–33.

Mandell, M. P. 2001. "The Impact of Network Structures on Community Building Efforts: The Los Angeles Roundtable For Children Community Studies." In *Getting Results Through Collaboration,* edited by M. P. Mandell 129–52. Westport, CT: Quorum Books.

———. 1994. "Managing Interdependencies Through Program Structures: A Revised Paradigm." *American Review of Public Administration* 24 (1): 99–121.

Mandell, M. P., and R. Keast 2009. "A New look at leadership in Collaborative Networks: Process Catalysts." In *Public Sector Leadership: International Challenges and Perspectives,* edited by J. A. Raffel, P. Leisink, and A. E. Middlebrooks, 163–78. Cheltenham, UK: Edward Elgar Press.

O'Toole, L. J. Jr. 1997. "Treating Networks Seriously: Practical and Research-Based Agendas in Public Administration." *Public Administration Review* 57(1): 45–52.

Steelman, T., and J. Carmin. 2002. Community Watershed Remediation: Connecting Organizational Resources to Social and Substantive Outcomes. In *Toxic Waste and Environmental Policy in the 21st Century United States,* edited by D. Rahm, 195–208. Jefferson, NC: McFarland Publishers.

Stewart, J. 2012. "Multi-case Methodology in Governance Related Research." *Public Management Review* 14 (1): 67–82.

Van de Ven A., and M. C. Poole. 1995. "Explaining Development and Change in Organizations." *Academy of Management Review* 20 (3): 510–40.

4 Building and Using the Theory of Collaborative Advantage

Siv Vangen and Chris Huxham

INTRODUCTION

In this chapter, we introduce the *Theory of Collaborative Advantage*—a practice-based theory about the management of collaborations, which focuses on the potential for collaborative advantage arising out of inter-organizational partnerships. We start with a brief introduction on how the theory is built, how it is structured, and what its purpose is. We then provide some conceptual examples that aim to illustrate the theory's contribution to knowledge, both theoretical and practical, about the management of collaboration in practice.

A THEME-BASED THEORY OF COLLABORATION

The development of the theory of collaborative advantage (TCA) is an ongoing endeavor that began in 1989. It has emerged out of research from very many and varied types of collaborative situations and involved individuals whose roles have ranged from heading up major partnerships to representing organizations that are involved as members. The types of collaborations have ranged from dyads to international networks, have been concerned with almost every aspect of the public and not-for-profit sectors, and have included Public, Private Partnerships (PPPs) that also span the commercial sector. They have addressed a wide range of areas including health, education, antipoverty, substance abuse, community development and planning, careers development, policing, economic development, and many more.

The TCA is a practice-based theory about the management of collaborations; it is derived from research involving practitioners on matters that are of genuine concern to them and over which they need to act. Also, it is structured in overlapping *themes* representing issues identified by practitioners as causing anxiety or reward. It seeks to depict what underpins the anxiety and reward in each area. While the focus is firmly on the impact of these themes on the practice of collaboration, the themes also include topics deemed important from policy considerations.

Collaborations are conceptualized as paradoxical in nature with inherent contradictions and mutually exclusive elements caused by inevitable differences between partners; differences that contain the very potential for collaborative advantage. Viz, the theory is also structured around a tension between *Collaborative Advantage*—the synergy that can be created through joint working—and *Collaborative Inertia*—the tendency for collaborative activities to be frustratingly slow to produce output or uncomfortably conflict ridden.

Contribution to knowledge is made through identifying and describing the complexity that underlies collaborative situations and the resulting challenges that are intrinsic to them. In this sense, implications for practice are regarded as an integral part of the theoretical conceptualizations and are presented in a nonprescriptive manner that informs both theory and practice. The idiosyncratic nature of actual collaborative situations is thus recognized as is the idea that there are practical tensions between positive and negative sides to alternative ways of managing. To that end, the TCA provides conceptualizations and frameworks that can be used as "handles to support reflective practice".

This chapter provides brief overviews of two new and two recent conceptualizations and frameworks relating to goals, trust, culture, and leadership. We introduce different ways of conceptualizing the issues, tensions, and challenges that underpin collaboration in practice and identify issues that need to be managed if collaboration is to yield advantage rather than inertia. In conclusion, we indicate how these four "themes" integrate with others that have not been included in this chapter, to provide an overall sense of the theory and practice of collaborative advantage (Huxham and Vangen 2005).

CONCEPTUAL FRAMEWORKS

Managing Goals

Agreement between partners on joint goals for a collaboration is usually seen as a requirement for success; the presumption is that collaboration goals cannot be enacted unless they are explicitly acknowledged by all partners (Agranoff and McGuire 2001; Ansell and Gash 2008). Goal congruence is therefore essential because it allows greater alignment between partners' goals and the joint goal for the collaboration, which in turn increases partners' commitment to it. Nevertheless, the reliance on congruent goals in collaborative contexts is problematic. In most situations, diversity of expertise and resources is essential to gaining truly synergistic advantage from collaborating and this, in turn, implies diversity of partners' goals. We can therefore locate a "goals paradox", which suggests that both congruence and diversity in goals influence success in collaboration. At the most basic level, this paradox suggests that congruence and diversity are in tension; goal congruence can make partners reluctant to cooperate and share information (Provan and Kenis 2008) whereas goal diversity leads partners to seek different and sometimes conflicting outcomes (Ansell and Gash 2008; Agranoff and McGuire 2001).

It is possible to unpack the complexity that underpins this problem through conceptualizing genuine goals for the collaboration as existing, if at all, in an entanglement of other, variously characterized goals that are both real and imagined. Our research suggests that goals that influence the actions and directions of a collaboration differ in type over six dimensions: level, origin, authenticity, relevance, content, and overtness as illustrated in Figure 4.1 below. A brief elaboration on each of these follows below.

Level

The first dimension relates to the level at which goals are recognized. It distinguishes between those that are about the collaboration, those that are about organizational purposes, and those that individuals wish to achieve. Goals expressed at the collaboration level relate to participants' views of what the collaborating partners aspire to achieve together. They are the public declaration of the sought after collaborative advantage. In contrast, organizational and individual level goals relate to the aspirations for the collaboration of each of the organizations and individuals involved. This distinction thus recognizes that goals at both the organizational and individual levels motivate and influence the actions of those who enact the collaboration in practice.

Origin

The goals in the first dimension mostly relate to the concerns of members of the collaboration. However, goals formulated by members are sometimes strongly influenced by the goals of organizations or individuals external to

DIMENSIONS	TYPES
Level	The Collaboration, The Organization(s), The Individual(s)
Origin	External Stakeholder(s), Members
Authenticity	Genuine, Pseudo
Relevance	Collaboration Dependent, Collaboration Independent
Content	Collaborative Process, Substantive Purpose
Overtness	Explicit, Unstated, Hidden

Figure 4.1   Dimensions of Goals

the collaboration. Government is perhaps the most common organizational stakeholder exerting pressure on collaborations and they frequently influence and shape them. Whether collaborations are mandated or constrained by government, nationwide policies as well as local priorities and interests tend to have an effect on the goals of the collaboration.

Authenticity

Goals expressed by members and external stakeholders may be genuine statements about what they aspire to achieve. However, there are many reasons why members may not identify with goals that are nevertheless publicly stated. For example, they may not subscribe to collaboration goals that have been imposed upon them by external pressure, or changes in the situation may have altered the relevance of previously genuine goals. Organizations may, for example, invent a jointly owned substantive goal that satisfies the specifications of a funding provider and which effectively disguises their real aim. Similarly, individuals may invent goals for their organizations to legitimize their own personal involvement in the collaboration. We characterize such possibilities as pseudo-goals.

Relevance

The identification of specific goals for each of the parties involved as well as the joint purpose is acknowledged as important if the collaboration is to succeed. Recognizing which organizational goals can reasonably be pursued through the collaboration is, however, not always straightforward. Other goals relating to the area remain to be addressed by the organization alone or perhaps through other collaborations. The fourth dimension thus recognizes that it can be hard to distinguish those goals that should or are intended to relate specifically to the collaborative agenda from those that are closely related but not explicitly a part of it.

Content

Many of the goals expressed by individuals are essentially concerned with what the collaboration is about, such as gaining access to resource and expertise, sharing risk, increasing efficiency, improving coordination in service provision, and learning. They relate to substantive outcomes and are obviously important in all collaborations. However, participants also— often implicitly—express goals that relate to how the collaboration will be undertaken. These goals can relate to any aspect of collaborative processes so might, for example, relate to modes of communicating, to kinds of relationship between members, or to a myriad of other possibilities.

Overtness

Finally, goals may be openly discussed and explicitly stated, but there are also many reasons why they may knowingly not be revealed to other participants, even if there is genuine goodwill between partners. Hidden agendas are endemic in collaboration. Deliberate concealing of goals is, however, not the only reason why they may not be clearly stated. In practice, there may be limited opportunities to explicitly discuss all potentially relevant goals in open forum; many goals go unstated even when there is no intent to hide them.

Taken together, these dimensions show that goals relevant to collaborations will relate to aspirations not only for the collaboration but also for the organizations and individuals involved; may have been generated by those involved but may also have been imposed or suggested by external stakeholders; may be genuine, but can also be manufactured to provide a reason for involvement in collaboration; do not always relate to the activities of the collaboration; can relate to substantive or processual concerns; and do not all appear overtly in the discourse of the collaboration.

It is the interplay among these goals that generates a problematic part of the paradox through producing major obstacles to achieving fully owned agreement of collaboration goals. The reasons for this can be summarized in four key points. First, it is highly unlikely that all the goals will be in harmony. Second, it is highly unlikely that any individual participant will know or understand more than a portion of the goals that are at play. This is a function of the sheer size and complexity of the entanglement, distractions caused by pseudo- and independent goals, and the masking effect of unstated or hidden goals. Third, differing perceptions on goals can lead to a low degree of mutual understanding even where there is individual knowledge or understanding. Fourth, because the entanglement is in a continuous state of flux as goals change over time, any mutual understanding of each other's goals—and hence any agreement over a collaboration goal—tends to be short-lived. This analysis does not challenge the notion that agreement on joint goals for a collaboration is important and desirable but it explains why that is inherently difficult to achieve and so questions the practicality of it as a *requirement* for success.

The goals paradox and the entanglement of goals suggest that there are real challenges associated with the management of goals in collaborations. The goals paradox serves as a reminder that there will be underlying tensions and that managerial responses need to incorporate these. The entanglement suggests that any managerial mechanism seeking to integrate congruent and diverse goals in collaborations should emphasize the importance of the paradox and its inherent tensions rather than seeking resolutions free of compromises or trade-offs. Accepting the paradox however, does not mean abandoning active management of goals. Rather, the entanglement provides participants with a handle for reflective practice by facilitating the consideration—and hence understanding—of their own and their partners' goals. It does not provide normative guidance on how to manage goals but aims to support participants in understanding their collaborative relationships and so allow them to devise their own management strategies (for a fuller account of this conceptual framework, see Vangen and Huxham (2012)).

Managing Trust

As with the issue of goals, trust is also seen as a necessary condition for successful collaboration (Lane and Bachmann 1998) yet the reality of many collaborations suggests that trust is frequently weak—if not lacking altogether. This particular paradox then suggests that there is a need to look at how trust can be built and maintained between partners in the context of collaboration.

Thus building can be conceptualized through a loop as depicted in Figure 4.2. This argues that two factors are important in initiating a trusting relationship. The first concerns the formation of expectations about the future of the collaboration; these will be based either on reputation or past behavior, or on more formal contracts and agreements (Gulati 1995). Given the difficulties of agreeing aims, as discussed previously, this is a nontrivial starting point. The second starting point involves risk-taking; partners need to trust each other enough to allow them to take a risk to initiate the collaboration (Gambetta 1998). If both of these initiators are possible, then, the loop argues, trust can be built gradually through starting with some modest but realistic aims that are likely to be successfully realized. This reinforces trusting attitudes and provides a basis for more ambitious collaboration.

This conceptualization of trust building aligns itself well with a "small wins" approach (Bryson 1988) within which trust can be built through mutual experience of advantage gained via successful implementation of low-risk initiatives. Trust can be developed over time moving gradually toward initiatives where partners are willing to take greater risks because

Figure 4.2   The Trust-Building Loop

a high level of trust is present. When risk and uncertainty levels are high, a strategy involving incremental increases in resource commitments may indeed be the preferred strategy. In many situations however, the collaborative advantage aimed for requires the collaborating partners to be more ambitious, and hence adopt a higher risk approach. The small wins approach may for example be in contradiction with the need to address major social issues rapidly or meet the requirements of external funding bodies for demonstrable output. More comprehensive ways of managing trust have different implications for initiating and sustaining the trust building loop. We will elaborate a bit further on this below.

Initiating the Trust Building Loop

FORMING EXPECTATIONS

Two structural features—ambiguity and complexity—that tend to characterize collaborations can act as barriers to the initiation of trust building. Whilst researchers have argued that "explicit" membership where the parties "know and agree on who is involved and in what capacity" is a key definitional element of collaboration, the surprising reality of many situations is the ambiguity about who the partners are. Typically, there are differences in views about who the central members are and what their roles or membership status are with respect to the collaboration. In practice it can be difficult to be certain about what organization, collaboration or other constituency (if any) individuals represent. Simply identifying with whom to build trust therefore can be very difficult and time-consuming.

Working out with whom trust should be built is not the only challenge in getting started in the trust building loop. As we have already discussed, practitioners continuously raise concerns over the establishment of joint aims. Seeking agreement on aims to effectively initiate the trust building loop can be problematic in practice.

MANAGING RISK

Gradually, as trust develops it becomes a means for dealing with risk. In situations where the small wins approach is not feasible however, the risk associated with the collaboration has to be managed as an integral part of trust building. Risk is usually associated with opportunistic behavior and vulnerability relating to apprehensions that partners will take advantage of collaborative efforts by for example claiming ownership of joint efforts. When the aim is to build trust however, risk management cannot be concerned with guarding against opportunistic behavior, e.g., via sanctions set out in contractual agreements. Instead, risk management must ensure that any future collaborative advantage can realistically be envisaged and is shared. This requires efforts associated with aims negotiation, structural ambiguity, clarification of expectations, willingness and ability to enact the agreed collaborative agenda in view of associated power, influence relationships, and so on. These activities are extremely resource-intensive and time consuming, and their management requires a great deal of skill and sensitivity. Hence the effort is only recommended where trust cannot be built incrementally.

Sustaining the Trust Building Loop
MANAGING DYNAMICS

Many collaborations are initiated so it must be presumed that expectations can be formed on the basis that either a minimal level of trust is present and/or there is a willingness to bear the associated risk. Sustaining the trust-building loop then requires the participants to work together, gradually becoming more ambitious, over time, in their joint endeavors. Unfortunately, while all organizations are dynamic in nature, collaborations are particularly so because they are sensitive to transformation in each of the partner organizations and therefore may change very quickly. Effort put into building mutual understanding and developing trust can be shattered, for example, by a change in the structure of a key organization or the job change of a key individual. Sustaining the trust-building loop therefore, requires continuous attention to trust relationships.

MANAGING POWER IMBALANCES

Even when careful and continuous attention is paid to trust building, the inherent fragility of the loop is evident. Alongside the issues relating to the dynamic nature of collaboration, power issues in particular seem to challenge efforts aimed at sustaining the loop. Imbalance in power and the inevitability that some partners will be more central to the enactment of the collaborative agenda than are others tend to dictate behaviors that get in the way of trust building. An appreciation of the inevitability of power imbalances as well as the ability to interpret any actions that members take in response to them may help prevent loss of trust. Furthermore, an understanding of the way in which balances of power tend to change during the life of a collaboration and indeed whether and how power imbalances can and should be deliberately shifted seems essential in sustaining the trust gained.

NURTURING THE COLLABORATIVE RELATIONSHIPS

Issues pertaining to the identification of partners, complexity and multiplicity of aims, risk and vulnerability, complexity and dynamics of collaborative structures, and power imbalances clearly all pose serious management challenges for building and sustaining trust. If not managed effectively, any one of these issues can prevent trust from developing or even cause loss of trust. Ideally therefore, all these issues need to be managed simultaneously and, due to the dynamic nature of collaboration, in a continuous manner. Failing to do so may cause the trust loop to fracture.

This framework has sought to illustrate in broad terms the contrast between two different approaches to the management of trust: small wins versus comprehensive management. Both approaches have their merits. The illustration of each intends to provide insight to inform the managerial judgment about the kind of trust-building activities that are appropriate to collaborative situations (for a fuller account of this conceptual framework, see Vangen and Huxham 2003a).

Managing Cultural Diversity

Cultural diversity in collaborations is also an issue that receives much attention from research and practice alike. Culture, in this context, is used broadly to refer to partners' "habitual ways of being and acting" that stem from the distinct professional, organizational, and national cultures to which they belong. Studies have shown that similar and compatible cultures yield greater connectivity and shared understanding between partners, which render the act of collaborating less problematic (Beamish and Lupton 2009). In practice, however, collaborations may necessarily span organizational, professional, and even national boundaries thus incorporating cultural diversity that may cause conflicts, misunderstandings, and points of friction (Bird and Osland 2006; Shenkar et al. 2008). Indeed, research has tended to focus on addressing such friction rather than treating culture as one of the resources that may lead to synergistic gains. However, as with goals, is it possible to locate a "culture paradox," which suggests that cultural diversity is both a source of stimulation, creativity, and reward and a source of potential conflicts of values, behaviors, and beliefs. Cultural similarity and diversity are thus in tension.

One way of addressing the "culture paradox" is to consider what specific management tensions need to be addressed if cultural diversity is to yield advantage rather than inertia. Our research points to three interrelated management tensions in this respect, each of which focuses on a particular interaction within collaboration. The first, termed "accommodation", addresses the interaction between organizations in a collaboration. The second, "agency", focuses on the individual actor and the quality of their orientation toward the collaboration and their host organization. The third, "quantity", analyzes the constitution of the collaboration regarding the quantity and extent of cultural diversity within it. A brief summary of each tension is provided below.

Accommodation Tension
In collaborations characterized by cultural diversity, flexibility at the organizational level is necessary to accommodate different operational procedures, and different ways of being, interacting, and working. Typically, partners have different structures and procedures (expressed through the organization but constituted additionally through professional practices or idiosyncrasies rooted in national cultures) that they deploy to meet their

own goals. When such distinct resources can be deployed jointly, they can be used to pursue collaborative goals. This joint pursuit however, usually requires some flexibility because partners' resources are oriented toward internal purposes rather than the goals of the collaboration and so is not designed to accommodate partners. Paradoxically, this need for flexibility may compromise those structures and processes that enable them to deliver their core business that enables them to make a contribution to the goals of the collaboration in the first place.

We thus identify an accommodation tension defined in terms of the poles of *flexibility* and *rigidity*. Flexibility in structures and processes and working through—and sometimes in spite of—difference is necessary to accommodate diverse cultures. Yet, a partner's established culture may be what enables it to make a contribution to the joint agenda in the first place; there is a need for a certain rigidity to preserve this resource.

Agency Tension

Following on from the accommodation tensions above, in culturally diverse collaborations, organizational representatives typically have to respond to cultural frictions at the interpersonal level within structures that are ill fit for that purpose. Typically, cultural frictions arise because individuals come to the collaboration with different expectations of what can be achieved within an organizational or collaborative context, with different ways of communicating and different etiquettes and norms. To anticipate or overcome these frictions, managers need to appropriately use their understanding of partners' culture—i.e., their partners' culturally embedded perceptions, behavioral characteristics, and professional expertise. However, managers express much frustration about not being in control of operational and strategic matters pertaining to the collaboration and the perception that they lack power, authority, or discretion to respond appropriately.

While it is entirely reasonable that managers should be supported and empowered to act on behalf of their organizations for the purpose of the collaboration, any individual autonomy needs to be exercised without leaving the individuals vulnerable and organizations at risk. We can thus identify an agency tension defined by the poles of *autonomy* and *accountability*—which can play out in a number of ways. In terms of generating advantage through cultural diversity, managers undoubtedly need enough individual autonomy to act on behalf of their organizations even to the extent of deviating from established organizational procedures. Yet protecting the organizations' interest and their inherent contribution to the collaboration requires individuals to maintain accountability toward their organization.

Quantity Tension

When collaborations span sector and/or national boundaries, the context within which partners operate and the organizational cultures and professional practices enacted in them can be very diverse. In the midst of this complexity, the quantity tension arises. It captures the sense in which increasing levels of complexity need to be embraced to secure advantage from cultural diversity. However such complexity requires an increasing level of control (and simplification) to militate against complexity-induced inertia.

Two common responses to handling complexity are suggested by our research. First, organizations seek to find partners with a similar culture or who are able and willing to compromise. This will yield connectivity and understanding between the partners and hence be easier to manage. Second, managers adopt practices that seek to control the impact that the activities of the collaboration have on their organizations' cultures. Typically they achieve such control by seeking to be the lead, thus effectively imposing their culture upon the collaboration, or by actively controlling the channels of communication between partners.

Notwithstanding the pragmatic need to control the complexity of collaborations, there is nevertheless a real opportunity cost associated with simplifying cultural diversity. Selecting partners that are culturally similar, insisting on being the lead partner, or limiting the number of individuals involved will effectively limit the potential for stimulation, creativity, and reward. Our data show many examples of managers reflecting on the value of communication in "avoiding thinking traditionally" and "gaining a richness of discussion" thereby genuinely tapping into partners' expertise. Similarly, they reflected on how greater diversity between their own organization and their partners would lead to greater opportunities to diversify rather than simply expanding their core business.

The quantity tension is thus defined by the poles of *complexity* and *simplification*. The essence of the tension lies in dealing with the complexities stemming from the number and cultural diversity of the partners that are involved. Retaining control is a necessary element of steering the joint agenda forward; however, embracing complexity is necessary if the collaboration is to generate advantage through cultural diversity.

The three interrelated management tensions identify seemingly opposing approaches to managing cultural diversity that may be used reflectively to support practice. They are intended to highlight areas of pertinent tradeoffs and compromises that should inform managerial judgment. As illustrated in Figure 4.3 below, the extremes on the left poles of the tensions treat cultural diversity as an inherent benefit to collaborative practice, in this mode managers embrace diversity through flexibility, autonomy, and accepting complexity. In contrast, the right poles of the tensions suggest that for cultural diversity to yield advantage, there needs to be substantial control. Here, the response is to simplify the extent and impact of diversity—organizations and individuals similarly show a bias with the collaboration to maintain their contributions. In practice, management interventions appropriate to moving the collaborative agenda forward will lie at some point between the two extremes. However, such intermediate positions do not "solve" the tension; in contrast, they operate *through* tension acknowledging the pull and

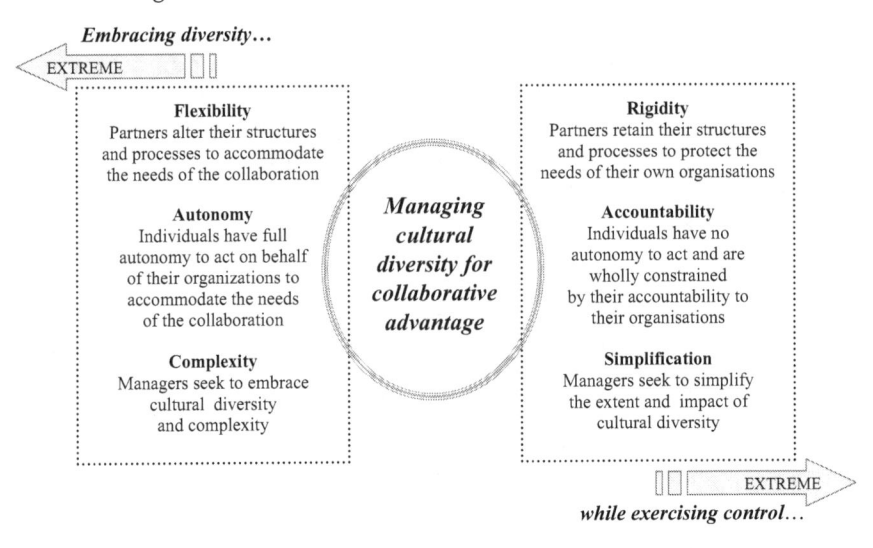

Figure 4.3 Managing Cultural Diversity Toward Collaborative Advantage

validity of each side (for a fuller account of this conceptual framework, see Vangen and Winchester 2013).

Leadership

Given the challenges inherent in collaborative contexts characterized by incongruent goals, lack of trust, cultural diversity, paradoxes, and tensions, concern for leadership is clearly important. A key question, in this respect, is what kind of leadership can most appropriately support the practice of collaboration? We will argue for an approach that departs from classical theories on leadership.

A presumption in much of the literature on leadership in organizations is that leadership is concerned with a *formal leader* who either influences or transforms members of a group or organization—*the followers*—by attaining alignment and commitment toward the achievement of some specified goals. Because hierarchical relationships generally do not feature in interorganizational settings, leadership that is centered on the formal senior business or public figures that are the subject of much leadership literature is likely to be found inadequate in collaborative context. Also, in collaborative contexts, enacting leadership can mean influencing whole organizations rather than just individuals. Given the inherent complexity and challenge and in particular the difficulty in specifying collaborative goals, it is far from straightforward to translate mainstream theories of leadership into the collaborative contexts.

However, some contributions to the theory on leadership are potentially relevant. Given the lack of traditional hierarchy in collaborative settings, it seems appropriate to focus on informal or emergent leaders (Kent and Moss 1994), decentering of leadership (Martin 1992) and distributed and shared leadership (Crosby and Bryson 2005). Researchers on leadership in collaboration have tended to emphasize relational leadership and processes for inspiring, nurturing, supporting, and communicating (Agranoff and McGuire 2001; Crosby and Bryson 2005). All of these views do not necessarily presume a leader—follower relationship and the focus tends to be on facilitating, empowering, and enabling rather than directing toward specified goals.

Our own approach incorporates these nurturing aspects of leadership and focuses on the mechanisms that *lead* collaborative activity and outcomes in one direction rather than another. Leadership is thus concerned with mechanisms for *making things happen* (note how this definition is much broader because it is no longer concerned with leadership being delivered by individuals only). Clearly this definition of leadership can include both visionary and more mechanistic aspects and therefore does not recognize as relevant the classic distinction between leaders and managers (Bryman 1996). We argue instead that in collaborations, *structures* and communication *processes* are *leadership media* that are as instrumental in leading to specific outcomes as is the behavior of the *participants* associated with it. This theoretical framework considers the three leadership media—structures, processes, and participants—and argues that all three are important to an overall understanding of leadership in collaborative situations. Leadership as it is *enacted by individuals* is considered within the *context* of the leadership influences of structures and processes. Below, we briefly describe the kinds of activities that occupy those who seek to enact leadership in practice.

Enacting Leadership

Much of what is done by those who try to make things happen is undertaken in *the spirit of collaboration*. Activities tend to be highly facilitative and concerned with *embracing, empowering, involving and mobilizing* partners. Finding the right partners may for example emphasize the inclusion of those with a stake in the collaborative issue. While such embracing of partners is an obvious initial task, it is also a continuous activity in practice. Due to the highly dynamic nature of collaborations, it typically entails continually looking out for alternative partners that are needed while also supporting those who want to be partners. Embracing members does not in itself empower them to have a voice in the collaboration or to contribute to the shaping of its agenda. Creating an infrastructure in which individuals and organizations can participate is an essential aspect. It may entail, for example, the design of a structure that will allow the community to act as a member alongside public organizations and to be empowered to play an active role. Yet, creating structures and support for involvement does not ensure the *involvement* of partners so leadership includes activities specifically aimed at overcoming hindrances to this. Problems arise because of the inevitability that some partners are more central than others, so managing the inequality between principal and subsidiary members frequently becomes an issue. Embracing, empowering, and involving members are essential leadership activities yet to *make things happen* and to influence individuals and whole organizations in support of the collaboration is seriously challenging. The issue of *mobilization* is closely linked to goals and aspirations and the recognition that partners need to get something in return for their efforts. Looking for levers for the activities that are shared to get partners to pay due attention to joint projects is one aspect of this role.

Leadership in collaboration thus implies much facilitative activity suggesting the need for relational skills such as patience, empathy, honesty, and deference. However, carrying through such an approach is far from straightforward and if collaborative inertia is to be avoided, more decisive tactics may be required.

To overcome the inevitability of working with individuals who are located in different organizations, perhaps even in different countries across different time zones; have different needs, values, perceptions, and levels of commitment; find communication difficult, and so on, those enacting leadership may engage in activities that, at face value, are much less collaborative. This may involve taking an active lead rather than facilitating agreement and joint implementation of the collaborative agenda. It may even involve *manipulating agendas* and *politicking*. The need to alter joint agendas can arise in many different ways, although typically it may be to avoid stagnation and collaborative inertia. Imposing an understanding of collaborative issues on others and influencing the agenda via stealthy behavior may be necessary tactics. Although collaboration is intended to be a sympathetic way of working, political maneuvering is often strongly evident. Those involved in collaborative activities frequently talk about probing the political undercurrents between and around individuals and finding ways of excluding those who are not "worth the bother".

These kinds of activities may be characterized as being *toward collaborative thuggery,* so called after the member of a city alliance who said that a collaboration he was involved with had been successful "because the convener is a thug ... if people are not pulling their weight he pushes them out". He was arguing that, thoughtfully adopted, this was a positive and effective mode of leadership.

Is this a case of high principles giving way to the pragmatism needed to get things done? We prefer to see it as another aspect of nurturing. In gardening, if you want to nurture an overgrown garden back to health, pulling up weeds and cutting back overgrown plants is all part of "tough love". So it is in collaborations. Those who lead more successfully seem to operate from both perspectives—in the spirit of collaboration with a healthy portion of collaborative thuggery—and to switch between them, often carrying out both types of leadership in the same act.

From the spirit of collaboration...

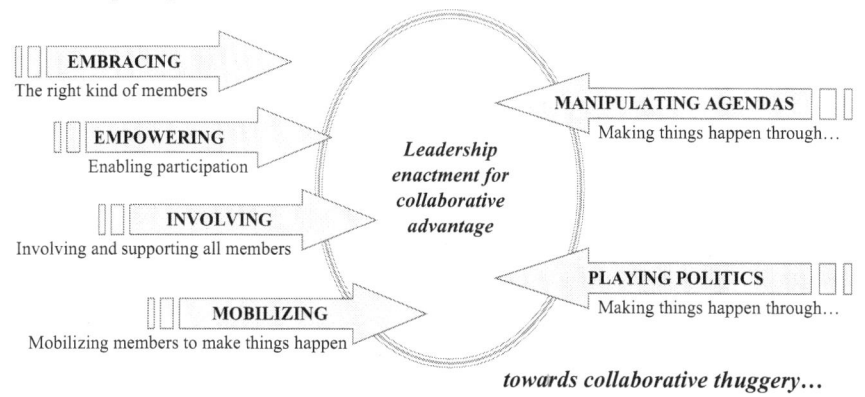

Figure 4.4 The Enactment of Leadership

The purpose of this framework is to highlight and legitimize the simultaneous enactment of both a facilitative and a directive leadership role. Both roles appear essential in making progress and should not be seen as alternative ways of leading but rather as alternative aspects of a leadership portfolio. Successful leadership seems to imply the ability to operate from both perspectives and to continually switch between them, often carrying out both types of leadership in the same act. As illustrated in Figure 4.4 below, the essence of the enactment of leadership for collaborative advantage would appear to involve the ability to lead in the "spirit of collaboration" while simultaneously drawing on "collaborative thuggery".

(For a fuller account of this conceptual framework, see Vangen and Huxham 2003b.)

CONCLUDING COMMENTS

In this chapter we have introduced the Theory of Collaborative Advantage through providing overviews of a selection of conceptualizations and frameworks pertaining to the management of goals, trust, culture, and leadership. These themes each present a part of the overall picture and, as we have alluded to, they interact with each theme affecting others. The theory of collaborative advantage is structured around many more of these themes but it is beyond the scope of this chapter to describe them all here. However, in terms of power for example, a key concern is that power sharing is important yet there are often both real and perceived power imbalances between partners that tend to have a negative impact on behaviors. Similarly, "membership structures" are frequently ambiguous, complex, and dynamic, which render issues concerning agreement on goals, building trust, managing power relationships, and cultural diversity infinitely hard. As a final example, success is not necessarily predictable and when it is achieved, is often not as anticipated. Knowing how to recognize key perspectives of success is nevertheless essential to facilitating the development of collaboration in practice.

Taking all of these themes together, it is clear that without careful intervention and management, collaborations are more likely to reach *collaborative inertia* than *collaborative advantage*. It is not surprising therefore that many fail. Nevertheless, there are many reports of success albeit that less may have been achieved than had been hoped for, some participants may be less pleased than others, the pace may have been slower than expected, yet the final outcome is perceived as better than would have been the case without the collaboration. Achieving such collaborative advantage requires careful reflection around the types of issues raised in this chapter and then careful attention to managing them.

The theory conveys that managing collaborations is a highly complex endeavor. It prescribes the kinds of issues that need attention. It does not however, tell the user which of the themes to focus on, when to do so, and how to use the information captured in them to guide them in their management actions. Knowing how to use the theory is in itself a matter for managerial judgment. Themes such as goals, trust, culture, and leadership provide sensible starting points to aid understanding about the management of collaboration in practice. The various conceptualizations and frameworks can then be used effectively as handles to support reflective practice.

ACKNOWLEDGEMENT

We wish to thank Nik Winchester for his work with Siv on the conceptualizations on cultural diversity—a brief summary of which is included in this chapter.

REFERENCES

Agranoff, Robert, and Michael McGuire. 2001. "Big Questions in Public Network Management Research." *Journal of Public Administration Research and Theory* 11: 295–326.

Ansell, Chris, and Alison Gash. 2008. "Collaborative Governance in Theory and Practice." *Journal of Public Administration Research and Theory* 18: 543–71.

Bird, Allan, and Joyce S. Osland. 2006. "Making Sense of Intercultural Collaboration." *International Studies of Management and Organization* 35: 115–32.

Beamish, Paul, W., and Nathaniel, C. Lupton. 2009. "Managing Joint Ventures." *Academy of Management Perspectives* 23: 75–94.

Bryman, Alan. 1996. "Leadership in Organizations." In *Handbook of Organization Studies*, edited by Stewart Clegg, Cynthia Hardy, and Walter, R. Nord, 276–92. London: Sage.

Bryson, John. 1988. "Strategic Planning: Big Wins and Small Wins." *Public Money and Management* 8: 11–5.

Crosby, Barbara, and John Bryson. 2005. *Leadership for the Common Good: Tackling Public Problems in a Shared-Power World.* San Francisco: Jossey-Bass.

Gambetta, Diego. 1988. "Can We Trust?" In *Trust: Making and Breaking Cooperative Relations,* edited by Diego Gambetta, 213–38. New York: Basil Blackwell.

Gulati, Ranjay. 1995. "Does Familiarity Breed Trust? The Implications of Repeated Ties for Contractual Choice in Alliances." *Academy of Management Journal* 38: 85–112.

Huxham, Chris, and Siv Vangen. 2005. *Managing to Collaborate: The Theory and Practice of Collaborative Advantage.* London: Routledge.

Kent, Russell L., and Sherry, E. Moss. 1994. "Effects of Gender and Gender Role on Leader Emergence." *Academy of Management Journal* 37: 1335–47.

Lane, Christel, and Reinhard Bachmann. 1998. *Trust Within and Between Organizations, Conceptual Issues and Empirical Applications.* Oxford: Oxford University Press.

Martin, Joanne. 1992. *Cultures in Organizations: Three Perspectives.* Oxford: Oxford University Press.

Provan, Keith, G., and Patrick Kenis. 2008. "Modes of Network Governance: Structure, Management, and Effectiveness." *Journal of Public Administration Research and Theory* 18: 229–52.

Shenkar, Oded, Luo Yadong, and Yeheskel Orly. 2008. "From 'Distance' to 'Friction': Substituting Metaphors and Redirecting Intercultural Research." *Academy of Management Review* 33: 905–23.

Vangen, Siv, and Chris Huxham. 2003a. "Nurturing Collaborative Relations: Building Trust in Interorganizational Relations." *The Journal of Applied Behavioral Science* 39: 5–31.

———. 2003b. "Enacting Leadership for Collaborative Advantage: Dilemmas of Ideology and Pragmatism in the Activities of Partnership Managers." *British Journal of Management* 14: 61–76.

———. 2012. "The Tangled Web: Unravelling the Principle of Common Goals in Collaborations." *Journal of Public Administration Research and Theory,* 22: 731–60.

Vangen, Siv, and Nik Winchester. 2013 "Managing Cultural Diversity in Collaborations. A Focus on Management Tensions." *Public Management Review,* Advanced Access DOI:10.1080/14719037.2012.743579.

5 The Democratic Potentials of Governance Networks in Intergovernmental Decision Making

Eva Sørensen

INTRODUCTION

Most models of democracy offer an intragovernmental approach to democracy that says little about how to democratize intergovernmental forms of policy making that involves more than one elected government despite the frequent occurrence of such policy processes in contemporary policy processes. Intergovernmental policy making brings together two or more democratically elected governments—be they transnational, national, or subnational—in processes of shared policy making. It can bring together governments at different levels in the political system such as for example the European Parliament, national parliaments, regional and municipal councils, and elected city and village councils and user boards, and it can involve governments placed at the same level of governance. The failure to address the question of how to democratically regulate intergovernmental policy making can be seen as a serious void in democratic theory that needs to be filled, and this void is becoming increasingly apparent due to globalization and recent governance reforms (Greven and Pauly 2000; Heffen, Kickert, and Thomassen 2000; Holden 2000; Hajer, 2003; Bache and Flinders 2004; Kersbergen and Waarden 2004; Bogason and Zølner 2007; Marcussen and Torfing 2007; Torfing et al. 2012). The unsettled debates among students of globalization and governance about the democratic implication of recent developments in the political system is a direct result of the profound lack of criteria for evaluating democratic quality of intergovernmental policy making (Klijn and Skelcher 2007; Pierre and Peters 2005; Sørensen and Torfing, 2005; Dryzek 2007).

The aim of this chapter is to propose that governance networks could be one of the cornerstones in developing an intergovernmental model of democracy. The democratic potentials of governance networks are directly related to the fact that they—given their particular constitutive form and functioning—provide an institutional framework for policy making that promotes the formulation of joint action in contexts characterized by nonhierarchical relations between interdependent but operationally autonomous actors with diverging views and interests such as, for example, different democratically elected governments. This framework encourages governments to commit themselves to intergovernmental negotiated agreements in a semiregulated context underwritten by interdependencies. Although the promotion of joint action between governments is not in itself a democratic attribute, the willingness to engage in collective policy making that reaches beyond the domain of the individual government is an important precondition for developing intergovernmental forms of democracy. As highlighted in the intense debate among governance theorists, governance networks are not necessarily democratic. They can also be a serious threat to democracy (Benz and Papadopoulos 2006; Hansen 2007; Torfing et al. 2012). I shall claim that the particular democratic contribution of governance networks depends on the degree to which they de facto promote intergovernmental policy making in ways that do not undermine but supplement and enrich the intragovernmental forms of democracy that has instigated the participating governments in the first place. They can become a valuable supplement to democracy by providing a much needed institutional framework for guiding governments' engagement in intergovernmental policy making without damaging the links to their respective constituencies. Governance networks can also *enrich* representative democracy through a destabilization of the sharp patterns of inclusion and exclusion that are direct products of intragovernmental forms of democracy (Connolly 1995).

In clarifying what governance networks can bring to the table in developing a model of intergovernmental democracy, valuable inspiration can be found in Mark Granovetter's (1973) famous argument about "the strength of weak ties". He points out how the presence of weak ties between groups constituted on strong ties is crucial for ensuring effective societal governance because weak ties stimulate an effective diffusion of information and influence as well as some degree of social cohesion in contexts characterized by considerable differentiation. Although Granovetter is more interested in effectiveness than in democracy and focuses on dyadic structures and not on the role and functioning of weak ties between multiple actors, his basic argument is also relevant in this context. The chapter aims to point out how weak ties can contribute to the development of an intergovernmental model of democracy and what role governance networks can play in establishing these ties. In relation to the latter question, I will discuss the extent to which the democratic quality of governance networks can be enhanced through acts of metagovernance.

The chapter starts out by giving a short description of the institutional void that exists in existing models of democracy and the growing concerns that this void gives rise to in light of current societal changes. Next, follows a brief outline of two case studies that illuminate the current need for a model of democracy that can guide efforts to enhance the democratic functioning of intergovernmental policy making. Then, the theoretical model is developed in more detail—the potential role that governance networks can play in this endeavor. The chapter concludes with an outline of how acts of metagovernance have an important role to play in ensuring that governance networks becomes a positive contribution rather than a threat to the development of an intergovernmental democracy.

THE INSTITUTIONAL VOID IN THEORETICAL MODELS OF DEMOCRACY

Existing models of democracy share an intragovernmental perception of democracy as a way of regulating political decision making processes within a given polity or community that places political power in the hands of the members of that polity i.e. the members of a city state or another kind of local community or a nation state (Held 1995). The main differences between different models of democracy concerns the question of how active a role the citizens play in making political decisions ranging from models of direct democracy to more or less elitist models of representative democracy that leaves policy making in the hands of an elected government as is the case in most modern liberal democracies (Lindblom 1965; Pateman 1970; Sartori 1987; Dahl 1956). Despite these differences, these models share the view that democracy is an intra-polis matter between a government and its citizens.

The reality of contemporary policy making is quite different from this neat intragovernmental modeling. Horizontal and vertical forms of intergovernmental policy making have become a frequent and integrated part of policy making in representative democracies. Horizontal forms of intergovernmental policy making bring together governments placed at the same level of governance. Nation states have always built alliances with each other (Stein and Turkewitsch 2012), but other levels of governance are increasingly doing the same. Big cities in different countries form partnerships in a joint effort to reduce global warming (Kern and Bulkeley 2009), and municipalities work closely together to coordinate their efforts to solve difficult policy problems (Sørensen et al. 2011). In vertical forms of intergovernmental policy, governments from different levels in the political system coordinate their attempts to solve complex governance tasks. This kind of joined-up government between levels is well known in federal as well as in decentralized unitary states (Blom-Hansen 2002; Braun 2012; Hallerberg 2012), and it plays a constitutive role in most transnational political systems such as the UN and the EU (Bogason and Zølner 2007; Enderlein et al. 2012; Zürn 2012). Intragovernmental models of democracy have particularly little to say about the democratic regulation of horizontal forms of intergovernmental policy making between nation states or, as we shall see later, between municipalities. They have more to offer in relation to vertical forms of intergovernmental policy making, but the main focus is on how to separate power between levels of government rather than on how to democratically regulate the complex interplay between them that characterizes practical political life.

The distance between the models of intragovernmental democracy and the real world of intergovernmental policy making has in recent years been further deepened as a result of political globalization (Held 1995; Zürn 2000; Holden 2000; Habermas 2001) and reform programs that blur the boundaries between different levels of governance (Kooiman 2003; Jessop 2004; Kersbergen and Waarden 2004; Pedersen et al. 2011). Hence, these reforms have given birth to a system of governance in which the autonomy of a government increasingly depends on its ability to meet standards defined at other levels of government and its influence is a product of its capacity to collaborate and coordinate with other governments (Abbott and Snidal 2000; Larner and Walters 2004; Sørensen and Triantafillou 2009). As envisaged by the two empirical case studies outlined below, the need to develop an intergovernmental model of democracy becomes more and more apparent.

EMPIRICAL MANIFESTATIONS OF THE DEMOCRATIC VOID

The results of two recent case studies of emerging forms of intergovernmental policy making can help to illuminate how the democratic void manifests itself empirically in actual governance processes. The first study focuses on a horizontal intergovernmental policy arena that brings together a number of Danish municipalities in joint policy making. The second study illuminates how vertical intergovernmental policy making is being institutionalized in an EU context. The two studies illustrate that intergovernmental policy making is an integrated, influential, and institutionalized aspect of contemporary policy making in representative democracies and that this kind of policy making suffers from a lack of democratic regulation.

Intermunicipal Policy Making in Denmark

A reform of the Danish political system that took place in 2007 resulted in an increase in horizontal intergovernmental policy making between the municipalities in each of five new regions. Although one of the defined goals of the reform was to reduce intermunicipal collaboration by constructing larger municipalities, the opposite happened. The now larger and stronger municipalities experienced a stronger feeling of interdependency in relation to a still more interventionist national government and a new regional level of governance (Sørensen forthcoming). This feeling of shared enemies triggered the formation of an arena for intermunicipal collaboration in each of the four regions—the so called Municipal Contact Councils (MCC). The MCCs are composed of the mayors and a selected number of political leaders from the opposition parties. A case study of the activities in the MCC in Region Zealand over a five year period from 2006 to the end of 2010 shows how the council, despite its informal status, is gradually becoming a more and more influential and institutionalized arena for intermunicipal policy making (see Sørensen forthcoming for more detail). It is noteworthy that although the MCC in Region Zealand has considerable political influence, few questions have been raised about the democratic functioning of the Council. The involved actors have been more concerned about how to coordinate and strengthen the ability of the MCC to make joint decisions that address pressing governance problems and enhance the willingness of the municipalities to stick together to develop and realize joint policy strategies. Members of the MCC, however, find it difficult to operate in the interface between their respective municipal councils and the MCC and search for ways to link and balance the policy making that goes on in the two arenas. Moreover, many of the involved municipal politicians note that although they fully accept the need for an MCC, they do not feel sure about what role it should play in the policy process and how it affects the policy making that takes place in the individual municipal councils.

Multilevel Policy Making in EU

The EU has developed several interesting vertical institutional mechanisms for bringing EU authorities and representatives from the member states together in processes of joint policy making. The Open Method of Coordination (OMC) is one of them. It is a method for joint policy making in policy areas where the EU does not have decision-making powers. The OMC is particularly interesting in this context because it lays out a procedure for formulating and implementing joint policy programs between autonomous but interdependent governments at different levels in a multilevel governance structure (Ansell 2000; Bohman 2005; Jessop 2004; Peters and Pierre 2004). A case study of the OMC process within the field of European employment policy from 2003 to 2009 shows how policy making is being exercised in complex intergovernmental policy processes that involves EU authorities as well as national and subnational governments. The study indicates that the ongoing dialogue between the European Commission and the national governments plays an important role in developing and implementing European employment policy (Bogason and Zølner 2007). Despite the important role played by intergovernmental policy making in European employment policy as well as in other policy areas, few questions have been raised about the democratic implications of the OMC method. One exception is the EU Parliament's critique of the so-called community model for escaping democratic control that the commission argues against in the whitepaper on governance (European Commission 2000) by categorizing the OMC as a mainly technocratic regulatory process of limited political relevance.

The two case studies mentioned above pinpoint the challenges we face in ensuring democracy in a world of intense horizontal and vertical intergovernmental policy making. We are largely on barren ground when faced with the task of guiding attempts to democratize horizontal and vertical instances of policy making that involves more than one government. The lack of guidance might in fact be what drives actors to focus on the regulatory aspects rather than the political aspects of intergovernmental policy making. Rather than putting the binocular in front of the blind eye however we should develop a model of intergovernmental democracy that gives answers to how such governance processes could be democratically regulated.

IN SEARCH OF AN INTERGOVERNMENTAL THEORETICAL MODEL OF DEMOCRACY

The search for an intergovernmental theoretical model of democracy could take departure in recent debates about what a global democracy might look like. Among those setting the agenda in this debate we find Davis Held (1995), who has developed a cosmopolitan model of democracy that draws the outline of a set of transnational political and legal institutions that are to function as a kind of world government. In my view, this model is problematic for two reasons. First, it seems unlikely to happen in any foreseeable future. Democratically authorized transnational political institutions do indeed have an important role to play in enhancing intergovernmental democracy but the willingness to leave political power in the hands of these institutions have proven to be limited. The hardships of the UN and other transnational political institutions are cases in point. Second, a cosmopolitan model of democracy does not provide the institutional set up needed to accommodate the kinds of situated and task-related intergovernmental policy making that are needed to cope with the complex, dynamic, and diverse problems of our time (Kooiman 1993; Elsig 2007).

A more promising place to start is in recent theories of democratic governance. Among the contributors to this debate we find Paul Hirst (2000) and Archon Fung and Eric Olin Wright (2003), who point out how interactive governance arenas that bring together national and subnational governments can promote democracy by improving the exchange of information between them. Manfried Elsig (2007) follows the same line of argument when he shows how interactive governance arenas that bring together national governments, such as the WTO, are able to position themselves as democratically legitimate arenas for intergovernmental policy making. By merging these insights with Mark Granovetter's social network analysis, we see the first contours of how and why governance networks have an important role to play in building an intergovernmental model of democracy. It becomes clear that the democratic promise of governance networks springs from the fact that they are constitutively different from institutions. Rather than establishing strong ties between individuals or groups such as is the case in an intragovernmental model of democracy, networks provide weak ties between them. These weak ties bring interdependent but operationally autonomous actors together in an effort to define and pursue shared goals without giving up their autonomy. What distinguishes governance networks from a political entity such as a government is that they are temporary formations that are held together by situated interdependencies rather than stable organizational units held together by codified rules and norms (Sørensen and Torfing 2007, chap. 1).

As pointed out in governance research, governance networks can serve as an effective institutional platform for promoting intergovernmental policy making because they are driven by interdependencies between the involved stakeholders. These interdependencies encourage the participants to commit themselves to defining shared goals and to engage in joint action (Elsig 2007; Slaughter 2003). Governance researchers are more divided in the question of whether governance networks can serve as a means to enhance democracy (Torfing et al. 2012). Some argue that governance networks can improve democracy to the extent that they allow those who are most intensely affected by a particular decision directly in the policy making (Dryzek 2007; Young 2000; Rhodes 2000) and contribute to the development of shared points of identification and joint action between actors despite differences in viewpoints and interests (Sørensen and Torfing 2003). Others point out that governance networks have a propensity to include strong rather than weak actors and therefore will produce systematic inequalities in political influence (Hansen 2007) just as they tend to be difficult to hold to account due to their opaque and often informal character (Pierre and Peters 2005).

In light of these democratic potentials and challenges, considerations about how to ripe the fruits and avoid the dangers of governance networks for democracy in intergovernmental policy making must focus on the extent to which intergovernmental governance networks: 1) distribute influence to the intensely affected governments and not only to those with most resources; 2) add to the development of shared points of identification and shared purpose among the participants that encourage collective action in recognition of the differences between them; and 3) diffuse information in ways that enhance the ability of the participants to hold each other to account. I shall return to how governance networks can be brought to serve these functions in the section on metagovernance. First, however, I consider in more depth why governance networks are particularly relevant as a tool for democratization of intergovernmental policy making.

HOW CAN GOVERNANCE NETWORKS DEMOCRATIZE INTERGOVERNMENTAL DECISION MAKING

As mentioned earlier, governance networks can become a supplement as well as enrichment of democracy because they are different than traditional forms of intragovernmental policy making. This difference means that they must be measured by other democratic standards than a government. While the democratic quality of a government relies on the degree to which it has close ties to its constituency, the democratic quality of governance networks depends on their ability to form weak ties between democratically appointed governments. In line with Granovetter's arguments, one might say that the particular democratic contribution of governance networks is their ability to establish weak ties between strong ties. The strong democratic ties between a government and its constituency advocated in models of representative democracy consist of formal procedures for ensuring equal political inclusion, a strong collective political identity and capacity for joint action ensured through clear boundaries to the outside world, and institutionalized mechanisms for holding governments in account. Such strong ties are not adaptable to a governance network that cannot function without a high degree of flexibility and capacity to reorganize itself in light of changing goals and ambitions, levels of interdependencies, and actor constellations. While the regulatory framework is fixed in intragovernmental models of representative democracy, it is under constant formation and transformation in processes of network governance.

Then, what is the particular democratic value of the weak ties between governments provided by governance networks? First of all, governance networks make it possible to *distribute political influence* more directly with reference to levels of affectedness. Hence, the democratic legitimacy of governance networks depends on the degree to which their members are recognized as representatives for stakeholders who are intensely affected by the policy problems that are being addressed by the network. To put it differently, governance networks pave the way for a flexible, situated, and problem-driven composition of intergovernmental democratic arenas that bring political influence into the hands of those governments who are most intensely affected. A further positive effect of introducing flexible and problem-driven intergovernmental governance arenas is a politicization of the question of who should be excluded and who should not. If pressure is put on intergovernmental governance networks to legitimize their position as influential policy makers on the grounds that they can be said to include the intensely affected governments, it is likely to have a spillover effect. Hence, it can increase the demand on the involved governments to actively reconsider and rearticulate the patterns of political inclusion and exclusion at play in their home communities. This internal destabilization and repoliticization of well-consolidated patterns of exclusion and inclusion can strengthen intragovernmental democracy if it widens the range of issues that can be made subject to political contestation (Dryzek 2000).

Second, by establishing weak ties between governments, governance networks can pave the way for the *construction of a particular pluricentric kind of democratic communality* between actors who subscribe to different collective political identities (Kersbergen and Waarden 2004). The significance of governance networks is that their ability to function well does not depend on the existence of a coherent collective political identity. Rather, they rely on a specific kind of relational storyline that stipulates the existence of a strong interdependency and shared destiny and need for joint action between actors with different collective political identities (Hajer 1995; Sørensen and Torfing 2003). In other words, governance networks add to the imaginary construction of a temporal, purposeful "we" that is constituted on difference. This kind of temporal political identification between members of different democracies is productive for democracy because it trains the participants in what Michael Sandel describes as the distinctive civic virtue of our time: *"the capacity to negotiate our way among sometimes overlapping, sometimes conflicting obligations that claims us, and to live with the tension to which multiple loyalties give rise"* (Sandel 1996, 350).

Intergovernmental networks place governments in situations where they have to deal with such tensions just as they offer a story line that legitimizes this course of action that is the image of governance networks as necessitated by interdependencies and driven by negotiated decision making between autonomous actors in ways that allow these actors to maintain their autonomy. By serving as a platform for coping with multiple and overlapping points of identification and the tensions that these complex obligations produce, governance networks have a central role to play in paving the way for the formation of a pluricentric communality that allows for the construction of situated and temporal collective political identities. This kind of communality is not only important for democracy because it allows for the establishment of an intergovernmental "we" that can set the agenda for the identification of shared political goals. It can also pave the way for a destabilization and reshuffling of strong and sedimented "we" and "they" ties within the individual democratic communities. Although such stabilizations are necessary for democracy, they are also dangerous because strong ties tend to block a permanent vibrant political contestation about what characterizes this "we" and who and what it includes. By bringing different and partly overlapping notions of political communality into dialogue with each other, and by training governments to shift between different points of identification, governance networks encourage self-reflection and political debate about the character of the political communality that forms the basis of a democratic community, and soften the boundaries between the included and the excluded. Thereby, governance networks help to reduce the totalizing tendencies that are inherent to the construction of strong collective identities (Connolly 1995; Dryzek 2000).

Finally, the weak intergovernmental ties provided by governance networks can be of great value to democracy because of their *capacity to ensure an effective diffusion of political information*. Hence, governance networks establish an environment in which governments can exchange information about facts, views, and ideas and diffuse this knowledge to their respective constituencies. It can be argued that the involved governments might chose to keep this information to themselves but the fact that the ties between the participants are weak makes it notoriously difficult for the participants to keep the aggregated information within the network. This capacity and propensity to diffuse information does not only increase the ability of the involved constituencies to hold intergovernmental governance networks to account for their actions, it also improves chances that the control and accountability mechanisms provided by the institutions of representative will be able to hold their promises. Models of representative democracy provide a series of mechanisms for diffusing political information to the citizens. There are laws granting citizens the right to obtain information about the actions taken by politicians and the public administration and the media have extended access to key policy arenas. Although these mechanisms for diffusing political information are crucial for democracy, intergovernmental governance networks expand the level of political information available to decision makers because governance networks function as sites for information exchange and information aggregation. Furthermore, intergovernmental governance networks can help to destabilize well-established alliances between powerful elites and hegemonic policy discourses that lay the ground for asymmetrical distributions of political power in representative democracies (Connolly 1995, 24). This ability to diffuse political information in ways that reduce the chances of closure make intergovernmental governance networks a valuable means to supplement and refine the control and accountability mechanisms provided by the institutions of representative democracy.

Having now outlined the potential role that intergovernmental governance networks can play in supplementing and enriching models of representative democracy, it should immediately be stressed that this potential is not released automatically. If governance networks are to serve this function, they must be actively constructed as democratic arenas through deliberate and strategic acts of metagovernance.

PROMOTING INTERGOVERNMENTAL NETWORK DEMOCRACY THROUGH METAGOVERNANCE

If intergovernmental governance networks are to serve as a positive contribution to democracy, they must be put under pressure to justify and legitimize their actions with reference to democratic norms and standards. More precisely, they must be able to show that they distribute influence with reference to levels of affectedness, provide a sense of shared destiny or communality constituted on the presence of plural collective points of identification, and diffuse political information in ways that promote the ability of the participating governments and the affected constituencies to hold the governance network to account.

Due to the self-governing character of governance networks, the pressure on them to live up to these standards cannot be exercised by means of hierarchical rule and control but must take the form of different strands of metagovernance. As extensively argued by governance researchers, governance networks can be governed in ways that grant the networks a considerable space for self-governance (Jessop 1998, 2004; Kooiman 2003; Meuleman 2008; Sørensen and Torfing 2009). Although most of this literature debates how acts of metagovernance can enhance the efficiency and effectiveness of governance networks, it has also been pointed out how metagovernance can make them more democratic (Sørensen and Torfing 2005; Torfing et al. 2012).

Governance researchers point to a number of ways in which governance networks can be metagoverned. Much of the debate concerns the regulatory powers of institutional design, and this debate tends to take departure from a neo-institutional understanding of what an institution is rather than an old-institutionalist approach focusing on formal rules and procedures (Sørensen and Torfing 2007, 30). Governance theorists who perceive human action as predominantly guided by a logic of consequentiality describe metagovernance through institutional design as the construction of incentives structures that motivate self-governing actors to act in particular ways (Scharpf 1994; Kickert, Klijn, and Koppenjan 1997). In contrast, researchers who view human action as guided by a logic of appropriateness view institutions as universes of meaning that form the identities and subjectivities of the involved actors (March and Olsen 1995; Foucault 1991). Seen from this latter perspective, metagovernance through institutional design is about forming the hearts and the minds of those members of governance networks. In my view, metagovernance through institutional design can be exercised both through the construction of incentives structures and through the formation of universes of meaning (Sørensen 2013). Among some of the tool kits for metagoverning governance networks proposed by governance researchers, we find funding schemes that encourage the formation of networks through the construction of interdependencies; story lines that produce convincing images of shared destiny; performance-based resource allocation; and evaluation schemes that put pressure on networks to justify and explain their activities (Sørensen and Torfing 2009). These tool kits can not only be taken into use in an attempt to enhance the effectiveness of governance networks, but also to enhance their democratic quality.

Then, who is in a position to metagovern governance networks? In governance research, the role as metagovernor has predominantly been viewed as a task to be performed by a step higher authority with the resources that this position entails. However, as pointed out by some (Kooiman 1993; Jessop 1998), metagovernance can be exercised by a wide range of actors. This view is supported by Christopher Hood's (1986) argument that the capacity to govern society can be performed by any political actor who has the nodality, authority, treasure, and organizational capacity to do so. In the case of metagovernance, it could be added that actors who are able to activate one or more of these capacities in ways that add to the formation of a desired institutional framing of intergovernmental governance networks can increase the pressure on these networks to legitimize themselves with reference to a particular set of democratic norms and standards. As such, this role can not only be taken on by strong governments, but also by transnational political organizations, other governance networks, by strong social and political movements, or by the media, including not least the new social media. Whether or not these actors will choose to use their resources as metagovernors to enhance the democratic quality of intergovernmental governance networks is another matter. It depends on the strength of democratic norms and patterns of action among the involved actors as well as the degree to which metagovernors are put under public and institutional pressure to legitimize and account for the outcomes of and procedures regulating intergovernmental influential governance networks.

CONCLUSION

The aim of the chapter has been to argue for the need to develop an intergovernmental model of democracy and to point out how weak ties between governments such as those provided by governance networks might play in developing such a model. Like social science in general, models of democracy have tended to celebrate the value of strong ties and thus overlooked the important democratic potentials of weak ties between governments. In consequence, the establishment of weak ties such as those provided by governance networks has been seen as a threat to democracy because these ties did not live up to the demands for strong ties of inclusion/exclusion, identification, and accountability. Globalization and recent public sector reforms, however, have illuminated the need to develop an intergovernmental model of democracy, and I have taken the first steps in exploring the role that governance networks might play in this context. By merging the contributions of recent governance research and Granovetter's social network analysis, it is pointed out that the potential contributions of governance networks is that they are flexible, ad hoc, driven by the commitments of the participants, and therefore have the potential to destabilize settled world images and fixed relationships and power structures.

It might be argued that it is problematic to expect governance networks to serve as a means to improve democracy in light of the many criticisms that have been raised against them for being a threat to democracy. I do not deny these criticisms, but I claim that they are not intrinsic to governance networks. Social network analysis indicates that governance networks do in fact enhance inclusion, social cohesion, and accountability due to their reliance on weak ties. In my view, the democratic problems pertaining to governance networks have to do with the fact that they—like intergovernmental policy making—have until now not been perceived as arenas for political decision making. This failure to view intergovernmental networks as democratic arenas is apparent in the two empirical cases mentioned earlier. They bear witness to the fact that even though intergovernmental networks have become an integrated and institutionalized governance practice, they are not expected to live up to democratic norms and standards. I can think of two reasons why they are not viewed as democratic arenas. First, governance theory has approached governance networks from a managerial perspective focusing on the extent to which they contribute to the provision of effective public governance. Second, the hegemonic position of the traditional intragovernmental approach to democracy has placed intergovernmental policy making outside the realm of democratic decision making. If, however, governance networks were to be viewed as democratic arenas, their full democratic potentials could be released. Put under pressure to legitimize their actions with reference to democratic norms and standards, they will be able to enhance the democratic character of intergovernmental policy making through the democratic division of influence between affected governments, through the construction of a pluricentric communality that celebrate attempts to formulate and realize shared objectives in the light of differences in political identity and interests, and through a broad diffusion of information about the actions of a governance network that makes it possible for the affected communities to hold governance networks in account. The effort to change the perception and image of governance networks from nonpolitical to political arenas in need of democratic regulation is currently the first and most important task for those who chose to take on the task as metagovernor of intergovernmental governance networks.

REFERENCES

Abbott, Kenneth, W., and Duncan Snidal. 2000. "Hard and Soft Law in International Governance." *International Organization* 54 (3): 421–56.

Ansell, Christopher. 2000. "The Networked Polity: Regional Development in Western Europe." *Governance. An International Journal of Policy and Administration* 13 (3): 303–33.

Bache, Ian and Matthew V. Flinders, eds. 2004. *Multi-Level Governance*. Oxford: Oxford University Press.

Benz, Arthur and Yoannis Papadopoulos, eds. 2006. *Governance and Democracy*. London: Routledge.

Blom-Hansen, Jens. 2002. *Den Fjerde Statsmagt?* Aarhus: Aarhus University Press.

Bogason, Peter, and Mette Zølner, eds. 2007. *Methods in Democratic Network Governance*. Basingstoke: Palgrave Macmillan.

Bohman, James. 2005. "From Demos to Demoi: Democracy across Borders." *Ratio Juris* 18 (3): 293–314.

Braun, Dietmar. 2012. "Multi-level governance in Germany and Switzerland." In *Handbook of Multi-level Governance,* edited by Henrik Enderlein, Sonja Wälti, and Michael Zürn. Cheltenham: Edward Elgar.

Connolly, William E. 1995. *The Ethos of Pluralization*. Minneapolis: University of Minnesota Press.

Dahl, Robert A. 1956. *A Preface to Democratic Theory*. Chicago: University of Chicago Press.

Dryzek, John S. 2000. *Deliberative Democracy and Beyond*. Oxford: Oxford University Press.

———. 2007. "Networks and Democratic Ideals: Equality, Freedom, and Communication." In *Theories of Democratic Network Governance*, edited by Eva Sørensen and Jacob Torfing, 262–73. Basingstoke: Palgrave Macmillan.

Elsig, Manfred. 2007. "The World Trade Organization's Legitimacy Crisis: What Does the Beast Look Like?" *Journal of World Trade* 41 (1): 75–98.

Enderlein, Henrik, Sonja Wälti, and Michael Zürn, eds. 2012. *Handbook of Multi-level Governance*. Cheltenham: Edward Elgar.

European Commission. 2000. *European Governance: A White Paper*. Brussels: European Commission.

Foucault, Michel. 1991. "Governmentality." In *The Foucault Effect*, edited by Graham Burchell, Colin Gordon, and Peter Miller, 87–104. Hemel Hempstead: Harvester Wheatsheaf.

Fung, Archon, and Erik Olin Wright, eds. 2003. *Deepening Democracy: Institutional Innovations*. London: Verso.

Granovetter, Mark S. 1973. "The Strength of Weak Ties," *American Journal of Sociology* 6 (78): 1360–80.

Greven, Michael T. and Louis W Pauly, eds. 2000. *Democracy Beyond the State? The European Dilemma and the Emerging Global Order*. Lanham Maryland: Rowman & Littlefield Publishers INC.

Habermas, Jürgen. 2001. *The Postnational Constellation*. Cambridge: MIT Press.

Hajer, M. 1995. *The Politics of Environmental Discourse: Ecological Modernization and the Policy Process*. Oxford: Clarendon Press.

Hajer, Maarten. 2003. "Policy without Polity? Policy Analysis and the Institutional Void." *Policy Sciences* (36): 175–95.

Hallerberg, Mark. 2012. "Multi-level Governance, Decentralization and Fiscal Federalism." In *Handbook of Multi-level Governance*, edited by Henrik Enderlein, Sonja Wälti, and Michael Zürn. Cheltenham: Edward Elgar.

Hansen, Allan D. 2007. "Governance Networks and Participation." In *Theories of Democratic Network Governance*, edited by Eva Sørensen and Jacob Torfing, 247–61. Hampshire: Macmillan.

Heffen, Oscar van, Walter J.M. Kickert, and Jacques J.A. Thomassen, eds. 2000. *Governance in Modern Society: Effects, Change and Formation of Government Institutions*. Dordrecht: Kluwer Academic Publishers.

Held, David. 1995. *Democracy and the Global Order*. Cambridge: Polity Press.

Hirst, Paul. 2000. "Governance and Democracy." In *Debating Governance,* edited by Jon Pierre, 13–35. Oxford: Oxford University Press.

Holden, Barry, ed. 2000. *Global Democracy: Key Debates*. New York: Routledge.

Hood, Christopher. 1986. *Administrative Analysis: An Introduction to Rules, Enforcement, and Organizations*. Brighton: Harvester.

Jessop, Bob. 1998. "The Rise of Governance and the Risk of Failure: The Case of Economic Development." *International Social Science Journal* 50 (155): 29–45.

———. 2004. "Multi-level Governance and Multi-level Metagovernance." In *Multi-level Governance*, edited by Ian Bache and Matthew Flinders. New York: Oxford University Press.

Kern, Kristine, and Harriet Bulkeley. 2009. "Cities, Europeanization and Multi-level Governance: Governing Climate Change through Transnational Municipal Networks." *Journal of Common Market Studies* 47 (2): 309–32.

Kersbergen, Kees V. and Frans V. Waarden. 2004. "Governance' as a Bridge Between Disciplines: Cross Disciplinary Inspiration Regarding Shifts in Governance and Problems of Governability, Accountability and Legitimacy." *European Journal of Political Research* 43: 143–71.

Kickert, Walter J.M., Erik-Hans Klijn, and Joop. F.M. Koppenjan, eds. 1997. *Managing Complex Networks: Strategies for the Public Sector.* London: Sage.

Klijn, Erik-Hans. and Chris Skelcher. 2007. "Democracy and Governance Networks: Compatible or Not?" *Public Administration* 85 (3): 587–608.

Kooiman, Joop., ed. 1993. *Modern Governance. New Government-Society Interactions.* London: Sage.

———. 2003. *Governing as Governance.* London: Sage Publications Ltd.

Larner, Wendy, and William Walters, eds. 2004. *Global Governmentality: Governing International Spaces.* London: Routledge.

Lindblom, Charles E. 1965. *The Intelligence of Democracy: Decision Making Through Mutual Adjustment.* New York: The Free Press.

March, James G., and Olsen, Johan P. 1995. *Democratic Governance.* New York: The Free Press.

Marcussen, Martin, and Jacob Torfing. 2007. *Democratic Network Governance in Europe.* Basingstoke: Palgrave Macmillan.

Meuleman, Louis. 2008. *Public Management and the Metagovernance of Hierarchies, Networks and Markets.* Heidelberg: Springer.

Pateman, Carole. 1970. *Participation and Democratic Theory.* Cambridge: Cambridge University Press.

Pedersen, Anne R., Karina Sehested, and Eva Sørensen. 2011. "Emerging Theoretical Understandings of Pluricentric Coordination in Public Governance." *American Review of Public Administration* 41 (4): 375–94.

Peters, B. Guy., and Jon Pierre. 2004. "Multi-level Governance and Democracy: A Faustian Bargain?" In *Multi-Level Governance,* edited by Bache, Ian and Flinders, Matthew, 75–92. Oxford: Oxford University Press.

Pierre, Jon., and B. Guy Peters. 2005. *Governing Complex Societies: Trajectories and Scenarios.* London: Palgrave Macmillan.

Rhodes, Rod A.W. 2000. "The Governance Narrative: Key Findings and Lessons from the ESRC's Whitehall Programme." *Public Administration* 78 (2): 345–64.

Sandel, Michael J. 1996. *Democracy's Discontent—America in Search of a Public Philosophy.* Cambridge: Harvard University Press.

Sartori, Giovanni. 1987. *Theories of Democracy Revisited.* Chatham: Chatham Publishers Inc.

Scharpf, Fritz W. 1994. "Games Real Actors Could Play: Positive and Negative Coordination in Embedded Negotiations." *Journal of Theoretical Politics* 61 (1): 27–53.

Slaughter, Anne-Marie. 2003. "Global Government Networks, Global Information Agencies, and Disaggregated Democracy." *Michigan Journal of International Law* 24: 1041–76.

Stein, Michael B., and Lisa Turkewitsch. 2012. "Multi-level Governance in Canadian and American Inter-governmental relations" In *Handbook of Multi-level Governance,* edited by Henrik Enderlein, Sonja Wälti, and Michael Zürn. Cheltenham: Edward Elgar.

Sørensen, Eva. 2013. "Institutionalizing Interactive Governance for Democracy." *Interpretive Policy Studies* 7 (1):72–86.

Sørensen, Eva, and Jacob Torfing. 2003. "Network Politics, Political Capital, and Democracy." *International Journal of Public Administration* 26 (6): 609–34.

———. 2005. "The Democratic Anchorage of Governance Networks." *Scandinavian Political Studies* 28 (3): 195–218.

———, eds. 2007. *Theories of Democratic Network Governance*. Basingstoke: Palgrave Macmillan.

———. 2009. "Enhancing Effective and Democratic Network Governance through Metagovernance." *Public Administration* 87 (2):234–258.

Sørensen, Eva and Triantafillou, Peter, eds. 2009. *The Politics of Self-Governance*. London: Ashgate.

Sørensen, Eva, Karina Sehested, and Anne Reff, eds. 2011. *Offentlig Styring som Pluricentrisk Koordination*. Copenhagen: DJØF Publishers.

Torfing, Jacob, B. Guy Peters, Jon Pierre, and Eva Sørensen. 2012. *Interactive Governance: Advancing the Paradigm*. Oxford: Oxford University Press.

Young, Iris M. 2000. *Inclusion and Democracy*. Oxford: Oxford University Press.

Zürn, Michael. 2000. "Democratic Governance Beyond the Nation-State: The EU and Other International Institutions." *European Journal of International Relations* 6 (2): 183–221.

———. 2012. "Global Governance as Multi-level governance." In *Handbook of Multi-level Governance* edited by Henrik Enderlein, Sonja Wälti, and Michael Zürn. Cheltenham: Edward Elgar.

6 Governance Network Performance

A Complex Adaptive Systems Approach

Christopher Koliba

INTRODUCTION

If we are to assess the performance of networks within a public administration and policy context, we must regard them as tangible, observable structures comprised of nodes (or agents) and ties that formally or informally, tightly or loosely, couple two or more nodes together. The kind of "network logic" that accompanies the study of networks bears a significant impact on our understandings of network performance. Although there is still likely room for debate, a comprehensive view of this network logic for the field of public administration and policy studies is emerging around a number of givens about multi-organizational networks found within the public administration and policy studies literature. These givens, however, are punctuated by a number of compelling methodological and theoretical challenges that may be best served by understanding network performance as an integral feature of a complex adaptive system. To describe and evaluate in such a manner, a comprehensive framework for categorizing network performance is needed.

We begin this chapter with a brief summary of the network logic that is presently in place. We then examine some of the seminal bodies of research and theoretical developments in network performance that have arisen over the past fifteen or so years, presenting a classification of types of current network performance research currently. Drawing upon the overarching network logic present in the first third of the chapter, and the survey of major network performance research in the second third, we conclude the chapter with some suggestions for integrating network research into a complex adaptive systems framework for network performance, accountability, and learning.

THE GIVENS OF NETWORK PERFORMANCE

There is a large and growing body of literature found within the public administration and policy studies journals and books drawing on network structures and metaphors to describe and evaluate administrative and policy practice. Although space precludes an in depth review of this literature, a number of efforts to synthesize this literature have been made (Kickert et al. 1997 Salamon 2002; Agranoff 2007; Provan et al. 2007; Koliba, Meek, and Zia et al. 2010) and are drawn on here. For brevity, the network logic that emerges out of this literature is provided in a series of summative statements. At the end of the explanation of each statement, a few references are provided that explain this logic in greater detail.

Networks Govern

Networks exist to carry out some facet or facets of the policy process and policy stream. Networks of multi-institutional arrangements are formed to carry out the full gambit of policy functions: framing problems, creating or advocating for policies, and implementing policies. Within the PA field, particular emphasis has been paid to the role of networks in *implementing* public policies. However, as classical policy systems theories remind us, public policy is carried out as coupled policy streams. Networks that exist to implement a given policy (regulate, contract, provide services, etc.) may also be actively involved in the framing of policy problems. The active participation of networks in carrying out one or more policy functions serves as the foundation of its governance functions (Kingdon 1984; Rhodes 1997; Salamon 2002; Sørensen and Torfing 2005; Bovaird 2005; Koliba, Meek, and Zia 2010).

Networks Exist Within All Policy Domains

As classical policy systems theories also suggest, networks exist within virtually every policy domain. If one is looking for them, networks are ubiquitous. Networks that persist within a single policy domain rely on that domain to set its boundary conditions and determine network structures and functions. Thus, we may begin to speak in terms of emergency management networks, social service networks, health care networks, transportation planning networks, etc. Although there is likely to be some cross boundary activities, these networks, are, by and large, discrete (Baumgartner and Jones 1993, 2002).

Networks Are Multi-Actor and Multiscalar

These domain-specific networks are comprised of agents spanning sectors, geographic scales, and social scale. These networks involve not only governments, but also for profit and nonprofit organizations as well. Contracting out and privatization of government services has required the establishment of loosely or tightly coupled networks of cojoined sectors. The kind of ties forged through contracting out and the formation of public-private partnerships are often linked to longstanding intergovernmental ties that link federal, state, regional, and local governments in complex networks of intergovernmental relations. Over time, the nature of these intergovernmental ties evolve, shaped by reforms to centralize or decentralize, and signified by trends toward devolution, federalization, deregulation, or reregulation (Salamon 2002; Bovaird 2004; Koliba, Meek, and Zia 2010).

Lastly, the multi-scalar features of these networks are marked by the nested complexity of social scale—as individuals form groups, which form organizations and institutions, and which ultimately give shape to interorganizational networks. Individual, group, organizational, and whole network goals may or may not align with one another. All of these features form the basis of a complexity that poses significant challenges to measuring and managing network performance (Gage and Mandell 1990; Koppenjan and Klijn 2004; Pierre and Peters 2005; Koliba, Meek, and Zia 2010).

Networks Are Usually Composed of Mixed Administrative Authorities

Although some have hung onto the notion that networks are managed exclusively through horizontal ties, the existence of networks that rely solely on such ties are hard to find. The kind of shared governance models outlined in the Proven and Kenis typology of network governance (2007) rarely exists at the level of interorganizational networks that carry out sustained policy functions. Instead, lead organizations or network administrative organizational structures are in place. These networks have been said to exist "in the shadow of hierarchy". However, networks are often shaped by principal-agent relationships that are decidedly vertical in nature. Thus, most networks of interest to public administration are comprised of mixed authorities, in which command and control arrangements persist for some administrative subsystems or assemblages, with more collaborative structures guiding other subsystems assemblages (Salamon 2002; Agranoff and McGuire 2003; Provan and Kenis 2007; Koliba, Meek, and Zia 2010).

Networks Are Complex

The multisector, multiscalar composition of network agents combines with mixed administrative ties to present a decidedly complex picture of network structure and function and network management. Although we will not explore the characteristics of this complexity in great detail here, it is important to note that a significant body of scholarship has been taking shape in the United States and Europe drawing on the parameters of complexity science to study and model these networks. The use of such modeling approaches will only be briefly touched on later. Suffice it to say, the nonlinearity, emergent qualities of this complexity poses significant challenges to measuring network performance (Katz and Kahn 1978; Baumgartner and Jones 1993; Rhodes 1997; Zia and Koliba 2011; Morcol 2012; Gerrits 2012; Koliba and Zia 2013).

Networks Are Governed

Despite the complexity of these networks, they are, to some large degree, governed. They are steered by the decision making of individual network managers, guided by laws, rules, and regulations enforced by institutions and shaped by the policy tools designed and implemented to address public interests and provide public value. To varying degrees, network governance is informed and determined by the explicit performance standards that are set by network governors, defined in legislation, and negotiated through interjurisdictional or partnership agreements. However, expectations about network performance are also implicitly held by any person with a vested stake in the network's activities. Therefore, networks are governed by explicit and implicit performance standards that are both endogenous and exogenous to the network. The extent to which these standards influence network structures and functions will vary. This observation has been the focus of many of those who have studied network performance thus far (Provan and Milward 1995; Frederickson and Frederickson 2006; Turrini et al. 2010; Koliba, Campbell, and Zia 2011; Kenis and Provan 2009).

Network Actors Can Use Performance Indicators to Guide Decision Making

As has been widely noted, performance goals and the standards put in place to measure and monitor them are only as good as the practices and systems put in place to use them. Within the nomenclature of performance management frameworks, the use of performance data to inform strategic decision making is suggested. Performance metrics are used in resource allocation, strategic planning, and tactical decision making. They are used to make a system or network responsive to the goals, desires, and ascriptions of certain agents—be they funders, regulators, or collaborators. Performance goals, explicitly or implicitly tied to performance indicators, may serve as inputs that guide endogenous or intranetwork decision making. Perceptions of network performance may also be held by agents who are exogenous to a network. For instance, citizens and elected officials may pressure network actors to respond to concerns and adapt to changing conditions. These agents may not formally reside within the network, but can exert influence over the selection and use of performance goals (Radin 2006; Frederickson and Frederickson 2006; Moynihan 2008).

Performance Standards Can Keep Networks Accountable

The use of performance measures to make decisions is guided by the kind of accountability ties that exist between members of a network, and between members of the network and those outside of the network. This kind of network accountability has been cast in terms of the ties that persist across and between network agents. For our purposes here, network accountability may be distilled down to a series of relations between those to whom account is rendered and those who render account. These networked accountabilities have been described as "hybrid accountability regimes" contribute to the governance and performance of networks (Mashaw 2006; Koliba, Mills, and Zia 2011). Differentiating between democratic, administrative, and market ties, this approach to network accountability takes into consideration the democratic anchorage of networks, the persistence of vertical and horizontal ties, and the existence of market accountabilities that not only shape the actions of businesses and firms, but also has increasingly influenced the actions of public and nonprofit organizations. The implications of these hybridized accountabilities for network performance are profound. It has been widely noted that the robustness of accountability ties within any kind of public administrative setting is important. As the number of network agents expand, the robustness of these ties can become diluted, and has a significant impact on how network performance is measured, evaluated, and monitored (Sørensen and Torfing 2005; Mashaw 2006; Radin 2006).

Performance Standards Are Contingent on the Value(s) Placed Upon Them

Contemporary views of public performance and accountability underscore the appreciation that perceptions of performance are the products of social construction. As Deborah Stone has so eloquently laid out in her book, *Policy Paradox: The Art of Political Decision Making* (2002), determinations around what to measure and how to measure it are ultimately political considerations. This view is endorsed by Beryl Radin who, in her book, *Challenging the Performance Movement: Accountability, Complexity and Democratic Values* (2006), situates the contemporary interest in performance management within this very context. The conclusion to be drawn here is that the management of performance within any public context, whether considered at the network level or not, is a political devise used to govern. Questions of performance are eminently informed by who has power. The extent to which this power is welded capriciously through some kind of political calculation, or through the use of more scientifically rendered, boundedly rational, decision-making processes. In either instance, the capacity of agents to learn from the use of performance indicators is important and becomes the basis for a systems view of network performance that can account for the role of politics and administrative science in managing performance.

It has been widely recognized that governance networks need to be particularly sensitive to adding "public value". The notion of public value has been posited as a central and virtually universal feature of contemporary, democratic governance theory. Stoker has noted that, "the judgment of what is public value is collectively built through deliberation involving elected and appointed government officials and key stakeholders. The achievement of public value, in turn, depends on actions chosen in a reflective manner from a range of intervention options that rely extensively on building and maintaining network provisions" (Stoker 2006, 42). Thus, we must both honor and be resigned to the fact that what passes for performance will ultimately be judged against whatever is defined as public value. For our purposes here, we will sidestep this critical, but highly normative, line of inquiry.

We may conclude two things from this assessment of our current state of thinking about networks: 1) Networks are complex structures that can be empirically studied and modeled; and 2) That a robust theoretical basis for studying these networks may exist if a network logic is combined with contemporary views of public performance and accountability.

NETWORK PERFORMANCE AS A SYSTEMS CONSTRUCT

To explain how networks perform and use performance standards to govern, we may draw on the basics of general systems theory, which describes systems in terms of stocks and flows of resources bound together through a series of correcting and reinforcing feedback loops. Patricia Ingraham and Amy Donahue have drawn on a systems lens to describe the classical policy/ performance process undergirding most conceptualization about how performance is understood.

This flow diagram (Figure 6.1) defines the major assumptions guiding the "managing for results" movement that has marked the past twenty years of performance management literature. In this diagram, Ingraham and Donahue's unit of analysis is the individual public bureaucracy or municipal government. They describe a "Government Management" process as a black box that needs to be unpacked and described if the relationship between resources and results are to be understood. They sought to analyze this black box in terms of management capacity that they define as, the "intrinsic ability to marshal, develop, direct, and control its [financial], human, physical, and information capital to support the discharge of its policy directions" (Ingraham and Donahue 2000, 294). They focus on the role of government agents, and their use of resources to produce results.

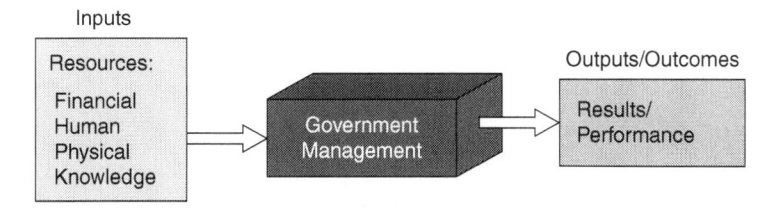

Figure 6.1 Classical Systems View of Managing for Results,
Source: Adapted from Ingraham and Donahue, 2000

Scaling up to the network level, the black box of network governance appears to be even more complex. Resources are still inputs and results are outputted. However, processes are guided by more agents with complementary, conjoined, or even competing agendas. Different network agents may have access to different kinds of financial, political, social, human, physical, and knowledge capitals. Construed in terms of networks, these capital resources flow between nodes in the network. Understanding the relationship between resource flows and a network's performance is critical. Ingraham and Donahue lay out a framework for how to track these resource flows and tie them to performance indicators for individual public sector organizations. Scaling up and across to the level of interorganizational networks is needed.

In the network performance literature, the black box of network performance management capacity is approached in one of three ways: 1) Network structure determinants: Those studies that focus on the relationship between network structures and network performance; 2) Performance management analysis: Those studies that focus on the use of performance data within networks; and 3) Organizational learning and knowledge management analysis: Those studies that examine the relationship between the use of performance data and network performance as instances of organizational learning and knowledge transfer. In essence, network management practices encompass all three facets. Network managers may have a hand in designing and executing network structures and functions, they may have a hand in determining which performance management indicators matter, and, they will most definitely need to have a hand in facilitating how the network learns over time from the use of performance data.

To build a theory of network performance that encompasses network determinants, performance management subsystems, and network learning and knowledge transfer, we must return to the givens outlined earlier in this chapter in which we situate performance management as a critical feature of governance. Theoretically, effective governance requires the conscious articulation of performance goals and the collection of data designed to assess the level of achievement of these goals. Effective governance requires some level of situational awareness of network governors—those agents within the network with some measure of steering power. As we have noted, the complexity of networks may prevent network governors from comprehending how their interorganizational networks operate. Effective network governors will possess the capacity to distill network properties into manageable units of analysis.

Donald Moynihan suggests that the location within a network where this distillation of network properties needs to take place is the "performance management system". Performance management systems are designed to take information from the environment, through consultation with the public, stakeholders, public representatives, and the array of stakeholders to whom networks are accountable. Performance management systems provide a means by which network governors engage in coding—interpreting and refining information from the external environment and internal stakeholders into a series of information categories such as strategic goals, objectives, performance measures, and targets. After this coding takes place, performance information can then be presented to decision makers and ultimately used to implement collective action (Moynihan 2008, 6).

The figure below provides an overview of the relationship between network inputs, processes, and outputs (the upper portion of the system model in Figure 6.2) and the collection and use of performance data (the lower portion of the system model in Figure 6.2). The transformation of performance data into knowledge that leads to decisions and actions, "closes the loop" of feedback—forming the basis of a systems view of network performance.

Drawing on this systems model of network performance, we can distill the prevailing body of network performance research into one of three categories:

1) **As pure studies of network performance undertaken with the goal of determining the optimal composition of network structures and functions within particular policy domains (and across policy domains when comparative analysis is rendered).** These studies and analytical frameworks focus on the relationship between inputs, processes (that are enacted through network structures and discrete acts of network management), and outputs/outcomes. In Figure 6.2, this relationship is signified in the upper set of arrows flowing from left to right.

2) **As studies of how networks manage performance through the establishment of performance management systems.** These studies and analytical frameworks concentrate on the definitions, collection and uses of performance data. These studies look at the role of performance

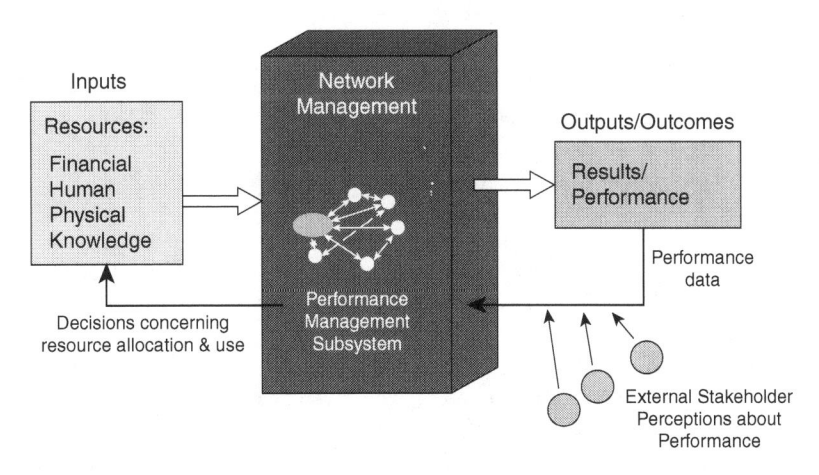

Figure 6.2 Network View of Managing Performance

data as inputs into a network's performance management subsystem and outputted as decisions concerning resource allocation and use. In Figure 6.2, this relationship is signified in the lower set of arrows flowing from right to left.

3) **As studies of learning and knowledge transfer that attempt to link network performance management systems to network outcomes.** Building on the organizational learning, knowledge management, and community of practice literature, these studies consider the relationship between network determinants, performance management subsystems, and network performance. Viewing the network in terms of learning and knowledge transfer can capture the nature of these complex governance networks. In Figure 6.2, this approach encompasses the system in its entirety.

Referencing some of the seminal pieces of network performance research, we describe the current thinking drawn from these three approaches to network performance research and theory. Studies of network structure determinants of performance are being fueled by the longstanding network performance research of Keith Provan and Brinton Milward (1995), whose research has primarily focused on social service networks. We will rely on a comprehensive review of this tradition recently conducted by Turrini and colleagues (2011) to summarize the current state of thinking regarding the relationship between network structure and network performance. In addition, the work of Kenneth Meier and Laurence O'Toole (2003; O'Toole and Meier 1999) fall into this category. Their extensive study of the Texas educational system has helped to clarify what we know and do not know about network structures, the kinds of management functions carried out across these structures, and network performance. Representing the studies that have empirically examined the use of performance management within complex governance networks, we summarize some the findings and theoretical frameworks of David and George Frederickson's study of health care networks (2006) and Koliba, Campbell, and Zia's study of congestion management networks (2011). Capturing the tradition of network performance research that looks at the role of organizational learning and knowledge transfer, we draw on Donald Moynihan's conceptualization of the relationship between organizational learning and network performance (2008) and Robert Agranoff's comparative case study analysis of network performance management (2007). There is a sizable and growing body of literature emerging around each one of these traditions. It is recognized that a much broader array of factors may be culled under each category. The purpose of this chapter is to pull out the distinguishing features of the network performance literature to provide the beginnings of a foundation for a fully explicated theory of network performance.

DETERMINANTS OF NETWORK STRUCTURE

The research teams of Provan and Milward and Meier and O'Toole are credited with having the most established research agendas on the "determinants of network effectiveness". With a focus on the performance of social service networks (Provan and Milward, 1995) and education networks (Meier and O'Toole 2003; O'Toole and Meier 1999), they have narrowed their attention to the relationship between network structure, network management, and network performance. Recently, Turrini and colleagues undertook a meta-analysis of the literature on network performance, relegating their review to studies that have focused on policy implementation—specifically, social service delivery (2010), following the research line laid out by Milward and Provan. By narrowing their focus to networks carrying these types of functions, they have, rightly, set initial boundary conditions that are essential to a meta-analysis of this nature. Their study resulted in the identification of concepts and variables that they coded for around client, community, and network level performance. Of the thirteen concepts that they found that had an impact on network performance, several stand out for closer review here.

- **Resource munificence.** The relationship between the existence of financial capital and network performance was a clear finding and underscores an observation that has long been assumed: that it takes money to produce results. In particular, Turrini and colleagues find that the role of local contributions to funding social service networks was critical to their positive performance, suggesting that in the case of social service network, at least, local agents need to have "skin in the game".
- **System stability.** Several studies in the meta-analysis by Turrini and colleagues focused on the relationship between the stability of the network and its capacity to perform. The conclusion is that social service networks tend to perform better when they have stable external and internal environments. That networks need to have established certain thresholds of homeostasis is an important finding and has a significant bearing on understanding the relationship between performance management and a system's feedback.
- **Existence of bridging and bonding mechanisms.** A key finding from their meta-analysis concerns the important role that collaborative capacity plays within social service networks. Turrini and colleagues define this collaborative capacity in terms of the cohesion and support from community and the existence of integrating tools such as the use of information technology and collaborative management tools to ensure network performance.
- **Intentional network steering processes.** Another key feature of this meta-analysis concerns the important role that the intentional steering

mechanisms of the network plays. Network performance is viewed to be positively influenced by the existence of network administrative organizations or lead organizations, suggesting here that within the context of social service networks, the exercise of vertical authority may be crucial to success.

The body of research surveyed by Turrini and colleagues focused on deriving determinants of network effectiveness by studying network properties that may, with some measure of certainty, be said to contribute to network performance. The challenges associated with this approach to network performance lies in the uncertainty associated with isolating the causal properties of these structures. The nonlinearity of network dynamics cannot be taken for granted, nor ignored. That said, this line of inquiry for network performance studies is crucial if we are to develop more sophisticated understandings of the black box of network process.

A second line of research into network determinants is worthy of mention here. Meier and O'Toole's long-term study of the Texas educational system has made major contributions to the network determinants literature (2003; O'Toole and Meier 1999). In particular, their research has focused on the role that certain network management strategies play in bringing about higher performing schools. Their research sheds light on the particular roles that network managers play in building and utilizing network structures to achieve functional aims. Two particular conclusions to be drawn from this research are provided below:

- **Network manager's capacity to bridge and boundary span.** Meier and O'Toole frame this capacity as the role of managers to pursue, "networking outward with multiple other actors and with frequency". Such activities have been shown to "strengthen program performance in the short run and also builds the baseline for future enhancements" (Meier and O'Toole 2003, 697).
- **Network manager's capacity to leverage network resources.** The capability to take advantage of the resources available as networks are built is carried out through the actions of network managers. Meier and O'Toole observe, "Network management helps to free . . . units from the constraints of existing routines and allows them to use selected available resources more effectively" (Meier and O'Toole 2003, 697). This capacity may be viewed as ensuring that the accomplishments of the whole network are more than just the sum of its parts.

The picture painted in this brief overview of the seminal works in the network determinants and performance literature is one in which both the network structures themselves, as well as the network manager's roles in building and leveraging network structures, serve as critical variables contributing to network performance.

PERFORMANCE MANAGEMENT ANALYSIS

The most extensive single set of cases studies of performance management systems operating within networks may be found in David Frederickson and George Frederickson's book, *Measuring the Performance of the Hollow State*, in which they provide a comparative case study analysis of health care delivery networks (2006). This body of work makes a substantial contribution to the literature on network performance because of its explicit focus on the role of federal performance management initiatives embodied in the Government Performance and Results Act (GPRA) and their impact on network structuration and performance management systems. They lay out a set of nine parameters that influence how the networks in their study collect and use performance data. Several parameters are highlighted here.

- **The level of third-party policy implementation.** Drawing on the notion of direct and indirect government, they situate each network along a continuum of "directness". This particular parameter draws our attention to the role of government as a lead organization within a network. It suggests that the performance goals ascribed to by government may, or may not, trump all other goals set forth by other network agents depending on the leverage that third-party providers possess within the network.
- **The characteristics of network performance goals.** Frederickson and Frederickson also classify performance goals using a logic model of systems dynamics, rightly suggesting that performance goals may be pegged to process, outputs, or outcomes. Presumably, performance goals that are characterized by inputs need to be considered as well. Their findings suggest that networks may be guided by different mental models of performance that are shaped by perceptions about where in the system performance goals need to be targeted.
- **Predilections toward the precision of performance measures.** Frederickson and Frederickson also find that the composition of viable performance measures along a continuum of qualitative/descriptive to quantitative/precise also varies among networks.
- **The level of goal and policy agreement.** The last parameter to highlight here concerns the level of goal agreement among network agents or between the network as a whole and its external stakeholders. Within the Frederickson and Frederickson model, goal agreement may range from incongruent to congruent. Presumably, goal congruence may ebb and flow over time, with some subassemblages of network agents reaching agreement around goals, while others may not.

Frederickson and Frederickson find that the use of performance goals and measures in network settings are influenced by two factors: the perceptions of individual agents and the network structures through which these perceptions are mediated. They conclude that effective network performance management systems need the support of key agency leadership, a shared commitment to a performance culture, and adequate funding for performance management functions (Frederickson and Frederickson 2006, 63).

In their comparative analysis of four congestion management networks, Koliba, Campbell, and Zia identify how and where performance management functions are taking place within four different networks (2011). They identified multiple assemblages of network actors using performance data to guide action in each case, suggesting that more than one performance management system may be operating within a given network. Applying Frederickson and Frederickson's parameters to their study, they found that goal congruence and performance measurement precision varied *within* networks, adding another dimension of complexity to the Frederickson and Frederickson model.

We conclude that instead of describing networks as whole networks operating under overarching network characteristics, we may need to begin to think of networks as compositions of subassemblages of networks that are linked together under one guiding function: "managing performance". Thinking in terms of networks as assemblages of smaller networks may, in the long run, provide a more precise and manageable way of conceiving of network performance. By breaking networks down into their subassemblages, we may then draw on Elinor Ostrom's conception of "action arenas" as spaces within networks where critical decision making occurs (1990). Within the architecture of network performance being proposed here, these action arenas are the spaces within the network where performance data are collected and used. These spaces within a network may be empirically observed, studied, and modeled. By focusing on the performance management systems of larger networks operating within particular policy domains, we may then study how or to what extent these performance management systems facilitate a network's capacity to transfer knowledge and learn. Considered in light of the network performance system outlined in Figure 6.2, the mediating structures are those performance management systems that intake performance data and export decisions about resource allocation and joint activities.

ORGANIZATIONAL LEARNING AND KNOWLEDGE MANAGEMENT ANALYSIS

In his book, *The Dynamics of Performance Management: Constructing Information and Reform*, Moynihan positions performance management systems as mediating structures that facilitate knowledge management and organizational learning. These mediating structures provide a space for "interactive dialogue routines" that are "specifically focused on solution seeking, where actors collectively examine information, consider its significance, and decide how it will affect action" (2008, 167). The kinds of cycles of inquiry that unfold in these mediating structures follow some semblance of a cycle of inquiry in which dialogue about performance inform decisions leading to actions or tasks. The loop is closed when those actions or tasks are evaluated. These evaluations then inform further dialogue undertaken within "communities of practice" (Koliba and Gajda 2009).

As mediating structures, performance management systems often involve groups of individuals who engage in dialogue about performance data. The extent to which these discussions lead to strategic decision making that, in turn, improves performance is predicated on a number of factors. The most comprehensive study of these factors has been undertaken by Robert Agranoff and his colleague Michael McGuire (2003). Their study of community development networks identified public action tools that can shape the structures and functions of a network's performance management system.

Extending these studies into other types of networks, Robert Agranoff offers us one of the first comparative case studies analyses across policy domains, including networks that engage in environmental management, community economic development, transportation planning, and telecommunications networks. In his book, *Managing within Networks: Adding Value to Public Organizations*, he lays out several characteristics of successful networks that he studied (2007). We distill these findings into three areas of most importance:

- **Space for problem identification and information exchange.** Agranoff observes that effective networks bring in those stakeholders that are necessary to approach an issue and devise sufficient spaces for the formal and informal exchange of information and the collective formulation of problems, solutions, and goals around performance and results. If executed well, these formal exchanges will lead to strategic planning and monitoring.
- **Adaptation and use of technology.** As a conduit through which information flows, Agranoff finds that successful networks effectively used technology as a tool to facilitate collaborative dialogue routines. These technologies may take the form of structured opportunities for face-to-face interactions and electronic exchanges, to computer-aided, data-based driven asset management and decision support tools.
- **Capacity building of network managers.** Agranoff finds that key agents in successful networks possessed a certain intentionality around building network capacity. He and others (see Meier and O'Toole) have begun to articulate the skills needed to build and run networks. He recognizes that the human capital of requisite skills and know-how forms the basis of a network's capacity to effectively manage performance and concludes that we need to understand more about how this kind of capacity is generated and sustained.

Agranoff offers a host of other observations about how spaces, technologies and network managers contribute to the actions of networks. Space precludes an extended discussion of his contributions to the identification of other determinants of network performance. He does conclude, as Turrini and colleagues do in their meta-analysis and Meier and O'Toole do in their Texas education dataset, that the existence of bridging and bonding functions is critical to network success. Agranoff's research takes this observation a step further by relating the existence of joint problem-solving tools to the building of a collective knowledge base that is used within effective networks. The observations of Turrini and colleagues regarding network stability are salient here because they found that network learning and knowledge transfer require some measure of network stability. System stability is generated through a combination of rich collaborative capacity and the existence of steering mechanisms in which somewhere, some subsets of agents are accountable for results.

The major conclusion to be drawn from this focus on network knowledge management and learning is that much more work needs to be done to study and model how network performance data is used and informs the learning and steering of networks. We suggest that to accomplish this, we must isolate where network performance data is collected and used, study those spaces as critical action arenas, and assess the relationship between their performance and the performance of the network as a whole. In some cases, such as small networks where the number of agents is relatively small, they are one and the same.

PERFORMANCE AS A PROPERTY OF A COMPLEX, DYNAMIC SYSTEM

The model of network performance highlighted in Figure 6.2 and explained in subsequent sections provides the beginnings of a classification scheme for framing network performance studies and guiding further theory development. Building on the "managing for performance" framework first introduced by Ingraham and Donahue, we explored how the black box of networks may be described using a network and systems logic that distinguishes between network structures and network management roles, performance management functions, and the integration of them within a knowledge management and learning context. Tying these properties together serves as the major contribution of this chapter to the literature.

The picture of network performance provided here is one predicated on the assumption that governance networks are complex adaptive systems. A complex adaptive systems is, "one whose component parts interact with sufficient intricacy that they cannot be predicted by standard linear equations; so many variables are at work in the system that its overall behavior can only be understood as an emergent consequence of the holistic sum of all the myriad behaviors embedded within" (Levy 1993, 34). Network structures, network managers' actions, the uses of performance data, and the capacity of networks to learn from performance data provide a basic architecture for describing network performance as an integral feature of a complex system. These systems are stochastic, meaning that they are inherently nondeterminant; e.g., nonlinear.

The overwhelming majority of research on network performance has relied on qualitative analysis to thickly describe networks. Qualitative case studies are contextually rich, but limited in their capacity to render generalizations. Measures of network resource munificence, network properties like centrality and betweenness, and qualitative comparative analysis have been used to quantify network properties. Linear regression analysis has proven to be powerful when key, high leverage variables can be isolated. All of these approaches are extremely useful in building theory. They are, however, limited by their assumptions.

All too often we are left trying to metaphorically find our lost keys under the lamp post. Our methods of inquiry shape the kinds of questions we ask and the kinds of theories we derive. These traditional methods tend to limit our imaginations to describing inherently unique phenomena, or reductionist, linear relationships between a few isolated variables. If we set our sights on too narrow of a plane or lean too greatly on contextual factors, we run the risk of not being able to say much about network performance in general. The persistent focus on the identification of linear, deterministic relationships drives much of network performance research to date. This pursuit is critical and drives most network determinant research. Such linear causal logic also persists in the performance management research as optimal systems design, data collection methods, and decision making tools are sought. In knowledge transfer and learning research, best practices around learning and innovation processes are considered with new theories developed around them.

When networks are viewed as being dynamic and complex, a persistent challenge is raised: What if the relationships between variables are not linear? Combinations of variables may have multiplier effects. Negative and positive feedback loops will likely exist. Emergent and novel results will likely arise out of simple interactions. Complex adaptive systems are inherently stochastic. New tools, methods, and theories need to be devised to accommodate this stochasticity (Koliba and Zia 2013).

Such nonlinearity may be captured using computer simulation modeling techniques such as system dynamics, agent-based modeling, social network analysis, and qualitative comparative analysis (Koliba, Zia, and Lee 2011). New data-mining programs are allowing large volumes of textual and numerical data to be analyzed for pattern identification. Inevitably, these data-mining techniques may be turned toward studying network performance data, network structures, and related traces of knowledge transfer. These newer modeling techniques require fresh approaches to theory development that account for nonlinearity, self-organization, and emergence. High leverage bifurcation points existing within the network may be identified, studied, and experimented with to devise optimal performance management systems for networks. These approaches to modeling complex systems can take into account nonlinear dynamics. For a theory of network performance to advance, attempts must be made to compare network structures operating within different policy domains. Larger "n" studies are likely needed and a standard typology of network structuration must emerge.

The model of network performance presented in Figure 6.2 contributes to our understanding of network structuration. By viewing the three features of network performance highlighted in this model as being interrelated, we can then begin to better understand how structures and functions work, how performance knowledge flows, and how complex systems evolve, adapt, and perform.

Those looking for some overarching conclusions to be drawn from this chapter might be disappointed in this articulation of what new theories can or should be derived. For a deeper exploration of the emerging terrain of "complexity friendly" theory development and testing, we refer the reader to a recent publication on this subject (Koliba and Zia 2013). This chapter is the result of an exercise in integration. Out of this integration lies a foundation on which to describe, model, and ultimately evaluate the dynamics of an inherently stochastic system.

CONCLUSION

With the rise of computational capacity, the extension of complexity science to the study of social phenomena, and the veritable explosion in network analytics, we sit at the threshold of a new era of theory development regarding network performance. The extent to which a grand theory of network performance is possible remains to be seen. There are a lot of reasons to remain skeptical about such a prospect. Our assertions about the prevailing network logic may be questioned. Disagreements regarding the extent to which any theory is generalizable across networks functioning across different policy domains may persist. Doubts about our capacity to study the evolution and emergence of networks over time may be caste. Our imaginations may also be limited by our reductionist tendencies and by the limits of our methodologies.

There is also room to be optimistic. If a feasible theory of network performance can be devised, we may use this theory to design more effective networks. We may be able to suggest which network configurations and subassemblages work best in which situations. To accomplish this, we will need to rely on more than our traditional social science research methods. To achieve such results, we will need to settle on some basic premises to guide a theory of network performance. In this chapter, we have attempted to set the table for such an undertaking.

REFERENCES

Agranoff, R. 2007. *Managing Within Networks: Adding Value to Public Organizations*. Washington, DC: Georgetown University Press.

Agranoff, R., and M. McGuire. 2003. *Collaborative Public Management: New Strategies for Local Governments*. Washington, DC: Georgetown University Press.

Baumgartner, F. R., and B. D. Jones. 1993. *Agendas and Instability in American Politics*. Chicago: The University of Chicago Press.

———, eds. 2002. *Policy Dynamics*. Chicago: The University of Chicago Press.

Bovaird, T. 2004. "Public-Private Partnerships: From Contested Concepts to Prevalent Practice." *International Review of Administrative Sciences* 70 (2): 199–215.

———. 2005. "Public Governance: Balancing Stakeholder Power in a Network Society." *International Review of Administrative Sciences* 71 (2): 217–28.

Frederickson, D., and H. G. Frederickson. 2006. *Measuring the Performance of the Hollow State*. Washington, DC: Georgetown University Press.

Gage, R. W., and M. P. Mandell, eds. 1990. *Strategies for Managing Intergovernmental: Policies and Networks*. New York: Praeger.

Gerrits, L. 2012. *Punching Clouds: An Introduction to the Complexity of Public Decision-Making*. Litchfield Park, AZ: Emergent Publications.

Ingraham, P., and A. K. Donahue. 2000. "Dissecting the Black Box Revisited: Characterizing Government Management Capacity." In *Governance and Performance: New Perspectives,* edited by C. Heinrich and L. Lynn, 292–318. Washington, DC: Georgetown University Press.

Katz, D., and R. Khan. 1978. *The Social Psychology of Organizations*. New York: Wiley.

Kenis, P., and K. Provan. 2009. "Toward an Exogenous Theory of Public Network Performance." *Public Administration* 87 (3): 440–56.

Kickert, W. J. M., E.-H. Klijn, and J. F. M. Koppenjan, eds. 1997. *Managing Complex Networks: Strategies for the Public Sector*. London: Sage Publications.

Kingdon, J. W. 1984. *Agendas, Alternatives and Public Policies*. Boston: Little, Brown and Company.

Koliba, C., E. Campbell, and A. Zia. 2011. "Performance Measurement Considerations in Congestion Management Networks: Evidence From Four Cases." *Public Performance Management Review*. 34(4): 520–48.

Koliba, C., and R. Gajda, 2009. "Communities of Practice as an Empirical Construct: Implications for Theory and Practice." *International Journal of Public Administration* 32: 97–135.

Koliba, C., J. Meek, and A. Zia. 2010. *Governance Networks in Public Administration and Public Policy*. Boca Raton, FL: CRC Press/Taylor & Francis.

Koliba, C., R. Mills, and A. Zia. 2011. "Accountability in Governance Networks: Implications Drawn From Studies of Response and Recovery Efforts Following Hurricane Katrina." *Public Administration Review* 71 (2): 210–20.

Koliba, C., A. Zia, and B. Lee. 2011. "Governance Informatics: Utilizing Computer Simulation Models to Manage Complex Governance Networks." *The Innovation Journal: Innovations for the Public Sector* 16 (1): Article 3.

Koliba, C., and A. Zia. 2013. "Complex Systems Modeling in Public Administration and Policy Studies: Challenges and Opportunities for a Meta-theoretical Research Program." In *COMPACT I: Public Administration in Complexity*, edited by L. Gerrits and P.K. Marks. Litchfield Park, AZ: Emergent Publications.

Koppenjan, J., and E. Klijn. 2004. *Managing Uncertainties in Networks*. London: Routledge.

Levy, S. (1993). *Artificial Life: A Report from the Frontier Where Computers Meet Biology*. New York: Random House Inc.

Mashaw, J. L. 2006. *Accountability and Institutional Design: Some Thoughts on the Grammar of Governance*. Cambridge: Cambridge University Press.

Meier, K.J. and L. J. O'Toole. 2003. "Public Management and Educational Performance: The Impact of Managerial Networking." *Public Administration Review* 63 (6): 689–99.

Morcol, G. 2012. *A Complexity Theory for Public Policy*. London: Routledge.

Moynihan, D. P. 2008. *The Dynamics of Performance Management: Constructing Information and Reform*. Washington, DC: Georgetown University Press.

Ostrom, E. 1990. *Governing the Commons: The Evolution of Institutions for Collective Action*. New York: Cambridge University Press.

O'Toole, L. J., and K. J. Meier. 1999. "Modeling the Impact of Public Management: Implications of Structural Context." *Journal of Public Administration Research and Theory* 9(4): 505–26.

Pierre, J., and B. G. Peters. 2005. *Governing Complex Societies: Trajectories and Scenarios*. New York: Palgrove Macmillan.

Provan, K., A. Fish, and J. Sydow, 2007. "Interorganizational Networks at the Network Level: A Review of the Empirical Literature on Whole Networks." *Journal of Management* 33: 479–517.

Provan, K. G., and P. Kenis. 2007. "Modes of Network Governance: Structure, Management and Effectiveness." *Journal of Public Administration Research and Theory*. 18: 229–52.

Provan, K.G., and H. B. Milward. 1995. "A Preliminary Theory of Interorganizational Network Effectiveness: A Comparative Study of Four Community Mental Health Systems." *Administrative Science Quarterly* 40 (1): 1–33.

Radin, B. 2006. *Challenging the Performance Movement: Accountability, Complexity and Democratic Values*. Washington, DC: Georgetown University Press.

Rhodes, R. 1997. *Understanding Governance: Policy Networks, Governance, Reflexivity and Accountability*. Buckingham: Open University Press.

Salamon, L. 2002. "The New Governance and the Tools of Public Action." In *The Tools of Government: A Guide to the New Governance*, edited by Salmon, L., 1–47. New York: Oxford University Press.

Sørensen, E., and J. Torfing. 2005. "The Democratic Anchorage of Governance Networks." *Scandinavian Political Studies* 28 (3): 195–218.

Stoker, G. 2006. "Public Value Management: A New Narrative for Networked Governance?" *American Review of Public Administration* 36 (1): 41–57.

Stone, D. 2002. *Policy Paradox: The Art of Political Decision Making*. New York: Norton.

Turrini, A., D. Cristofoli, F. Frosini, and G. Nasi. 2010. "Networking Literature About Determinants of Network Effectiveness." *Public Administration* 88 (2): 528–50.

Zia, A. and C. Koliba. 2011. "Climate Change Governance and Accountability: Dilemmas of Performance Management in Complex Governance Networks," *Journal of Comparative Policy Analysis*. 13 (5):479–497.

7 Governing Through Networks
A Systemic Approach

Deborah Rice

INTRODUCTION

Although the past two decades have taught us much about the emergence, management, and performance of governance networks, theoretical approaches to network governance have only been formulated more recently (for example, Klijn 2008; Klijn and Koppenjan 2012; Sørensen and Torfing 2007a, 2007b). When taking a closer look at existing conceptualizations of network governance, two major strands of literature can be identified. The first strand focuses predominantly on the coordination of interests within governance networks, asking questions such as under what conditions does network governance perform better than hierarchical steering mechanisms, how can cross-sector governance networks be managed effectively, and what might be the side effects of governing through networks (such as a loss of accountability or legitimacy, for example). The second strand focuses less on the steering challenges associated with network governance and more on its societal impact, inquiring about a possible metamorphosis of the bureaucratic state into a "society of networks" (Raab and Kenis 2009; see also Castells 2000).[1]

In this chapter, an attempt is made to bridge the two approaches to network governance by outlining theoretically how governance networks, as a specific type of organization, can affect complex, large-scale societal systems. To this end, the first part of the chapter presents a systemic view on networks that draws on the wider conceptual network literature. In the second part of the chapter, this systemic view is then applied to network governance, seeking to answer the question whether cross-sector cooperation among state actors, business actors, and civil-society organizations has the potential to change the state as we know it.

A SYSTEMIC VIEW ON NETWORKS

As it is often remarked, the term 'network' is used in a variety of meanings in the academic literature (Borgatti and Foster 2003, 995–6; Isett et al. 2011, i160; Van Alstyne 1997). Although this is usually regarded as problematic, it can also serve as a fruitful starting point for a systemic perspective on networks. After all, if one manages to first disentangle and then systematize various uses of the term "network", this may yield some valuable insights into the way different network types operate across different planes of societal existence. As a starting point, it is proposed here that networks can be (and have been) described in structuralist, functionalist, and institutionalist terms, with structuralism inquiring mainly about actor constellations and power relations within networks, functionalism focusing on the efficiency and effectiveness of networks in reaching certain objectives, and institutionalism building a conceptual bridge between (interpersonal) microlevel networks, (organizational) mesolevel networks, and (complex systemic) macrolevel networks as encompassing the entire spectrum of societal life. Yet even within each of those three perspectives, the term "network" is not used as a uniform concept. In the following, it will be discussed in more detail which network ideal types can be distinguished from a structuralist perspective, which functions the respective network types perform from a functionalist perspective, and how the institutional logics binding networks together are translated from the interpersonal (micro-) level, where they first emerge, to the meso- and macrolevels.

Networks from a Structuralist Perspective

Structuralism provides a useful starting point for describing networks in terms of their size, degree of integration, and internal power structures. A look through the structuralist lens yields three different conceptualizations of networks, all of which are subsumed under the network header in the academic literature. First, the term network (I) refers to interpersonal social networks as juxtaposed with abstract relations in complex social systems. Second, in between the two poles of interpersonal and abstract connections lies the organizational realm where people are interlinked in suprapersonal but not yet completely abstracted relations. Within this realm, the network (II) concept stands opposite not complex systems but organizations, with organizations implying "complete" formal relations among their members and networks implying either informal or formal "partial" organizational relations (Ahrne and Brunsson 2011; compare also Isett et al. 2011; Keast et al. 2004). Third, both the networks (I)-systems axis and the networks (II)-organizations spectrum can be subdivided into a network (III) and a hierarchical sphere, where interpersonal networks, partial or complete organizations, and complex systems are either characterized by horizontal (i.e. "symmetrical" and "egalitarian") power relations or by vertical ("superior-subordinate") power relations (Keast, Mandell, and Brown 2006, 35; Provan and Kenis 2007, 235).[2]

Figure 7.1 summarizes how the three network ideal types identifiable from a structuralist perspective relate to each other in a broader systemic context. The left half of Figure 7.1 pertains to social structures in which individuals have personal contact with each other, either within "primordial" networks such as families and friendships, or based on "rationalized" identities and roles in formal or informal, partial or complete organizations. The right half of Figure 7.1 pertains to the systemic realm where structural ties are abstract and complex, as in commodity markets and nations. Note that all horizontally structured systems correspond with the ideal type of markets because interaction within them proceeds along voluntaristic and egalitarian lines whereas all vertically structured systems can be labeled ideal-typical "polities" because interaction within them is based on cultural identities that assign to each member a specific place and status in the system. Finally, as Figure 7.1 also shows, organizations inhabit a middle ground between interpersonal networks and complex social systems, representing rationalized mirror images of interpersonal networks while also possessing systemic qualities—meaning that organizations have a raison d'être that is independent of their individual members.[3]

As a side effect, the systemic network perspective presented here partly rearranges or modifies the well-established trichotomy of networks, markets, and hierarchies (Powell 1990; Williamson 1985). Thus, from a systemic perspective, hierarchies are indeed to be regarded as inherently different from networks (III) but organizations (that are often equated with hierarchies; see Powell 1990, 303) are not in all cases because organizations can be structured both vertically and horizontally. Moreover, networks

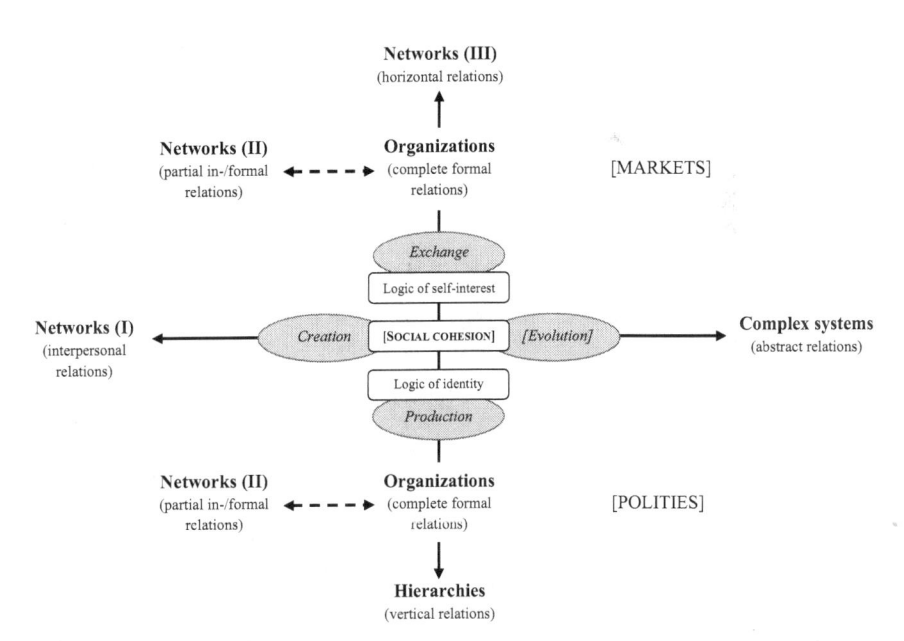

Figure 7.1 Networks from a Structuralist (black font), Functionalist (grey circles), and Institutionalist (white boxes) Perspective.

(I and II) are indeed to be regarded as inherently different from markets because the former are built on interpersonal relations while the latter are systemic (compare Van Alstyne 1997, 88); however, interpersonal networks (I/II) together with organizations can be juxtaposed not only with markets but also with polities. Finally, the networks (I/II)-social systems continuum should be regarded simultaneously as an asymptote symbolizing the entry point of formerly atomized individuals into two analytically separate worlds of social cohesion (networks [III] versus hierarchies),[4] with each of the upper and lower halves of Figure 7.1 covering a wide range of relatively more horizontal or vertical structural arrangements. For example, within the upper right square of Figure 7.1, monopoly markets would be much closer to the hierarchical end of the spectrum than perfect polypoly markets.

Networks from a Functionalist Perspective

A functionalist perspective on networks builds forth on the structuralist perspective. However, because both interpersonal networks (I) and complex social systems do not perform functions in a rationalized sense of the term, the functionalist network perspective pertains only to the organizational realm.

As a pioneer in functionalist organizational (and network) analysis, Mintzberg (1980) made the basic observation that hierarchical task organizations are best suited for streamlined production processes whereas relatively more egalitarian organizations perform better when production requires creativity and autonomous thinking. The reason for this, according to Mintzberg, is that hierarchical organizational structures subdue individuals' personal preferences and creative impulses to standardized production processes whereas egalitarian network (III) structures facilitate unconstrained creative exchange. When held against the analytical mirror of the structuralist network perspective presented above, it appears that Mintzberg's conceptualization operates across both the network (III)-hierarchy axis and the networks (II)-organizations spectrum. When analytically separating the functionalist implications of both, two more general insights emerge from Mintzberg's model. On one hand and regarding the network (III)-hierarchy axis, organizational hierarchies serve a primary production function, relying on functional differentiation and the standardization of roles to produce material or immaterial goods (such as cars or policies, for example). Organizational networks (III), in contrast, perform a secondary production function by providing a platform for the exchange of material or immaterial resources needed for production (like steering wheels or ideas) among a set of relatively autonomous individual or corporate producers (Keast et al. 2004; Klijn and Koppenjan 2012, 588–9; Podolny and Page 1998, 59 and 62–6; Provan and Kenis 2007, 240). The secondary production function performed by networks (III) also explains why organizational networks (III) are often comprised of producer organizations rather than private individuals (Agranoff and McGuire 2001, 296; Keast et al. 2004, 369). On the other hand and regarding the networks (II)-organizations spectrum, partial organizations perform a tertiary production function by creating informal or formal relations that did not formerly exist and that enable the exchange of hitherto inaccessible resources or the coproduction of hitherto nonproducible goods. The less "common ground" for creating such new relations exists in terms of knowing or trusting each other, the more informal the network (II) must be to fulfill that purpose, relying first and foremost on the social skills of individual persons to create a shared space for coproduction or exchange.[5] Figure 7.1 illustrates how the structuralist and functionalist network perspectives intersect: Next to the primary and secondary functions of production and exchange on the network (III)-hierarchy axis, the tertiary function of the creation of social relations stands opposite the "super-function" of systemic evolution on the networks (I)-systems axis.

As a final remark, it should be taken into account that not only hierarchies, networks (III), and partial or complete organizations, but also production, exchange, and the creation of social relations are ideal-typical concepts. In empirical reality, those ideal types are bound to intersect not only within each of the four squares of Figure 7.1, but also within each and every organizational configuration. For example, within a software company, one is likely to find a relatively horizontally structured development department where developers act as quasi-autonomous producers next to a hierarchically structured factory floor where DVDs are prepared for distribution. In other words, the four analytical poles of Figure 7.1 can be used to map not only the interactive boundaries of societies or societal sectors, but also single organizations as encompassing both eye-level and hierarchical relations alongside internal markets and polity (meso-) systems.

Networks from an Institutionalist Perspective

Having looked at networks from a structuralist and functionalist perspective, we are now ready to approach the question through which mechanisms networks—and in particular governance networks—can affect large-scale societal structures. To this end, an institutionalist perspective on networks is added here because institutionalism provides explanations for what holds human relations together in the first place and how such relations are mediated between the micro-, meso-, and macrolevels of society. The basic institutionalist argument put forth in this section is two-fold: first, that there are only two primary relational logics from which all other relational logics are derived; and second, that those two relational logics and their derivatives first emerge in interpersonal networks (I), travelling from the micro- to the meso- and macrolevels of society only to the degree that (very) large numbers of individuals share and enact them. This will be explained in more detail below, before the second part of the chapter addresses the question of whether governance networks have the potential to affect and possibly change state systems.

Two Basic Relational Logics: Identity and Self-Interest

From an institutionalist perspective, any type of social order—whether interpersonal, organizational or systemic—requires a glue that makes human relations stick beyond the timeframe of a single moment (Podolny and Page 1998, 59–60). The original source of all social cohesion lies in interpersonal networks (I) that emerge once two or more individuals perceive or experience a common ground between them. Such common ground may arise from two potential sources: either feeling connected with each other based on preconceived notions of who each person is (for example, Bolivian or father/child), in which case the network (I) is imbued with a cultural logic of identity; or being drawn to each other based on what each person has to offer (for example, kindness or a stamp collection), in which case the network (I) is infused with a logic of "needs" or more generally, self-interest (Schumpeter 1983, 12). However, it should be kept in mind that this is an ideal-typical description; in empirical reality, self-interested relations are never entirely free from the influence of identity because cultural identities influence strongly what one finds desirable and what not (such that a whitening body lotion may be a top seller in Manila but a shelf warmer in a Bavarian village, for example).

By definition, interpersonal networks that are rooted in a reciprocated logic of self-interest are accompanied by horizontal power structures because they are only sustainable if—and for as long as—all members benefit from interacting with each other (Jung and Lake 2011, 980). Interpersonal networks that are rooted in cultural identities, in contrast, always carry within them the seeds for hierarchical relations (albeit to varying degrees) because setting markers of identity such as ethnicity or hairstyle means defining a standard for who is "in" and "out" of the identity group, alongside an implied spectrum of varying degrees of membership (such that both a married woman and a single woman can be members of a patriarchal clan, yet with one being more equal than the other, to paraphrase Orwell's *Animal Farm*). Another implication of the logics of identity and self-interest being associated with different ideal types of human interrelation is that identity-based interpersonal networks tend to be more deeply integrated and stable than interpersonal networks grounded in a logic of self-interest, because self-interested behavior (commonly imprecisely associated with markets) immediately scouts for a new host and therefore makes network (III) relations unsustainable once no more benefits accrue from a network relation; conversely, interpersonal hierarchies remain stable for as long as the identities of their members do not change, irrespective of the functional efficiency of a hierarchical relation in production terms.

The Mediation of Relational Logics Between
the Microlevel and Mesolevel

Mesolevel rational organizations mimic and appropriate primordial identities and self-interests that emerge out of interpersonal family/clan, friendship or exchange relations for the achievement of shared strategic goals (compare Börzel 1998, 264; Merton 1940, 565; Raab and Kenis 2009; Ronfeldt 1996). As organizations grow larger, their cohesive grid becomes increasingly decoupled from any personal relations among their members and hence also from the identities and self-interests of individual members. Although every organizational configuration is characterized by at least a rudimentary organizational identity and self-interest, the logic of self-interest ideal-typically predominates in egalitarian exchange configurations whereas the logic of identity predominates in hierarchical producer networks (II) and complete producer organizations.

However, it should not be forgotten that although all forms of organization rationalize the behavior of their members by way of overwriting organizational interests and identities on personal interests and identities (at least during working hours), the individual members of organizations continue to be private persons as well. This means that internal and external organizational relations can never be rationalized entirely, as personal friendship ties, identity communities, and "serendipitous" encounters among individual members or individual members and non-members run parallel to and relativize or even undermine formal organizational structures and goals, thereby opening up entry points for new relational logics and consequently organizational change (Jung and Lake 2011, 975; Merton 1940, 567–8; Raab and Kenis 2009, 201; Schreyögg and Sydow 2011).

The Mediation of Relational Logics Between the Microlevel, Mesolevel, and Macrolevel

As was elaborated above, identities and self-interests are multilayered. First, every individual is born with intrinsic self-interests (both universal ones like a need for food and individually specific ones like a love for cooking) that could be described as the hardware of social cohesion because individuals need others for their intrinsic self-interests to materialize. Second, socialization into primordial identity communities leads to the emergence of acquired self-interests (such as preferring spicy food) that provide a cognitive operating system for entering into nonprimordial relations. Finally, as individuals join organizational configurations for specific purposes, their primordial identities and associated self-interests are complemented with rational interests (like being on time for work) and possibly identities; however, similarly to software that can easily be installed and uninstalled under a stable operating system, rational identities and interests are more prone to change than primordial ones because they are tied to restricted strategic objectives.

A defining characteristic of the postmodern era is that the principle of rational organization has spread into all spheres of societal life (Meyer, Boli, and Thomas 1987). As a result, even primordial identities and self-interests have become partly rationalized, being habitually subjected to the scrutiny of a rational producer logic (*status differentiation must have a purpose*) or exchange logic (*giving and taking must be in balance*). In addition, rational organizations provide a platform for individuals with very different primordial backgrounds to meet and thereby get in touch with alternative primordial identities and self-interests, which can lead to a rediscovery of intrinsic self-interests that have remained unaddressed or even been suppressed within a dominant primordial frame of reference. Such a view of the rationalization of interpersonal relations crushing the primordial buffer between intrinsic self-interests and relatively generalizable rational self-interests and identities explains not only why the emergence of complex social systems is a postmodern phenomenon, but also points to some mechanisms through which complex social systems might evolve and change. Most fundamentally, as was indicated above, polity and market systems will expand when formerly separate primordial relational logics become subsumed under a more general rational logic; however, the reverse is also possible, i.e. systemic contraction and fragmentation effectuated by a primordial backlash against rationalization processes. Another possible catalyst of systemic evolution lies in aggregated reciprocal effects between changing identities and interests at the microlevel, as when changing identities lead to a changed perception of the value of certain goods and hence to the expansion or contraction of market systems, or when changed interests lead to interaction across identity boundaries and hence to a possible amalgamation of hitherto separate polity systems. It is exactly on these grounds that some observers have voiced concerns about governance networks potentially transforming the state system as we know it: By establishing formal and informal relations among public and private actors, governance networks might affect the interests and identities not only of the involved individuals but also of the organizations they represent, thereby weakening public values and interests vis-à-vis private values and interests even at the systemic level (compare Börzel 1998, 265).

A SYSTEMIC VIEW ON NETWORK GOVERNANCE

In the second part of this chapter, the systemic network perspective developed above is used as a conceptual matrix for systematizing various ideal types of governance networks and identifying some possible mechanisms by which governance networks may affect large-scale societal systems, in particular the state system. This is important to investigate because networks among public and private actors have been described especially by critical institutionalists as diminishing the state's neutrality toward its citizens, although networks between first- and third-sector actors are generally viewed more positively than networks between first- and (profit-driven) second-sector actors (Agranoff and McGuire 2001, 319; Börzel 1998, 262–3; Löffler 2009, 219; Peters and Pierre 1998, 241; Salamon 2002, 38; Sørensen and Torfing 2007a, 5–6; Sørensen and Torfing 2007b, 38–41). Functionalist scholars, conversely, have been leaning toward a more pragmatic interpretation, seeing the shift toward network governance as "less fundamental than . . . tactical", with new governance mechanisms being merely "added" to "public governance within a hierarchical system" (Hill and Lynn 2004, 189; see also Klijn 2008, 509). In the following, both perspectives will be assessed more systematically, starting out from a structuralist categorization of the most common forms of governance networks.

Governance Networks from a Structuralist Perspective

Analogously to the systemic network perspective developed above, structuralism provides the basic starting point for answering the question whether governance networks have the capacity to change large-scale societal systems and if so, through which mechanisms. Figure 7.2 shows how some of the most common types of governance networks could be classified according to the analytical framework proposed earlier. First, Figure 7.2 illustrates that both first-sector organizations such as state agencies, second-sector organizations such as enterprises, and third-sector organizations such as nongovernmental organizations (NGOs) are to be classified as complete hierarchical organizations, although they are often (analytically imprecisely) associated with the hierarchy, market, and network forms of social order, respectively. Furthermore, Figure 7.2 also suggests that quasi-markets should be seen as sophisticated network (II) arrangements rather than systemic market structures because they represent formalized partial exchange

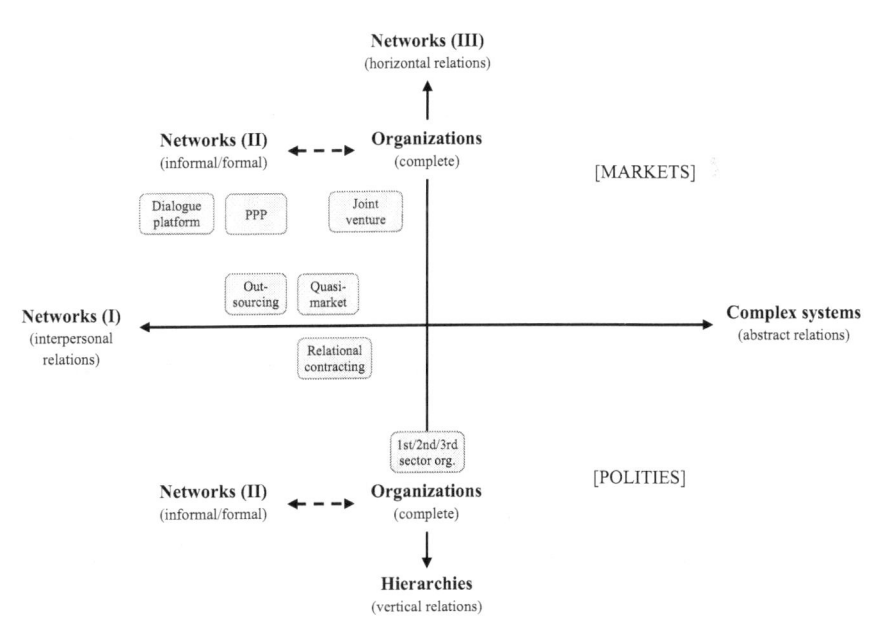

Figure 7.2 A Structuralist Matrix of Governance Networks.

relations among identifiable public and private actors (Podolny and Page 1998, 60; compare also Le Grand and Bartlett, 1993). Finally, although one might be inclined to classify outsourcing relationships as hierarchical networks (II), the integrated network perspective developed here would suggest that until principal-agent relations evolve into relational contracting arrangements grounded in at least a rudimentary shared identity, they remain in the sphere of relatively unstable exchange/network (III) relations (compare Agranoff and McGuire 2001, 311–2; Bertelli and Smith 2010; Bovaird 2006; Williamson 1985).

Governance Networks from a Functionalist Perspective

As indicated above, functionalist scholars tend to interpret governance networks rather pragmatically as exchange relationships serving a secondary or tertiary function in the "production of public purpose" (Sørensen and Torfing 2007a, 10; see also Hill and Lynn 2004, 176; Löffler 2009, 224–8; Osborne and Gaebler 1992; Rhodes 1996, 660; Salamon 2002). In this line of argument, first-sector organizations enter into relatively egalitarian and/or partial organizational relationships with companies or civil-society organizations to access previously inaccessible resources, or coproduce previously nonproducible goods (examples include the procuring of better wheelchairs through a quasimarket or the acquisition of shielded knowledge through a dialogue platform with private stakeholders). The fewer prerequisites for a formalized relationship of coproduction or exchange exist in terms of shared perceptions, trust, etc., the more relation-creating and hence informal a governance network must be to fulfill a—tertiary—production function for public producer organizations.

However, as is frequently pointed out, governance networks among first-, second-, and third-sector organizations also involve costs and risks that must be weighed against the benefits accruing from network governance. Most crucially, monitoring and other transaction costs increase substantially as governance networks move from the egalitarian and voluntaristic network (III) pole toward the production-oriented half of Figure 7.2 (compare Coase 1937, 388–9; Williamson 1985). Furthermore, regarding the networks (I)-systems axis, governance networks are characterized by a trade-off between creative capacity and steering capacity: The more formalized and complete a governance network is, the higher the steering capacity of the involved public actors and hence the transparency and democratic legitimacy of the network; simultaneously, however, the chance for any positive externalities to arise in the form of new insights, new projects, new strategies, etc. is much higher in informal and partial than in formal and more complete governance network configurations (see Keast, Brown, and Mandell 2007; Peters and Pierre 1998; Salamon 2002, 38; Stoker 1998, 23). Another steering dilemma associated with the networks (I)-systems axis is that exchange relations become more all-encompassing if network integration within successful governance networks deepens over time, whereas it is still possible to delimit exchange relations to a particular (set of) core resource(s) in partial governance networks. As a result, relative power positions are likely to shift gradually within successful governance networks because differential resource endowments in areas not foreseen by the original planners are likely to gain importance as network integration becomes more complete. Fully integrated cross-sector governance organizations are therefore a risky undertaking for both public and private actors and are only likely to occur when radical societal changes block established ways of doing things, making it necessary for public and private actors to work closely together even while knowing that their primary production functions and relative power positions will shift in that process, with unknown consequences (compare Merton 1940, 564).

Governance Networks from an Institutionalist Perspective

Whereas the functionalist analytical toolkit allows us to investigate the potential influence of governance networks on the productive capacity of first-sector organizations, the institutionalist repertoire enables us to inquire about the possible systemic repercussions of governing through cross-sector networks rather than hierarchical government bureaucracies (only). As was already mentioned, critical institutionalist scholars have pointed out that network governance may form a potential threat to state neutrality, first because corporate institutional logics are likely to become entangled with public institutional logics in governance networks, leading to a potential amalgamation of public and private (organizational) identities and interests; and second because first-sector organizations work together with civil-society actors and even private citizens within governance networks, thereby blurring the boundaries not only among the first, second, and third sectors of society but also between the state and individual citizens.[6] The latter could potentially provide a stepping stone toward a form of "governmentality", i.e. the "attempt of an increasingly reflexive and facilitating state to mobilize and shape the free actions of self-governing actors" (Sørensen and Torfing 2007a, 19; see also Foucault 1991). From the systemic network perspective presented above, such a scenario seems indeed possible. Because complex societal systems are held together by the identities and self-interests of individuals at the microlevel of society, aggregated and mediated through mesolevel organizations, it is possible for new micro- and mesolevel identities/interests to diffuse into—and thereby change—large-scale societal systems. However, based on the above-developed framework, four important qualifications must be added to this view that somewhat relativize the critical institutionalist assessment of the revolutionizing impact of network governance.

First, the systemic repercussions of changed identities and interests at the micro- and mesolevel are not unidirectional. More concretely, the diagnosed move toward governmentality and hence a spilling over of state identities and interests into the private sphere are accompanied not only by NPM (new public management)-informed drives towards "less" state but also by citizen-backed initiatives to strengthen the state vis-à-vis nested corporate interests, as the recent Occupy movement exemplifies (compare Ronfeldt 1996, 31). Therefore, the mechanisms by which microlevel identities and interests are translated into systemic structures and back should be seen not as linear but as dialectic, always carrying within them the seeds for opposing societal trends. Second, as we have seen above, network governance as a societal phenomenon encompasses a large variety of organizational configurations whose capacity for affecting the self-interests and identities of their members varies considerably. For instance, governance networks in the policy-making domain are likely to have a much larger systemic impact than service-oriented and relatively bureaucratic governance networks (Börzel 1998, 255; Klijn 2008, 511; Klijn and Koppenjan 2012, 588–9). Third, it should not be forgotten that governance networks are not the only transmission belt for new identities and self-interests into the public sector; for instance, changing public sector logics may also enter through the staff of state organizations who are, after all, not only organizational representatives but also private individuals embedded in manifold social life worlds. Finally, the above-developed framework suggests that if micro- or mesolevel changes spread across so many individuals and organizations that large-scale societal systems are affected, the reverberations of such systemic changes back to the microlevel will force all individuals and organizations embedded in the respective systems to adapt their identities and self-interests to the changed circumstances—profit-oriented companies, civil-society organizations, and state actors alike. This gives some hope that if the "society of networks" is really here or coming, there is going to be reshuffle for everyone.

CONCLUSION

This chapter sought to develop an analytical framework for answering the question whether, and if so how, governance networks are able to affect and change complex societal systems, in particular the state system. To this end, it was deemed necessary to first introduce a systemic theoretical perspective on networks more generally, combining structuralist, functionalist, and institutionalist insights on how different network ideal types function and how the cohesive glue tying interpersonal networks together is transposed to the complex systemic level via the transmission belt of rational organization. In the second part of the chapter, the systemic framework developed in the first part was then applied to governance networks more specifically. It appeared that governance networks do indeed have the potential to serve as transmission belts for changing identities and interests in large-scale and complex systemic environments. However, not all forms of governance networks have that capacity to an equal degree, and not only (governance) networks have that capacity but so do individuals, hierarchical forms of organization, and nongovernance networks. For that reason, the systemic impact of governance networks should not be overrated. It is theoretically even thinkable that governance networks will infuse public identities and interests into the private sector to the same degree that private-sector logics take hold in the public sector, so that the way in which societies organize their economic and social life will change just as much as the mechanisms through which citizens are governed in the era of network governance.

NOTES

1. A third literature strand defines network governance as the management of interorganizational networks (Jones, Hesterly and Borgatti 1997; Provan and Kenis 2007; Tuunanen et al. 2011). Because the current chapter is concerned specifically with public-sector governance, however, that literature is not addressed here.
2. A fourth, very broad definition juxtaposes networks with individual atomism; from this perspective, any human relation or system could be called a network (see Jung and Lake 2011, 973, footnote 7; Borgatti and Foster 2003, 992; Podolny and Page 1998, 59).
3. The "serendipitous networks" discussed by Provan and Kenis (2007) and Raab and Kenis (2009) would be positioned in between interpersonal networks and in-/formal organizational networks on the axis between interpersonal networks (I) and social systems, because although serendipitous networks belong to the organizational realm, they emerge "opportunistically" rather than strategically.
4. Because the interpersonal networks (I)-systems axis serves as an asymptote for networks (III) and hierarchies, Figure 7.1 would take the form of a torus rather than a ball in three-dimensional space.
5. A similar logic is reflected in the "3Cs" of cooperative, coordinative, and collaborative informal networks identified by Keast, Brown, and Mandell, 2007 (see also Powell 1990, 326).
6. Peters and Pierre (1998, 241) make the interesting point that states with a strong etatist tradition run a lower risk of succumbing to private-sector identities and interests than states with weak political institutions.

REFERENCES

Agranoff, Robert, and Michael McGuire. 2001. "Big Questions in Public Network Management Research." *Journal of Public Administration Research and Theory* 11: 295–326.

Ahrne, Göran, and Nils Brunsson. 2011. "Organization Outside Organizations: The Significance of Partial Organization." *Organization* 18: 83–104.

Bertelli, Anthony M., and Craig R. Smith. 2010. "Relational Contracting and

Network Management." *Journal of Public Administration Research and Theory* 20: i21–40.

Borgatti, Stephen P., and Pacey C. Foster. 2003. "The Network Paradigm in Organizational Research: A Review and Typology." *Journal of Management* 29: 991–1013.

Börzel, Tanja A. 1998. "Organizing Babylon: On the Different Conceptions of Policy Networks." *Public Administration* 76: 253–73.

Bovaird, Tony. 2006. "Developing New Forms of Partnership with the "Market" in the Procurement of Public Services." *Public Administration* 84: 81–102.

Castells, Manuel. 2000. *The Rise of the Network Society: Economy, Society and Culture*. Cambridge: Blackwell.

Coase, Ronald H. 1937. "The Nature of the Firm." *Economica* 4: 386–405.

Foucault, Michel. 1991. "Governmentality." In *The Foucault Effect: Studies in Governmentality*, edited by Graham Burchell, Colin Gordon, and Peter Miller, 87–104. London: Harvester Wheatsheaf.

Hill, Carolyn J., and Laurence E. Lynn Jr. 2004. "Is Hierarchical Governance in Decline? Evidence from Empirical Research." *Journal of Public Administration Research and Theory* 15: 173–95.

Isett, Kimberley R., Ines A. Mergel, Kelly LeRoux, Pamela A. Mischen, and R. Karl Rethemeyer. 2011. "Networks in Public Administration Scholarship: Understanding Where We Are and Where We Need to Go." *Journal of Public Administration Research and Theory* 21: i157–73.

Jones, Candace, William S. Hesterly, and Stephen P. Borgatti. 1997. "A General Theory of Network Governance: Exchange Conditions and Social Mechanisms." *Academy of Management Review* 22: 911–45.

Jung, Danielle F., and David A. Lake. 2011. "Markets, Hierarchies, and Networks: An Agent-Based Organizational Ecology." *American Journal of Political Science* 55: 971–89.

Keast, Robyn, Kerry Brown, and Myrna Mandell. 2007. "Getting the Right Mix: Unpacking Integration Meanings and Strategies." *International Public Management Journal* 10: 9–34.

Keast, Robyn, Myrna Mandell, and Kerry Brown. 2006. "Mixing State, Market and Network Governance Modes: The Role of Government in 'Crowded' Policy Domains." *International Journal of Organization Theory and Behavior* 9: 27–50.

Keast, Robyn, Myrna P. Mandell, Kerry Brown, and Geoffrey Woolcock. 2004. "Network Structures: Working Differently and Changing Expectations." *Public Administration Review* 64: 363–71.

Klijn, Erik-Hans. 2008. "Governance and Governance Networks in Europe." *Public Management Review* 10: 505–25.

Klijn, Erik-Hans, and Joop Koppenjan. 2012. "Governance Network Theory: Past, Present and Future." *Policy & Politics* 40: 587–606.

Le Grand, Julian, and Will Bartlett, eds. 1993. *Quasi-Markets and Social Policy*. Basingstoke: Macmillan.

Löffler, Elke. 2009. "Public Governance in a Network Society." In *Public Management and Governance*, edited by Tony Bovaird and Elke Löffler, 215–32. London and New York: Routledge.

Merton, Robert K. 1940. "Bureaucratic Structure and Personality." *Social Forces* 18: 560–8.

Meyer, John W., John Boli, and George M. Thomas. 1987. "Ontology and Rationalization in the Western Cultural Account." In *Institutional Structure: Constituting State, Society, and the Individual*, edited by George M. Thomas, John W. Meyer, Francisco O. Ramirez, and John Boli, 12–37. London: Sage.

Mintzberg, Henry. 1980. "Structure in 5's: A Synthesis of the Research on Organization Design." *Management Science* 26: 322–41.

Osborne, David, and Ted Gaebler. 1992. *Reinventing Government: How the Entrepreneurial Spirit Is Transforming the Public Sector*. Reading, MA: Addison-Wesley.

Peters, B. Guy, and Jon Pierre. 1998. "Governance without Government? Rethinking Public Administration." *Journal of Public Administration Research and Theory* 8: 223–43.

Podolny, Joel M., and Karen L. Page. 1998. "Network Forms of Organization." *Annual Review of Sociology* 24: 57–76.

Powell, Walter W. 1990. "Neither Market Nor Hierarchy: Network Forms of Organization." *Research in Organizational Behavior* 12: 295–336.

Provan, Keith G., and Patrick Kenis. 2007. "Modes of Network Governance: Structure, Management, and Effectiveness." *Journal of Public Administration Research and Theory* 18: 229–52.

Raab, Jörg, and Patrick Kenis. 2009. "Heading Toward a Society of Networks: Empirical Developments and Theoretical Challenges." *Journal of Management Inquiry* 18: 198–210.

Rhodes, Richard A. W. 1996. "The New Governance: Governing without Government." *Political Studies* 44: 652–67.

Ronfeldt, David. 1996. Tribes, Institutions, Markets, Networks: A Framework about Societal Evolution. RAND Paper P-7967. Santa Monica: RAND.

Salamon, Lester M. 2002. "The New Governance and the Tools of Public Action: An Introduction." In *The Tools of Government: A Guide to the New Governance*, edited by Lester M. Salamon, 1–47. Oxford: Oxford University Press.

Schreyögg, Georg, and Jörg Sydow. 2011. "Organizational Path Dependence: A Process View." *Organization Studies* 32: 321–35.

Schumpeter, Joseph A. (1983). *The Theory of Economic Development*. New Brunswick and London: Transaction Publishers.

Sørensen, Eva, and Jakob Torfing. 2007a. "Governance Network Research: Towards a Second Generation." In *Theories of Democratic Network Governance*, edited by Eva Sørensen and Jakob Torfing, 1–21. Basingstoke: Palgrave-Macmillan.

———. 2007b. "Theoretical Approaches to Governance Network Dynamics." In *Theories of Democratic Network Governance*, edited by Eva Sørensen and Jakob Torfing, 25–42. Basingstoke: Palgrave-Macmillan.

Stoker, Gerry. 1998. "Governance as Theory: Five Propositions." *International Social Science Journal* 50: 17–28.

Tuunanen, Mika, Josef Windsperger, Gérard Cliquet, and George Hendrikse, eds. 2011. *New Developments in the Theory of Networks: Franchising, Alliances and Cooperatives*. Heidelberg: Springer.

Van Alstyne, Marshall. 1997. "The State of Network Organization: A Survey in Three Frameworks." *Journal of Organizational Computing and Electronic Commerce* 7: 83–151.

Williamson, Oliver E. 1985. *The Economic Institutions of Capitalism: Firms, Markets, Relational Contracting*. New York: Free Press.

8 Developing Network Management Theory through Management Channels and Roles

Joris Voets

INTRODUCTION

In the age of New Public Governance (Osborne 2009), where high levels of complexities and interdependencies demand intergovernmental and public-private collaboration as problem-solving strategies (O'Toole 1997), the study of network governance and network management in particular becomes more important (Provan and Lemaire 2012).

Research on network management provides valuable insights, such as showing that network management matters (Meier and O'Toole 2003), the nature of network management activities (Klijn and Teisman 1997; McGuire 2002), how these activities differ from management of single organizations (Agranoff and McGuire 2001), different network management roles and styles (Agranoff 2003; Mandell and Keast 2007), who undertakes management roles (Rethemeyer and Hatmaker 2008; Voets and De Rynck 2011), and the skills and capabilities of network managers (Blomgren-Bingham, Sandfort, and O'Leary 2008).

A main challenge is to develop research on network management, as one of the three main research traditions or roots of what Klijn and Koppenjan (2012) identify as governance network theory, into network management theories. Network management theory starts from the basic idea that management is a process involving relationships between actors that need to be managed actively to achieve results (Klijn and Koppenjan 2000, 139).

The impressive amount of literature on network management, however, does not mean consensus or coherence in network management theories (Bevir and Richards 2009). The obvious explanation is that network management research is done by scholars from different disciplines and traditions (e.g. policy science, public administration, organization science), different epistemological positions (e.g. positivist, grounded, or antifoundationalist perspectives), with increasingly varied designs and methodologies used, making it hard to ensure coherent theory development (Lewis 2011).

The complexities and dynamics associated with networks and network management demand network management theories to be firmly grounded in empirical studies (McGuire 2002, 602). Agranoff and McGuire, for instance, contributed to network management theory over the past decades by systematically observing and mapping network management activities and behavior, mainly in in-depth case studies, also showing the importance of context to understand what network managers do and why they do it (Agranoff 2007; McGuire 2002; McGuire and Agranoff this volume). Other relevant contributions, like the work of Mandell and Keast (Keast et al. 2004; Mandell 1994; Mandell and Keast 2009) or Huxham and Vangen's theory on collaborative advantage (2005, this volume), are also grounded in in-depth observation of what actually happens in collaborative arrangements. Huxham and Vangen for instance identified and developed main themes such as resources, power, trust, and leadership, that help to understand and manage network dynamics, without however claiming simple causations between variables.

In the same tradition, this paper seeks to add to the theory of network management by drawing on a semigrounded theory study[1] of two policy networks that involved discussions with professionals and from insights from recent literature. It addresses two research questions: How do network managers try to make network strategies and activities effective? Which different management roles are required to make network management effective?

First, the paper discusses how networks, network management, and network managers are conceived. Next, the methodology and cases used to ground our insights are discussed. The paper then introduces the network management theory that centers around four management channels and five management roles. The first research question is addressed by introducing the concept of management channels, explaining how network managers develop and use them for network management strategies like activation or mobilizing, and formulating a number of propositions. The second research question is addressed by defining a set of network management roles that help to explain why network management is successful, including a set of related propositions. The paper concludes with reflections on how to develop the network management theory in future research.

POLICY NETWORKS, NETWORK MANAGEMENT, AND NETWORK MANAGERS

The nebulous nature of the network literature requires us to define first what is meant in this paper by networks, network management, and network managers.

A *network* can be defined as "*structures of interdependence involving multiple organizations or parts thereof, where one unit is not merely the formal subordinate of the others in some larger hierarchical arrangement*" (O'Toole 1997, 45). In a public context, such networks join actors concerned with issues of service delivery or policy, although Rethemeyer and

Hatmaker (2008) argue from their research experience that networks often feature degrees of both. In this paper, we focus on intergovernmental policy networks concerned with developing and implementing a policy agenda to develop specific focus areas. Such policy networks are important, because they try to achieve joint action that cuts across intergovernmental tiers and policy sectors, to develop certain areas and regions.

Network management concerns strategies and actions aimed at *"mediating and co-ordinating interorganizational policy making"* (Klijn and Koppenjan 2000, 136). Through network management, network managers try to achieve collaborative advantage and overcome or avoid collaborative inertia (Huxham and Vangen 2005; Rethemeyer and Hatmaker 2008, 630).

Researching network management then means focusing on the actual behavior of network managers. This includes their actions that can have an operational or strategic character (McGuire 2002), their focus on goal formation or goal achievement, their use of strategies focused on content or process (Kickert et al. 1997), and their ability to influence the resource dependencies and acquiring the resources needed for their organizations (Park and Rethemeyer 2012).

Network managers are those actors trying to achieve the network goals through purposeful action. The fact that they direct their efforts to achieve the network or collaborative goals distinguishes them from other network members that only act to achieve their personal or organizational agenda, without consideration of the network goal or even at the expense of others (Hjern and Porter 1981)[2]. In policy networks, the network managers are typically public officials (Rhetemeyer and Hatmaker 2008).

Network management research then focuses on three analytical levels and the interplay between them: 1) management at the level of policy games within the network, 2) the level of the network in operation (Klijn and Teisman 1997), and 3) the level of the network environment as the institutional context in which the policy games and networks operate (e.g., the impact of political/cultural context, Mandell and Steelman 2003). In this paper, management channels and roles cut across all three levels.

METHODOLOGY

This paper draws mainly on a study designed to understand how intergovernmental relations are actively managed in networks (Voets 2008). Two networks—the Project Ghent Canal Area (PGCA) and the Park Woods Ghent (PWG)—were studied using a grounded theory-based case study methodology utilized by Agranoff (2007). This methodology involves an adapted grounded theory method, allowing the analyst to start from literature-based major concepts that are then developed, refined and complemented through a series of case studies.

Data were drawn from documents, plans, site visits, and a broad set of semistructured, face-to-face interviews (27 PGCA, 25 PWG), which were transcribed and coded. After completing the study in 2008, the main conceptual insights on network management presented in this paper on management channels and roles were developed and validated in four annual (2009, 2010, 2011, 2012), two-day training courses on network management for public professionals (varying between 12 and 20 participants).

INTRODUCING TWO NETWORKS

Although space prevents full presentation of the two cases, a brief introduction sets the stage. Both are policy networks in Flanders (Belgium), involving different resources held by a range of actors: three local governments; different departments and agencies of the provincial, regional Flemish and Belgian federal governments; various interest organizations (e.g., main economic interests in the areas, environmental organizations); companies; and citizens.

Project Ghent Canal Area

The PGCA is concerned with developing a complex area, involving many stakeholders. The city of Ghent has a port linked to a canal that includes parts of the municipalities of Evergem and Zelzate. The intense economic activities in that maritime-industrial area bring with it a considerable environmental nuisance, while a number of residential areas historically present in the area became increasingly entangled with the maritime-industrial activity. The main objective of PGCA is to improve the environmental and living qualities while increasing economic development prospects by drawing up a joint vision on the future development of the canal area and an action program to achieve that vision. Main elements include reduction of soil, water, and air pollution; buffering housing and industry; linking residential areas; decoupling residential and economic traffic; expropriating housing in unliveable areas; developing and reorganizing water, road, and railways; and relocating companies. PGCA was supported by a network secretariat from the beginning.

Park Woods Ghent

The PWG is a policy network to develop a multifunctional park in the south of the urban region of Ghent. The focus area covers territorial parts of three local governments: the city of Ghent, and the municipalities of De Pinte and Sint-Martens-Latem. The issues and ambitions in the focus area are complex; it is an open landscape, pressured by the urbanization in the greater Ghent region. Different claims (heritage, science park, agriculture, recreation, housing, nature, etc.) need to be matched with the ambition of a substantial forest development in the focus area. Much energy was put in developing a spatial implementation plan (and currently implementation of it) that could accommodate these different interests. After a vision on the future development of the site was jointly developed, an action program was defined and a network secretariat was also set up.

MANAGEMENT CHANNELS

Knowledge of management strategies and activities is important, and listings thereof organized in different categories based on focus or level are plentiful—see Rethemeyer and Hatmaker (2008, 637) or Beach, Keast, and Pickernell (2012, 613) for an overview. However, how network managers actually put these strategies to work in networks and policy games remains a rather murky area that requires more research. Practitioners also demand such knowledge: in training sessions with network managers, the introduction of management strategies and activities by the trainer is always followed by the question of participants as to how to put them into practice and make them work. This paper tries to shed some additional light on this process through the concept of the management channels.

Defining Management Channels

We define *management channels* as the relational pathways or process routes created and used to deploy certain network management strategies. Such channels help network managers to exert interactive or within network power to get things done in terms of management. These channels can be seen as an elaboration of the concept of social structural resources (SSRs) defined by Rethemeyer and Hatmaker (2008). SSR's involve ties between actors and are a resource that *"owners can exploit and others can seek to control"* (634).

Network managers need to map such ties held by network members with other network members or relevant actors outside the network. They also have to create them consciously. These channels are used for a variety of network management strategies, such as network activation and deactivation, or for mobilizing to access such material-institutional resources as money and competences (Rethemeyer and Hatmaker 2008). *These channels are considered a relational backbone or an essential communication infrastructure that is a prerequisite for network managers to succeed in deploying at least part of their network management strategies.*

Such channels can be mapped systematically through social network analysis, in-depth interviewing, and document analysis, or a mixed method approach (see Alexander, Lewis, and Considine 2011). In this study, four channels, based on in-depth interviewing and document analysis, are distinguished.

Four Channel Types

The first type concerns *personal channels*: network members know other members or actors outside the network because they have personal ties (e.g., old friends, family ties). Many actors interviewed in both cases stressed the importance of these relations: *"those relations you have to identify, that is the use of the PGCA"* (interview quote PGCA). Most personal ties existed before the network was created, but part of them developed along the way. Interviewees pointed to friendships and acquaintances used as informal channels to discuss canal matters in the PCGA or issues for the PWG but also to carry out active lobbying, thus supporting Agranoff (2007) who also identified such behavior.

The second type is *professional channels*: network members know other members or actors outside the network through professional contacts. Such ties stem from their job or membership in professional associations, which was clearly the case for spatial planners involved in both cases.

The third type concerns *philosophical channels*: network members know other members or actors outside the network because they share philosophical relations (e.g., member of same church or freemason lodge). Well-informed interviewees were convinced such relations were present and used. This type of channel is linked to politicians of different parties, civil servants, entrepreneurs, etc., presenting informal pathways to discuss PGCA or PWG matters, to influence actors' positions, to help acquire resources, etc. While these people are connected because they share certain belief systems at a philosophical level, this does not mean that they make up an epistemic community and share beliefs regarding the development of the focus area[3]. It proved impossible however to analyze their precise use or role in more detail, because those who have access to such channels are very secretive about it and real power tends not to reveal itself (Arts and Van Tatenhove 2004)—only one interviewee admitted his access to and use of that type of channel.

The fourth type involves *party political channels*: network members adhere to the same political party or faction as certain other members or actors outside the network, providing access to relevant party members and policy-makers. While Wright and Krane (1998) argue that party politics is of limited relevance in studying intergovernmental networks, they were essential for network managers to achieve results in this study, especially in acquiring resources for goal attainment: money, legal decisions, permits, etc. Network management is not only about good interactions within the network, but also a matter of power and control over public resources located in the network environment, where politicians ultimately have the ability to compel resource provision (Saidel 1991). As in many countries, in Belgium those politicians are linked to political parties who provide channels to access decision making for (other) public and private actors.

The party political relations with ministers through ministerial cabinets[4] in particular present a black box to acquire key decisions regarding resources. Playing this black box is crucial for network managers to achieve results: *"Depending on the dossier, we use the red, blue or green line[5]"* (interview quote PGCA). The quote illustrates how these party political channels are strategically used by network managers depending on the policy games at hand.

While the third and fourth type of channels are the hardest to determine, they are crucial for policy-making in countries like Belgium (Dewachter 1992) with a strong party political tradition, a history of political actors being socialized in a particular philosophical tradition, joined by a culture of political appointment throughout the civil service[6] (Voets and De Rynck 2008). This context makes network management much more political, and researchers need to be aware of that, requiring a much stronger political researchers' eye. The challenge then is to learn which channels matter for which strategies, to get the right channels involved in the network, and how to use them strategically.

Using Channels

Channels are used to implement a wide range of single management strategies, including mobilizing and activation or deactivation of actors (Scharpf 1978). For instance, in the PGCA, the Flemish administration of road infrastructure did not want to participate in the network. The network then used a number of channels to convince the ministerial cabinet competent for public infrastructure to suggest the department head to get involved in the network: *"X and Y at the cabinet have played an important role in making that administration more responsive"* (interview quote PGCA). X and Y were not part of the network, but approached by a number of network members through personal and political channels.

Channels are also used for combined management strategies (Agranoff 2007). In the PGCA network, for instance, network activation and deactivation were done simultaneously through the same channel: one unit of the administration for water infrastructure was deactivated and replaced with another unit of that administration because the former was not considered to be active or supportive enough by the network managers: *"We muddled along with that representative for a long time, but then I solved the problem by asking for someone else in Brussels myself"* (interview quote PGCA).

To implement network management strategies, network managers can use single or multiple channels as they see fit: *"Well, there are two options: you want to do something about the issues in the area, or not. If you want to do something about it, there are two conditions. First of all, you need the required contacts, politically, at a higher level. Secondly, you have to be willing to use them for your aim. Conversely, you have to accept that they also try to use you for their aims. But that is part of the game"* (interview quote PGCA).

The latter part of the quote is also important for network management: the use of channels is not free of charge, and reciprocity is often expected in one way or another by the actors accessed on behalf of the network agenda. There is a certain amount of channel currency available in any situation, and network managers need to make trade-offs regarding the extent to which the expected benefits outweigh the costs, and for which policy game or network issue that currency is most important.

Coping with Contingencies

These channels can be affected by a number of contingencies, most notably turnover of people representing network members or relevant actors outside the network can prove to be advantageous or disadvantageous. For example, elections were major change events leading to the loss of existing channels or creating opportunities and new channels because certain persons entered or left the arena.

In the PWG, for instance, the competent minister of the Green Party was pushed into opposition after elections and replaced by a Christian-Democratic minister less inclined to support the network, hampering access to important material-institutional resources. In the PGCA, after subsequent election, the access of the network improved because a new minister in the Flemish government had its political home base in the Ghent region and, unlike its predecessor, actively supported the network agenda. Smart network managers deal with or even anticipate such events (see second proposition below).

Formulating Propositions

To make the concept of channels useful for network management theory, a number of propositions are presented, allowing for future development and testing:

> *Proposition 1: The density of channels matters—The higher the number of channels available to network managers, the more likely network management will be effective.*

This proposition can be linked to Provan and Milward's (2001) definition of a key aspect of quality of relations between actors in a network, namely density: the more channels or linkages available in the network, the more effective that network managers can be. More channels can allow network managers to use more network strategies, or to have more alternative pathways to a certain goal, thus increasing the potential substitutability of various channels.

> *Proposition 2: The multiplexity of channels matters—The more variation in any existing channels, the more likely network management will be effective.*

This proposition builds on Provan and Milward's (2001) notion of multiplexity. It means here that having a number of different types of channels at the disposal of network managers is better than the availability of just one or two types, or having only limited variation within a channel type. Striving for such variation is also a form of risk management by network managers.

We illustrate this for the party political channel. First, in a multiparty and federalized political system like Belgium, political personnel changes frequently because of elections and politicians moving across federal, regional, and local positions. Second, multiparty governing coalitions make it less evident for a single party to be in power all the time at all levels during a policy networks' life cycle. In the multilevel and intergovernmental networks studied, the situation frequently occurred that a certain party was part of a governing coalition at one level, but not at another level.

By ensuring channels to all political parties via different network members, the impact of political changes and the risk of party political competition over the network was mitigated by the network managers. In both cases, the main network managers ensured channels in and to all relevant political parties: "*That is another reason why it was sensible to take the municipality of Evergem on board: there was a Christian-Democratic government for years. I also saw that they included the provincial government. The governor [known to be a Social-Democratic] consciously brought in a Liberal-Democratic or Christian-Democratic member of the provincial executive, I saw him watch over that very carefully. So, from the local angle, we all made sure that the different parties were involved*" (interview quote PGCA).

Both propositions can be refined further by adding two additional propositions.

> *Proposition 3: Network type matters—the optimal mix of number and variation of channels for network management is dependent on the type of network.*

Although Rethemeyer and Hatmaker (2008) argue that the distinction between policy and collaborative networks, for instance, is not very useful to advance network management theory, it can be hypothesized that different network types require different management channels.

Keast, Brown, and Mandell (2007) distinguish three network types. For cooperative networks, focused only on sharing of information and/or expertise, one can assume that network managers have less or no use for party political or philosophical channels as the issue of power and requiring other resources is absent or less salient. For coordinative networks, in which actors try to achieve better coordination between their individual efforts for improved service delivery, professional channels might be more important because accomplishing tasks is the primary goal. Finally, in collaborative networks, which join actors to solve complex issues that they cannot solve on their own, philosophical and party political channels might be more important to build new types of relationships and to acquire various resources.

> *Proposition 4: Network development stage matters—the optimal mix of number and variation of channels for network management depends on the phase of the network.*

Networks are not static and evolve through time. Depending on the network management issues at hand in a certain development stage, the relevant channels can also vary. During the phase where a policy network goal still needs to be defined, personal and professional channels for instance might be more important to bring in people and ideas. If the network becomes more mature, moving into a phase where it requires policy decisions or budgets, and an action program becomes tangible, the party political and philosophical channels might prove to be much more relevant for the network managers.

MANAGEMENT ROLES

Typically in networks, there is no single manager and network management activities are deployed by a range of actors (Agranoff 2007). The extent to which network management is shared among network actors might even be regarded as an indicator for success.

Analysis of network management strategies and activities and the actors using them enables us to define different management roles or functions. Network research so far has identified a number of roles (see Agranoff 2003; Mandell 1990) but they need to be refined and developed further. A more fine-grained set can help us identify which network management roles are required for certain management strategies and how the absence of certain roles might explain network success or failure.

We define five distinct management roles that could well provide a basis to build on. They originated from our study and were validated by other network professionals during the training courses on network management. They recognized the roles, supported their relevance, and often stated that lacking one or more roles was part of the explanation why their network management was not always effective.

Five Management Roles

Agranoff (2003, 18–20) coined three important roles: network promoter, network champion, and vision keeper. Although we use his roles, we defined them differently based on our study and add the roles of network operator and creative thinker.

A *network champion* refers to those people whose main function is to scan, develop, and access the management channels developed in the previous section. Such people are likely to be more senior in terms of age and position in their organization, because building and gaining access to channels requires time and experience, but also a sufficiently high position in the parent organization to gain access to top civil servants and politicians. Network champions are the main spiders weaving and managing the network's webs. In both cases, their channels spanned across tiers and across the political and administrative realm. Network champions perform a range of network management strategies, but most notably selectively (de-)activating and mobilizing actors, two main management behaviors defined by Agranoff and McGuire (2001). They are very active in boundary-spanning or brokering as they create and use different management channels on behalf of the network. They are intergovernmental scale-crossing brokers (Ernstson et al. 2010), taking up a multilateral brokerage role (Mandell 1990), able to connect different governmental tiers and crossing policy silos.

A *network promoter* refers to persons considered as the face of the network, taking up a visible leading role. They promote the network in the outside world but also ensure binding actors within the network. Network promoters are able to put the network agenda first, safeguarding a certain level of neutrality to transcend and mediate between different interests in the network. In doing so, network promoters help to manage some of the uncertainties in the network (Koppenjan and Klijn 2004) by ensuring relational trust and a safe environment for actors to participate. Network promoters possess moral authority, derived from reputation outside of the network and for their reputation-building within the network, thus sharing features with the concept of sponsor' of Crosby and Bryson (2005) as individuals with considerable prestige and authority. While network promoters also engage in (de-)activation and mobilizing, they are crucial in framing and synthesizing, facilitating participants' roles by developing rules of the game and network values and helping to create conditions that enhance interactions in the network resulting in added value (McGuire 2002, 602). In both cases, the provincial governor was the main network promoter. His institutional position as commissioner of the Flemish government, competent to coordinate complex policy efforts in the province, provided him with authority to bring actors to the table, assuring them that their interests would be taken seriously. The personality of the governor as a former political heavyweight also gave him status and legitimacy in the network.

The role of *vision keeper* involves people keeping track of the main agenda of the network. The vision keeper is a strategic rather than operational role, monitoring to what extent the network develops in the desired direction, if the vision or action program agreed upon in the network is followed or not. They act or intervene when they detect inside or outside threats to the network agenda. In PGCA, one vision keeper was a leading civil servant who helped to set up the network and kept monitoring it from a distance after his position in his parent organization had shifted. In PWG, one vision keeper was a senior planner who played a very active role in developing the spatial structure plan, but who remained a network enthusiast (Sullivan and Skelcher 2002, 117) afterward, monitoring the network from a distance.

Hence, this network role can be played by people inside or outside the network, for instance because they move to a different position in a different organization but remain committed and interested in the network because they have become a loyal supporter.

The role of *network operator* refers to those people focused on ensuring the practical functioning of the network: preparing, organizing, reporting meetings, contacting relevant actors, taking care of communication, etc. The network operator thus takes up the more practical tasks for framing and synthesizing, while the network promoter is more engaged in the strategic tasks in this respect. The PGCA has a full-time network operator supported by a back office of provincial civil servants. In the PWG, this role was shared and shifted over time until a full-time operator was hired at a later stage.

The final role identified is that of *creative thinker*. Those playing this role are not identified with a single sectoral interest (similar to the network promoter) and provide ideas and try to change perceptions or even to reframe the mindsets of network members about which games to play and what the network is about (Klijn and Teisman 1997). Their main management activities involve providing technical, conceptual, and methodological capacity to enable framing and synthesizing. The key creative thinker in both cases was a consultancy firm, hired to help set up the process, to provide input by drawing up plans, concepts, etc. In the PGCA, for instance, they introduced the concept of coupling areas, providing a neutral wording for the difficult challenge of buffering housing from industry, while safeguarding farmers' activities and developing some ecological sections within those buffer zones. Creative thinkers provide, so to speak, the intellectual lubricant for the network to function.

Formulating Propositions

Based on these five roles, a number of propositions can be added to the previous propositions. Together they provide the basis for the development of this theory of network management.

> *Proposition 5: If the five management roles are present in a policy network, network management is more likely to be effective than if one or more management roles are absent.*

The five management roles are considered to be complementary pieces of the management puzzle. We assume that if the five management roles are played well in a policy network, the probability that network management is effective increases, and the reverse.

While the five management roles were present and well developed in the PGCA, the PWG experienced problems with two roles. For many years, the PWG network lacked a full-time coordinator and the network operator role had to be shared or alternated between different network members. This situation weakened the network, limiting the capacity for network management. Also in contrast to the PGCA, which had a network promoter from the beginning, the PWG lacked a network promoter for a long time. Actors either were not accepted in that role by other actors (because not considered sufficiently neutral), or possible candidates were not interested (because of the risks associated with the issues in the focus area or having other priorities). Only years later, the provincial governor took up the role of network promoter in the PWG. Many interviewees claimed the lack of a network promoter and a strong network operator limited the scope and effectiveness of network management actions, like the input of creative thinkers.

> *Proposition 6: The relevance of the management roles depends on the developmental phase of the network.*

The importance of certain functions can fluctuate over time, depending on the development stage of the network. It is likely that the role of the network operator is rather continuous throughout the networks' life cycle, but that the role of the creative thinker is only important in certain stages, for instance when the network tries to develop its policy goals or needs specific input for a complex policy game. The vision keeper is likely to gradually emerge and become more important as the network progresses, while the network promoter can be crucial from the beginning to provide the network with a sufficient level of credibility and trust to get started. The role of network champions, mastering the management channels, is likely to require a minimal and continuous level of management activity, with peaks if certain resources need to be obtained or if expected and unexpected changes in the network's membership or representation (e.g., after elections) need to be managed.

CONCLUDING REMARKS

As network management research is booming, network management theories gradually develop as well. Two main questions in this respect include how network management strategies and actions are put into practice, and that of the relevant management roles for network management to be effective. Drawing on case study research and sessions with network professionals, the study casts light on these questions. It shows how network managers use four types of channels to achieve strategies and actions like (de-)activation and mobilizing. Network managers not only use personal and professional ties with network members or relevant actors outside the network, but also access philosophical and party political channels, for instance to acquire relevant resources. Network managers use existing channels but also develop or create new channels, for instance by bringing in new actors. We also show that a major contingency is staff turnover that can be managed to a certain extent. We argue that having a high number and a high variety of channels increases the probability for network managers to be effective, but also that the relevance of the channels depends on the type of network and the stage of the network.

Furthermore, this chapter developed five management roles that help to refine the existing role menu and bridge the gap between knowledge about types of network activities and strategies and knowledge concerning who network managers are. We argue that if these five management roles are present in a policy network, network management strategies and actions are more likely to be effective, but that the relevance of these roles can depend on the stage of the network.

Next steps are to test and develop these propositions further. To do so, we might benefit from bridging network management with leadership theories, following up on the demand for researching leadership in networks that Silvia and McGuire (2010) have voiced and that Mandell and Keast (2009) try to capture with their concept of process catalysts. To what extent do these management roles fit the concept of process catalysts? Can we develop the five management roles by linking them to the three types of network leadership behavior (people-oriented, task-oriented, and organization-oriented) of Silvia and McGuire? Are certain leadership behaviors related to certain management channels as defined here? To what extent can we link management roles to personal skills and capacities and/or institutional positions of actors? There is considerably more to be investigated.

NOTES

1. See methodology section.
2. A fit between the goals of network members and the network goals is considered essential if a network is to succeed.
3. An epistemic community (Haas 1992, 3) *"is a network of professionals with recognized expertise and competence in a particular domain and an authoritative claim to policy-relevant knowledge within that domain or issue-area"*, sharing beliefs regarding the latter.
4. In Belgium, federal and regional ministers have substantial personal staff called ministerial cabinets (up to 50 people per minister) that prepare and follow-up on policy. These staff members are often civil servants loyal to the ministers' political party.
5. green = Green Party, red = Social-Democratic Party, blue = Liberal-Democratic Party.
6. Nowadays mostly restricted to top positions.

REFERENCES

Agranoff, Robert. 2007. *Managing Within Networks: Adding Value to Public Organizations*. Washington, DC: Georgetown University Press.

———. 2003. *Leveraging Networks: A Guide for Public Managers Working Across Organizations*. Arlington: IBM Endowment for the Business of Government.

Agranoff, Robert, and Michael McGuire. 2001. "Big Questions in Public Network Management Research." *Journal of Public Administration Research and Theory* 11 (3): 295–326.

Alexander, Damon, Jenny M. Lewis, and Mark Considine. 2011. "How Politicians and Bureaucrats Network: A Comparison across Governments, *Public Administration* 89 (4): 1274–92.

Arts, Bas, and Jan van Tatenhove. 2004. "Policy and Power. A Conceptual Framework between the 'Old' and 'New' Policy Idioms." *Policy Sciences* 37 (3–4): 339–56.

Beach, Sandra, Robyn Keast, and David Pickernell. 2012. "Unpacking the Connections between Network and Stakeholder Management and their Application to Road Infrastructure Networks in Queensland." *Public Management Review* 14 (5): 609–29.

Bevir, Mark, and David Richards. 2009. "Decentring Policy Networks: A Theoretical Agenda." *Public Administration* 87 (1): 3–14.

Blomgren-Bingham, Lisa, Jodi Sandfort, and Rosemary O'Leary. 2008. Learning to Do and Doing to Learn: Teaching Managers to Collaborate in Networks. In *Big Ideas in Collaborative Public Management*, edited by Lisa Blomgren-Bingham and Rosemary O'Leary, 270–86. Armonk, NY: M.E. Sharpe.

Crosby, Barbara C., and John M. Bryson. 2005. *Leadership for the Common Good: Tackling Public Problems in a Shared-Power World*. 2nd ed. San Francisco: Jossey-Bass.

Dewachter, Wilfried. 1992. *De Mythe van de Parlementaire Democratie*. Leuven: Acco.

Ernstson, Henrik, Stephan Barthel, Erik Andersson, and Sara T. Borgström. 2010. "Scale-Crossing Brokers and Network Governance of Urban Ecosystem Services: The Case of Stockholm." *Ecology and Society* 15 (4): 28.

Haas, Peter M. 1992. "Introduction: Epistemic Communities and International Policy Coordination." *International Organization* 46 (1): 1–36.

Hjern, Benny, and David O. Porter. 1981. "Implementation Structures: A New Unit for Administrative Analysis." *Organizational Studies* 2 (3): 211–37.

Huxham, Chris, and Siv Vangen. 2005. *Managing to Collaborate. The Theory and Practice of Collaborative Advantage*. London: Routledge.

Keast, Robyn, Kerry Brown, and Myrna P. Mandell. 2007. "Getting the Right Mix: Unpacking Integration Meanings and Strategies." *International Public Management Journal* 10(1): 9–34.

Keast, Robyn, Myrna P. Mandell, Kerry Brown, and Geoffroy Woolcock. 2004. "Network Structures: Working Differently and Changing Expectations." *Public Administration Review* 64 (3): 363–71.

Kickert, Walter J.M., Erik-Hans Klijn, and Joop F.M. Koppenjan. 1997. "Introduction: A Management Perspective on Policy Networks." In *Managing Complex Networks. Strategies for the Public Sector*, edited by Walter J.M. Kickert, Erik-Hans Klijn, and Joop F.M. Koppenjan, 1–13. London: Sage.

Klijn, Erik-Hans, and Joop F.M. Koppenjan. 2012. "Governance Network Theory: Past, Present and Future." *Policy & Politics* 40 (4): 187–206.

———. 2000. "Public Management and Policy Networks: Foundations of a Network Approach to Governance." *Public Management* 2 (2): 136–58.

Klijn, Erik-Hans, and Geert R. Teisman. 1997. "Strategies and Games in Networks." In *Managing Complex Networks. Strategies for the Public Sector*, edited by Walter J.M. Kickert, Erik-Hans Klijn, and Joop F.M. Koppenjan, 98–118. London: Sage.

Koppenjan, Joop F.M., and Erik-Hans Klijn. 2004. *Managing Uncertainties in Networks: A Network Approach to Problem Solving and Decision Making*. London: Routledge.

Lewis, Jenny M. 2011. "The Future of Network Governance Research: Strength in Diversity And Synthesis." *Public Administration* 89(4): 1221–34.

Mandell, Myrna P. 1994. "Managing Interdependencies Through Program Structures: A Revised Paradigm." *The American Review of Public Administration* 24 (1): 99–122.

———. 1990. Network Management: Strategic Behavior in the Public Sector. In *Strategies for Managing Intergovernmental Policies and Networks*, edited by Robert W. Gage and Myrna P. Mandell, 29–54. Westport Connecticut: Praeger.

Mandell, Myrna P. and Robyn Keast. 2007. "Evaluating Network Arrangements: Toward Revised Performance Measures." *Public Performance & Management Review* 30 (4):574–97.

———. 2009. "A New Look at Leadership in Collaborative Networks: Process Catalysts." In *Public Sector Leadership: International Challenges and Perspectives*, edited by Jeffrey A. Raffel, Peter Leisnik, and Anthony Middlebrooks, 163–78. Cheltenham: Edward Elgar.

Mandell, Myrna P., and Toddi A. Steelman. 2003. "Understanding What Can Be Accomplished Through Interorganizational Innovations." *Public Management Review* 5 (2): 197–224.

McGuire, Michael. 2002. "Managing Networks: Propositions on What Managers Do and Why They Do It." *Public Administration Review* 62 (5): 599–609.

Meier, Kenneth J., and Laurence J., Jr. O'Toole. 2003. "Public Management and Educational Performance: The Impact of Managerial Networking." *Public Administration Review* 63 (3): 689–99.

Osborne, Stephen P. 2009. *The New Public Governance? Emerging Perspectives on the Theory and Practice of Public Governance*. London: Routledge.

O'Toole, Laurence J., Jr. 1997. "Treating Networks Seriously: Practical and Research-Based Agendas in Public Administration." *Public Administration Review* 57 (1): 45–53.

Park, Hyun Hee, and Karl R. Rethemeyer. 2012. "The Politics of Connections: Assessing the Determinants of Social Structure in Policy Networks." *Journal of Public Administration Research and Theory* (Advance Access): 1–26.

Provan, Keith G., and Robin H. Lemaire. 2012. "Core Concepts and Key Ideas for Understanding Public Sector Organizational Networks: Using Research to Inform Scholarship and Practice." *Public Administration Review* 72 (5): 638–48.

Provan, Keith G., and H. Brinton Milward. 2001. "Do Networks Really Work? A Framework for Evaluating Public-Sector Organizational Networks." *Public Administration Review*, 61 (4): 414–423.

Rethemeyer, Karl R., and Deneen M. Hatmaker. 2008. "Network Management Reconsidered: An Inquiry Into Management of Network Structures in Public Sector Service." *Journal of Public Administration Research and Theory* 18 (4): 617–46.

Saidel, Judith R. 1991. "Resource Interdependence: The Relationship between State Agencies and Nonprofit Organizations." *Public Administration Review*, 51 (6): 543–53.

Scharpf, Fritz W. 1978. "Interorganizational Policy Studies: Issues, Concepts and Perspectives." In *Interorganisational Policy Making*, edited by Kenneth I. Hanf and Fritz W. Scharpf, 345–70. Beverly Hills: Sage.

Silvia, Chris, and Michael McGuire. 2010. "Leading Public Sector Networks: An Empirical Examination of Integrative Leadership Behaviors." *Leadership Quarterly* 21 (2): 264–77.

Sullivan, Helen, and Chris Skelcher. 2002. *Working Across Boundaries: Collaboration in Public Services*. Basingstoke: Palgrave.

Voets, Joris. 2008. *Intergovernmental Relations in Multi-Level Arrangements: Collaborative Public Management in Flanders*. Leuven: KU Leuven.

Voets, Joris, and Filip De Rynck. 2011. "Exploring the Innovative Capacity of Intergovernmental Network Managers: The Art of Boundary Scanning and Boundary Spanning." In *Innovation in the Public Sector. Linking Capacity and Leadership*, edited by Victor Bekkers, Jurian Edelenbos, and Bram Steijn, 155–75. Houndmills, Basingstoke: Palgrave MacMillan.

———. 2008. "Contextualising City-regional Issues, Strategies and their Use: the Flemish Story." *Local Government Studies* 34 (4): 453–70.

Wright, Deil S., and Dale Krane. 1998. "Intergovernmental Relations. In *International Encyclopedia of Public Policy and Administration*," Vol. 2, edited by Jay M. Shafritz, 1168–76. Bolder: Westview Press.

Part III
Putting Theory into Practice

9 Network Management Behaviors
Closing the Theoretical Gap

Michael McGuire and Robert Agranoff

INTRODUCTION

It is generally understood that managers operate differently in collaborative entities than in hierarchies. This has been clear from the early years of interorganizational network consciousness. Standard "line management" organizational approaches, e.g., POSDCORB, do not fit into the highly interactive cross-organization processes that seek to create a new *holism* out of the brokered contributions of organizational representatives operating in goal-directed networks. One groundbreaking work (Kickert and Koppenjan 1997, 47) conceptualized network management as "the steering of interaction processes". They posited steps like mobilizing, organizing, and brokering favorable conditions as mechanisms for governing joint action. Agranoff and McGuire (2001) built on these ideas by suggesting a series of four behaviors that might capture the essential steps in network management: activating, mobilizing, framing, and synthesizing. These four steps have subsequently been raised by others as a means to describe network management processes (Keast and Hampson 2007; Page 2008; Rethemeyer and Hatmaker 2008; Beach, Keast, and Pickernell 2012; Saz-Carranza 2012; Silvia 2011). Although the Agranoff and McGuire framework has been heavily cited, a complete empirical analysis that examines this four-step process in detail has heretofore not been undertaken. Here we attempt to cross that bridge.

Observation of managerial behavior is one mechanism for more accurately documenting how managers match behavior with environmental constraints (McGuire 2002). In an empirical challenge of sorts, McGuire maintains that the preliminary classification of the four behaviors "should be tested and refined, even rejected, if sound data are collected from managers for this purpose", adding to both theory and practice (608). We seek to meet this challenge with data from a study of Metro in Columbus, Ohio, a math and science high school that is organized and operated by network rather than as a typical board governed school. This study seeks to add to the theory of network management by taking a deep look into the formation and operation of Metro, which is an action type network that is actively engaged in developing operating policies and programs as well as carrying out its agreements and decisions (Agranoff 2007). Analytically, our concern is with managerial process, bringing out the assumptions regarding the grouping of network management behaviors in practice as network actors organize and operate.

The data analysis in this paper is taken from a multimethod study of the Metro High School network formation and operation[1], and of the school's culture and community (Hunter et al. 2008). The research design included field-based data-gathering to understand the four network management phases within the Metro network. The guiding research question for this part of the larger Metro study is thus: Is the Metro school network formulated and operated by collaborative management processes involving activating, mobilizing, framing, and synthesizing?

The study is organized into five sections. The first section describes the four network management behaviors first suggested by Agranoff and McGuire. Second, the empirical setting is discussed as a means to demonstrate that the Metro school is indeed a networked entity. The third section describes the grounded theory methodology used by the researchers. The fourth section forms the heart of the empirical analysis and shows how the four behavior framework fits into the Metro school experience. Finally, the implications of these findings and modifications are presented.

FOUR NETWORK MANAGEMENT BEHAVIORS

In general, *activation* refers to the set of behaviors used for identifying and incorporating the persons and resources needed to achieve program goals. The skills, knowledge, and resources of these potential participants must be assessed and tapped. Activation can be a critical component of management "because resources like money, information, and expertise can be integrating mechanisms of networks" (McGuire and Silvia 2009, 39).

In addition to activating the network, Agranoff and McGuire proposed that managers often must induce individuals to make and keep a commitment to the network. *Mobilizing* behaviors are used to develop support for network processes from network participants and external stakeholders. Publicizing the network's accomplishments and using incentives to motivate network participants are a few of the behaviors undertaken by network managers.

The Agranoff and McGuire framework posited that network managers attempt to frame the structure and the norms and values of the network as a whole. Referring to this behavior as *framing*, the argument is that managers undertake behaviors designed to arrange and integrate a network structure by facilitating agreement on participants' roles, operating rules, and network values. Facilitating agreement on network roles, helping to establish an identity and culture for the network, assisting in developing a working structure for the network, developing a shared vision for the network, changing the network structure when appropriate, and altering the perceptions of participants to understand the unique characteristics of working with persons in contexts without organizational mechanisms based in authority relations are hallmark behaviors associated with framing (McGuire 2002).

The fourth category of network behavior posits that managers use *synthesizing* behaviors intended to create a collaborative environment and to enhance the conditions for productive interactions among network participants. Synthesis also facilitates managers' ability to create and maintain trust among network participants as a means to build relationships and interactions that result in achieving the network purposes. Along the path to synthesis, successful network management achieves results-based collaboration between network participants while minimizing and removing informational blockages to cooperation.

STUDY SETTING

The research that supports this analysis of network management behaviors emanates from a study of Metro High School, Columbus, Ohio, which is an accelerated science, technology, engineering and math (STEM) school that is uniquely operated as a network of public and private agencies as the equivalent to governing by a public or voluntary organized school board. Metro's major partners include the Educational Council (superintendents of Franklin County's 16 county school districts), The Ohio State University (OSU), national and state Coalitions for Essential Schools (CES) (Knowledge Works in Ohio), and Battelle Memorial Institute, a non-profit research and development foundation that operates on a business model. As Figure 9.1 indicates, there is much more to this operation, including linkages to important learning centers or sites where students have internships, projects, field placements, and classes; relationships with the PAST Foundation, which organizes research, field learning, and dissemination of STEM learning to the 16 school districts; contractual arrangements with OSU for student counseling; access to OSU leadership and educational resources; and linkages with other community resources such as industry/educator curricula taskforces and the use of the OSU Library as the Metro Library.

In a sharp distinction from hierarchical governance, Metro is governed and operated on a multipartner basis, that is, by network. Metro is officially "governed" by the Education Council (EC) Project, upon the advice of the Metropolitan Partnership Group (MPG), a multiparty steering group administered by the Metro School administration and the Education Council staff. The school admits about 100 students for each class, by interview and lottery, apportioned by school district population among the 16 districts. It operates on an accelerated basis and is oriented to subject mastery.

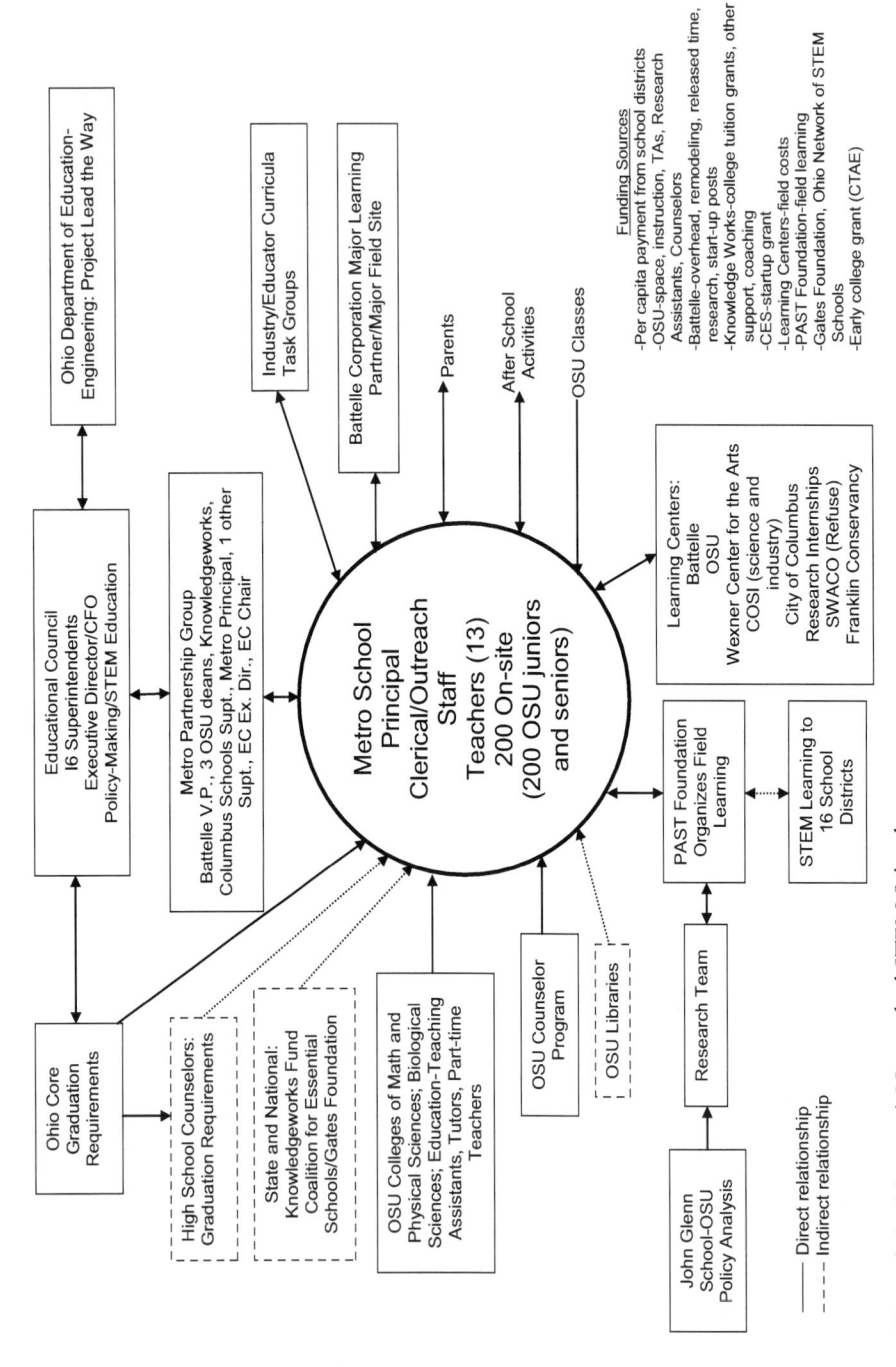

Figure 9.1 Metro—A Networked STEM School

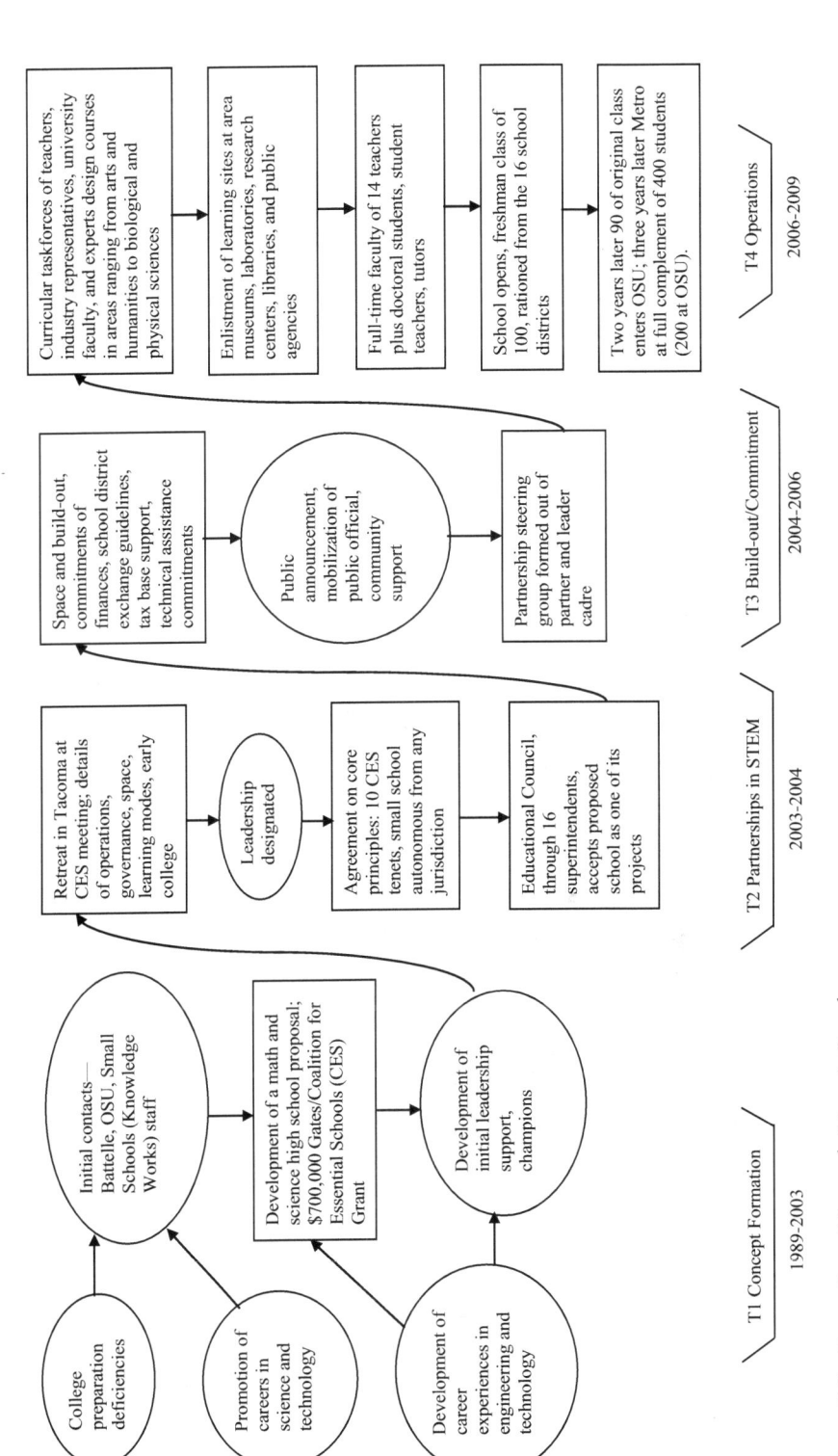

Figure 9.2 Event-State Network–Metro's Development

The development of Metro is an interesting story in network formation. The field investigation allowed us to develop a sequence of its formative events, summarized and highlighted in Figure 9.2. Of particular note at this point is that Metro's founders did not set out to create the network structure that emerged; like many such entities, it began as a form of an organic, loose partnership among Battelle, OSU, and the Educational Council. As the group proceeded, its operating principles became built on a set of agreed principles related to small size, autonomy from a school system, and personalized, performance-based development of "habits of the mind." What began as a loosely coupled partnership in the end led the steering group to organize as a network.

METHODOLOGY

This study was conducted by a *grounded theory* method as adapted for dealing with complex structures like networks and organizations. As such, it is an inductive study, in which the research design is intended to generate theoretical propositions from the data gathered. Grounded theory thus means theory that was derived from the data, in this case primarily qualitative, systematically collected and gathered, and analyzed throughout the research process (Glazer and Strauss 1967; Corbin and Strauss 2008). Basically, it provides a way to look at the Metro network empirically from the perspectives of those immersed in the network. The grounded theory approach taken in this study "puts the qualitative researcher somewhere between designs based on deductive quantitative . . . testing of explicit theoretical propositions and descriptive and casual inference, and thick analysis of nominal data analyzed by inference" (Agranoff 2007, 39). Its three distinguishing features include coding of verbal data that ultimately leads to theoretical sampling, constant comparison of data to theoretical categories, and focus on the development of theory via theoretical saturation of categories rather than substantive verifiable findings (Bryant and Charmaz 2010, 13).

Pure grounded theory begins without any preconceived theoretical frameworks in mind, allowing theory to emerge from the data. Recent practice has modified this type of approach, calling for utilizing previous research to formulate a preliminary conceptual framework, as well as the use of pretheoretical applications to frame the important questions (Corbin 2009). Miles and Huberman (1994, 34) recommend designs that pay prior attention to a conceptual framework, as well as to research questions, sampling, and instrumentation that have a "focusing and bounding" role within an area of study. It is thus standard grounded theory practice to begin with a framework such as the four previously identified managerial processes.

Data creation began with literature-based concepts posited by Agranoff and McGuire (2001), McGuire (2002), and others who have investigated the four network management behaviors. In addition, preexisting textual material, including project progress reports, grant applications, Partnership and Educational Council meeting minutes, and other written materials were read. Together this led to the creation of a discussion guide, identifying key network actors, making contacts, and holding extended (one to two hours) discussions with 29 core persons. Discussions were supplemented by observations of key meetings and task force sessions. In turn, the discussions and written materials led to the creation of a working text that led to NVivo coding of the text.

The coding process followed the standard grounded theory process: 1) open coding, breaking data apart and delineating concepts to stand for blocks of raw data; 2) axial coding, cross-cutting or relating concepts to one another; 3) conceptual saturation, acquiring sufficient data to develop categorical themes; 4) comparative analysis, comparing responses for similarities and differences; and 5) theoretical sampling, seeking concepts that are relevant to the emergent analytical "storyline" (Corbin and Strauss 2008, 195). It is a long and tedious process, going back and forth from the raw data to NVivo, where the latter is most useful to develop the open coding and axial coding stages.

The second research activity involved analyzing the coded discussion data by bringing out cross-respondent patterns through looking for similarities and differences, selecting categories, finding respondent pairs, data triangulation, and looking for "pre-concepts. Next, data analysis included the process of clustering to support relationships, themes, and trends, along with data reduction for confirmation and then delineation of the deep structure that supports our explanatory framework. Fourth, data displays include the tables and figures documented in this paper as well as flow charts, figures, time-ordered matrices, and sequential event displays reported in the project report (Hunter et al. 2008) that have now become standard in qualitative and/or multimethod research. This theoretically focused and bounded inductive approach proved to be well suited to study network formation and operation where previous research offered only conceptual speculation and guidance, but little empirical evidence.

In general, following the advice provided in one of the leading methods guides for mixed methods research (Teddlie and Tashakkori 2009, 294–296), the research met the following standards:

1. Prolonged engagement, that is, research team members in the field for one and one-half years.
2. Persistent observation, particularly by two of the research team members, along with intermittent observation by the principal researchers.
3. Data triangulation among coded discussions, printed reports, meeting minutes, and observation notes by the multiple researchers involved in the project.
4. Peer debriefing to principal leaders, administrators, and project funders for participant reactions.
5. Member checks by key participants to document the accuracy of the themes, interpretations, and conclusions.

These actions supported the research team's interpretations of reality, allowed for consistency of the data collected, guarded against replication breakdown, and allowed for the development of working hypotheses that reflect situation-specific conditions. These multiple techniques supported our quest for insight, richness, depth, variation, and, most important, applicability (Corbin and Strauss 2008, 305–306).

THE FOUR BEHAVIORS OF NETWORK MANAGEMENT IN METRO

The primary results are reported in Table 9.1, which provides summary "identifiers" of Metro activities that constitute the management of the network. Table 9.1 is divided into four distinct phases of Metro's development: concept formation, developing the STEM partnership, build out and commitments, and school operations, roughly over the 10-year period from 1999 to 2009. The previously identified event-state flow chart in Figure 9.2 (Miles and Huberman 1994, 116) created from the coded data was developed prior to the creation of Table 9.1. Each event related to the network formation and operation was coded into the four time sequences. The data were then coded by the four network management behaviors. Table 9.1 makes clear that not only do many different network management behaviors comprise each of the four phases, but also that they are continuing management behaviors throughout the life of the network. There was some tendency for activating and mobilizing activities to be prevalent at the early stages, with framing as most notable in the middle stages, and with a great deal of synthesizing near the latter stages, but never was any one of the four exclusive to any time period. It suggests the recurrent nature of these activities.

Activating

A look at the activation phase in the first column of Table 9.1 demonstrates the near constant need to enlist champions and vision-keepers, then resource bearers, then those with expertise, and finally for outreach and client support. It began with basic ideas that Knowledge Works had for creating small high schools in Ohio, along with early OSU interest in a downtown school, and discussions among the two network champions, the OSU president and Battelle's Chief Executive Officer. These critical organizational representatives moved the project forward, as the potential partners—OSU deans, Battelle vice president, COSI's director, two Knowledge Works staff, the Columbus Schools' superintendent and the CEO of the Educational Council (EC)—all met at a Coalition for Essential Schools conference in Tacoma, Washington, for nearly one week to explore potential commitments and general ideas. All but COSI, which returned to the fold later, became the

Table 9.1 Metro Stages through Network Management Behaviors

Time Frame/Behaviors	1. Activation	2. Mobilization	3. Framing	4. Synthesis
1. Concept Formation 1989–2003	• Knowledge Works/CES • First Gates Foundation Grant-small high schools • OSU interest in downtown school • Initial champion discussions OSU President/Battelle CEO	• Initial, informal search for space and sponsors • OSU downtown school feasibility exploration • Champions sell idea: 1) internally, 2) key community groups/organizations	• 10 CES principles • Agreement: 1) public/private, 2) scalable, 3) sustainable without grants, 4) general access—not gifted and talented only	• From gifted and talented to broad enrollment • Science and technology emphasis • Would not be another charter school
2. Partners in STEM 2003–2004	• Invitations to Tacoma Meeting: OSU, Battelle, COSI, Knowledge Works, Columbus Schools, Education Council • Education Council enlisted—Executive Director first administrator • Enlistment of multiple network managers	• Tacoma meeting/workshop • Community support building • Second Gates grant for small science and math school • Organization commitments of Battelle, OSU, Education Council, Columbus schools • MOU solidifies major partner organizations	• Basic triangle: small, autonomous, ten CES principles • Education Council agrees to be governing body; Executive Director—CFO • Principal designated	• STEM concept adopted • Hybrid organizing scheme across school districts • Partner reciprocity, resource sharing risk sharing emerges • Operations within multiple hierarchies

(Continued)

Table 9.1   *(Continued)*

Time Frame/Behaviors	1. Activation	2. Mobilization	3. Framing	4. Synthesis
3. Build-out and Commitment 2004–2006	• OSU/Battelle architects assigned • OSU scientists design special classrooms • Contractor remodeling • Contacts with field sites • Lead teacher sought • Contacts with learning sites	• OSU commits to space • Battelle funds remodeling • Knowledge Works—technical education consultant on small schools, staff committees • Enlistment of OSU deans • Knowledge Works $1 million startup expenses and college tuition	• Formalizing of Partnership advisory group representing partners/vision keepers • Rules of student admission/retention progress • Education Council—school district levies/funding • Mastery adopted as progress measure	• Partnership explores, recommends policies • Education Council sets broad inter-district policies • Public announcement • External contracts: food, counseling, special classes • Curricular task forces in six areas, language arts and physical sciences
4. Operations 2006–2009	• New Learning Centers/links added: Mayor's office, SWACO, museums and libraries, COSI • Students and parents involved • PAST Foundation—export of STEM to 16 districts • COSI brought back into core partners	• Internships and projects at Battelle and other learning centers • Curricular, counseling and credit links with the school districts • Finding transportation, special education, and school lunch resources	• Interoperable systems established: crediting, project equivalents, records, reporting • Student recruitment from 16 districts • Network philosophy solidified	• Teacher hiring • Student recruitment • Instructional policies • Learning site agreements • OSU graduate students • Partnership Group meetings • School at full compliment • Classes at OSU • Expansion of classes at COSI

guiding forces or vision-keepers. Activation at the later stages involved preparing the OSU donated site for the school, finding internship and learning sites, and during operations, finding new learning centers such as museums, libraries, and public programs. Students, teachers, and the 16 school districts were also activated for STEM learning. At different times, Metro needed a host of actors to establish and maintain the network. It also was a continuing process to identify and sustain these disparate actors in the joint venture.

Mobilizing

Mobilization is also a continuing activity. Indeed, the second column of Table 9.1 shows it to be the "busiest" of the four, which should be of no surprise for those who understand that networks rarely, if ever, have the legally based legitimacy as those of most hierarchical organizations. Mobilization amounted to the continuing search for network legitimacy through cultivating broad community support and the resources needed to operate networked operations. In spite of the fact that management is a collective process, to maintain commitment to the network's viability and mobilize external support for the network's activities, most network operations require one or more persons who are catalytic leaders and have a passion for the collaborative undertaking, and thus can make things happen. Despite the fact that authority is dispersed and shared in networks, someone still needs to emerge and help orchestrate a vision, see that plans are being followed, orchestrate contacts among key partners, and command a reasonable measure of resources. These are the champions of the partnership-related undertaking.

Metro was fortunate to have two primary champions. The most visible champions were clearly the Battelle CEO and the OSU president. In addition, the support of former U.S. Senator John Glenn and the OSU provost were very important. Together, the Battelle and OSU leaders provided oversight and monitoring of the process. These key champions did not become involved in the details, but instead provided a rallying point for mobilizing support and giving legitimacy to the endeavor.

The mobilization role of the champions was two-fold. First, the champions had to sell the basic idea of a STEM school with CES principles to their respective organizations. The champions had to convince internal parties that it was a worthwhile investment of organizational resources. For OSU, this meant convincing external actors (e.g., the Board of Trustees) and internal actors (e.g., the colleges), and in particular the three colleges that ultimately became investors. It was said to mean a lot of "mountain moving" in the large, slow, OSU bureaucracy. For Battelle, it was working with administrative staff to support the effort and to convince them that investing in STEM education was a wise new "business start".

The second role of the network champions was working with leaders in the community by selling the idea before civic groups, trade associations, city and county elected officials, legislators and state agency personnel, and to the business community. One person referred to the champions as "ice cutters who helped move the obstacles out of the way." Their role was mainly in connecting and trying to get people to move forward. The two prime champions kept in regular contact. Their roles were in no way operational, but to support all of the parties involved in more direct issues and to reinforce the disparate resource commitments, drawing on their established networks in the larger Columbus community.

Mobilizing also included cementing in the vision-keepers at the Tacoma workshop, followed by continuously building community support. Also key was a $200,000 Gates Foundation/CES grant that the Tacoma group received to plan for a small science and math school in or around Columbus. About the same time, the Educational Council agreed to take on the Metro idea on an interim basis, initially serving as the fiscal and operational vehicle, thus making the small school idea one of their several countywide projects. This, in effect, meant that the 16 school district superintendents (and their boards) were behind this idea, a most important legitimacy and resource bearing step that brought in 15 additional suburban school districts to join with Columbus schools. The result of these specific commitments of the other partners was a Memorandum of Understanding by the three major partners and investors—OSU, Battelle, and the Educational Council—which in effect "chartered" the network.

Mobilization during build-out included OSU's commitment to donate a three-year lease worth $1.2 million in retail value, loan out of OSU architectural staff, and development of an agreement among multiple deans to provide $1 million in university funding for nine graduate teaching assistants. Battelle pledged its support by providing an initial contribution of $600,000 per year for the first three to four years, plus the loan of several critical personnel, donated staff time, and coverage of some contracted services. At the same time, Knowledge Works began consulting and organizing key committees, and also committed $1 million in startup expenses and for college tuition funding for advanced students.

In the operations phase, mobilization involved establishing a commitment by Battelle with other centers to establish learning opportunities through internships and projects. For example, several students began working on robotic engineering research at Battelle and others were at the local solid waste district working on chemical treatments. Most important, operational mobilization included support from routine linkages with the 16 school districts, primarily over student credits, conduct issues, and counseling, along with establishing contractual resources and agreements with the various learning centers. While network building is multifaceted and constant, the mobilizing frame suggests gradual movement from finding ideas and supporters to committing resources

Framing

Framing involves the practices and decisions that hold an interorganizational group together. The third column in Table 9.1 makes this clear, as the core ideas for Metro began with the Coalition for Essential Schools ten Common Principles, that focus on developing habits of the mind, mastering a limited number of skills areas and knowledge, personalized teaching and learning, student self-teaching, establishing a tone of decency and trust, and incorporating nondiscriminatory and inclusive policies, programs, and pedagogies. Early agreements among the champions and other leaders also specified that: 1) the school would involve public-private partnerships and other collaborative working relationships; 2) the project was to be scalable, in that more than one ought to come out of this effort; 3) it needed to be sustained without philanthropy; and 4) the school needed to be public and one that was general access—not an elite or private school—but with comparably high standards.

As the partners formed these principles and forged agreements, the concept of Metro was transformed into a basic ideology. As one of the Metro founders explained, the basic Metro concept "was based on a triangle of issues". At the apex was "start small, stay small". One leg involved "autonomy" from a school district or some other form of organization or jurisdiction. The other leg involved the CES principles. Inside the triangle was the project goal: "To create a small, highly personalized, intellectually vibrant school". These became the grounding issues.

The next important framing step involved the Educational Council officially becoming the governing body and fiscal agent for the school. It was decided that it would adopt network policies and oversee operations, officially select administrators, and so on. Very soon after, one of the CES consultants, a former suburban high school principal, was designated as Metro principal. As build-out was beginning, the partnership advisory group of vision-keepers was formalized. It was to recommend policy to the EC and work out details of an interorganizational nature. Most important in this regard were rules of student admissions/retention/programs based on the adopted principle of mastery. Students would advance when they demonstrably understood and could apply learning concepts. Also, the EC adopted a fee schedule. School districts that sent students to Metro would pay a per capita fee that was roughly equivalent to the per pupil state aid formula. During the operations phase, student recruitment plus various Metro school district interactive mechanisms for student records, crediting, and reporting were established. Thus, from basic ideas, to general policies, to administrative systems, framing is also a continuous process that is essential to establishing network operations.

Synthesizing

The synthesizing phase is outlined for Metro in the fourth column of Table 9.1. From basic agreements with regard to issues of emphasis—broad enrollment, science and technology, and a new form of school—the STEM concept was adopted. STEM is based on the idea that business and industry leaders, policy makers, and educators need to converge around advocacy for strong science, technology, engineering, and math education as essential for the future of the country. STEM education is based not solely on pedagogy, but on new strategic approaches and different forms of public and private partnerships at the local level with support from state and national resources. From here the idea of a hybrid structure to support the STEM idea evolved that would include but not be directly part of any school district, setting aside any consideration of the charter school idea. It was near universally agreed that authority should be shared and based on partner reciprocity–resource sharing and risk sharing. In the build-out phase, policies were explored and recommended by the partnership, educational council policies were delineated, public support was solidified by public announcement, and support services contracts were negotiated. Most important, the lead teacher and designated content-area leaders worked with a series of curricular planning teams from Battelle, OSU, PAST Foundation, and area high schools. These "open to anyone" task forces met weekly for three months and the results of the meetings went first to the Metro Partnership Group and then on to the Educational Council to ensure that the innovative curriculum was also aligned with Ohio Educational Standards within each content area.

Synthesizing operations involves a series of administrative activities that are illustrated in the lower right-hand cell of Table 9.1. Each serves the internal operation of Metro as well as transorganizational relationships, which involved the operations and policies of some other entity. For example, most Metro teachers are not Metro hires but on temporary assignments from the school districts, meaning that the labor contract of the sending school district applies. At the time of the field study, Metro was dealing with eight different union-management agreements. Also, students are recruited from the 16 districts with "slots" allocated by school population proportion. Finally, non-OSU classes for third and fourth year students were located at the Columbus Organization of Science and Industry. College credit articulation involved triangulation between school district curriculum people, OSU instructors, and Metro officials. In other words, synthesizing the network at the operational phases involves an overwhelming number of transactions and their accompanying costs. This is because the operations of the network are interdependent; one entity must rely on the resources, knowledge, and authority of the other.

Bringing It Together and New Insights

The preceding analysis was conducted with the guidance of the Agranoff and McGuire (2001) model of network management. Together the four behaviors initially postulated more than a decade ago emerged in the real world of the Metro situation. The research suggests that the frequently used set of network management behaviors indeed can be used to guide future research and practice.

The Four Behaviors in Summary

Activation was at the heart of the development of Metro's network. The idea for a new school emerged from a single grant program and slowly progressed through a process of adding individuals to the mix who possessed the resources necessary to create the school. Prior working relationships grew, knowledge was exchanged and applied, new social and professional connections were established, financial commitments emerged, and, overall, the size and scope of the network evolved into a fully activated entity.

In addition, one of the most successful but difficult managerial activities of Metro was that of the early participants' awareness of the importance of external support. Indeed, many discussants noted how involving the executives of Battelle and OSU during the summer of 2005 (three years before Metro opened) changed everything. Framing the network was performed almost from the beginning. The Coalition for Essential Schools common principles were the guiding norms for establishing Metro and were viewed as being "unequivocal", said one discussant. Decision making processes and organizing principles were also developed early. As one participant in the Tacoma group stated, it was in Tacoma where "we developed the parameters, divided up roles and responsibilities, and built process agreements that allowed us to come out with a sense of trust". Later, the Metro Partnership Group was formed as the operational network "manager" to deal with issues of school operation, giving general advice, providing insights, brainstorming, and discussing potential grants.

Information dissemination throughout the Metro network has been paramount to the network's success. Task forces were created to encourage negotiation and deliberation, and the Metro network remains transparent. Also, the central participants in the network obviously value cooperation between the network participants. Metro is highly successful at facilitating productive linkages among the broad array of network participants. Rather than becoming insular over time, the discussants conveyed that the Metro network managers continue to seek advice, invite guidance, and plan within the steering groups.

Multiple Managers

Research in the Agranoff and McGuire tradition speaks consistently of a singular network manager, and typically this refers to the government actor (Silvia and McGuire 2010). However, recent scholarship, as well as the findings presented here, suggest that a focus on a singular actor may not be appropriate at times. Rethemeyer and Hatmaker (2008) assert that the introduction of multiple network managers into a given network context implies that each network manager does not perform all of the functions identified by Agranoff and McGuire. Saz-Carranza and Ospina (2011) state that leadership in networks is "a collective achievement rather than the property of individuals" (406). It is clear that the formation and operation of Metro involves multiple "managers", each performing a role at any given time, but also each undertaking involves multiple network management behaviors across time. There may in fact be several "initiators" in a network who may take action at the same time (de Bruijn and ten Heuvelhof 2008, 7; Beach, Keast, and Pickernell 2012).

Simultaneity of Managing

Previous attempts to operationalize the framework depicted the four behaviors in linear terms, as if the manager passes through each behavior distinctively from one to the other in the order discussed (McGuire 2002). The behaviors were viewed independently and as exclusive events. The study discussed here suggests that this depiction of linear behaviors must be modified. This is made clear in Table 9.1, where each of the four behaviors appears and reappears throughout concept formation, partnering, build-out, and operations. Indeed, the data show overwhelmingly that network management behavior is simultaneous. Consistent with the previous point about the existence of multiple network managers, each of the four behaviors was undertaken at various points in time by various actors fulfilling multiple goals. For example, at the same time that the curricular design was being forged, the Tacoma group of leaders met regularly to work out the location, physical plant, OSU contributions, philosophy, how to differentiate the four grades, overall size, and so on. The educational council became involved in the details of how students were to be chosen, as well as school financing. OSU and Battelle took the lead on the physical plant, building issues, that is, along with an OSU architect who was loaned to design classrooms/laboratories.

The Importance of Managing Both Networks and Organizations

Network management involves a shift or change in the role of the single, "home" organization, but not the elimination of the importance of that organization. Certainly, bureaucratic agencies of the state that participate in networks are being challenged operationally to accommodate collaborative activity. However, while the public agency has changed to meet the challenge of networked activity, it has not disappeared (McGuire and Agranoff 2010). Managers work both for and in the state, and for and in the network. They increasingly operate with agents and organizations external to the agency, which has changed what they do and how they operate. However, the "home" organization, be it a public agency or a nongovernmental organization, typically remains the primary focus of network managers (Agranoff forthcoming).

As the decision support of the superintendents on the Metro education council or the tasks performed by the champions and the Metro partnership group suggests, it is clear that networks allow public entities to work together but are not necessarily replacing hierarchies. This appears to be contrary to what some observers have argued (Castells 1996). Although it is certainly true that mutual dependency is leading to an increasing number of horizontal relationships crossing many boundaries, lateral connections seem to overlay hierarchies rather than acting as replacements for them (Agranoff 2011; McGuire and Agranoff 2011). According to the managers in the study, there is a premium on the ability to function across boundaries, but this skill has not necessarily replaced the need for internal skills.

CONCLUSION

We have provided a detailed roadmap of how networks are managed by empirically looking inside one of them from the perspective of its practitioners. Scholars have been conceptually wrestling with network management for decades now, and its importance is likely to increase as a growing array of public programs rely on networks instead of traditional hierarchies to deliver services (Kettl 2009). While the documentation of one contemporary network as offered here is not the be all or end all for the field's knowledge about managing in network settings, the Metro study does reveal and categorize the basics of what actors do in such settings. Despite the usual caveats about the single case study, we conclude that the Agranoff and McGuire framework serves as a useful research framework. Before "frequency" can be established, it must be preceded by "phase"; that is, identification of particular characteristic states (Dyke 2006, 289). Activating, mobilizing, framing, and synthesizing are useful descriptors of network management. These descriptors provide us with a vocabulary of tasks or behaviors: accessing resources, motivating participants, facilitating agreement, and enhancing interactions that reflect the theory in practice (See also Keast and Hampson 2007). It represents early steps in a more complete picture of the network manager and his/her actions.

It should also be noted that the current research as reported allowed for notable modifications to our earlier assumptions. As indicated, these activities demonstrate that network management appears to be less linear than was originally understood by the authors. Networks appear to involve simultaneous activity among the four categories in overlapping phases. The research demonstrated that there is no single network manager, but many, who undertake varying managerial actions over long periods of time. Moreover, the idea of a network culture based upon a set of negotiated and agreed upon principles proved to be important in order for managers to focus on operational issues. Finally, we were able to lend support to the contention that the work of each home organization remains important. That is, the network does not replace them, as hierarchical organizations program and transact within networks (Agranoff 2007, 219).

In conclusion, the practitioners that have informed this study make clear the importance of extensive looking into the structure of how public managers operate across boundaries. Kettl (2006) underscores the importance of changing boundaries related to mission, resources, capacity, responsibility, and accountability, that, when subjected to today's inter-organizational service networks, vastly complicate administration. Kettl argues that one of the basic dilemmas of public administration is "devising new strategies to bring public administration in sync with the multiorganizational, multisector operating realities of today's government. It requires a 'collaborative, network-based approach' " (2006, 17). It is not enough to casually identify the importance of approaches like "negotiating practices", "mutual understanding", "interdependent operation", or "moving beyond hierarchical boundaries" as the essence of management in these emergent entities (Agranoff 2012). Network research must step deeper into processes and approaches.

NOTE

1. The quantitative phase of the study involved a study of network structure and patterns of interaction.

REFERENCES

Agranoff, Robert. Forthcoming. Reconstructing Bureaucracy for Service Innovation in the Governance Era. In *Positive Innovation through Collaboration and Design*, edited by Chris Ansell and Jacob Torfing. London: Routledge.

———. 2007. *Managing within Networks: Adding Value to Public Organizations.* Washington, DC: Georgetown University Press.

———. 2011. Collaborative Public Agencies in the Network Era. In *The State of Public Administration: Issues, Challenges and Opportunities*, edited by Donald C. Menzel and Harvey L. White, 272–294. Armonk, NY: M. E. Sharpe.

———. 2012. *Collaborating to Manage: A Primer for the Public Sector.* Washington, DC: Georgetown University Press.

Agranoff, Robert, and Michael McGuire. 2001. "Big Questions in Public Network Management Research." *Journal of Public Administration Research and Theory* 11(3): 295–326.

Beach, Sandra, Robyn Keast, and David Pickernell. 2012. "Unpacking Connections between Network and Stakeholder Management and their Application to Road Infrastructure Networks in Queensland." *Public Management Review* 14(1): 1–21.

Bryant, Antony, and Kathy Charmaz. 2010. "Grounded Theory Research: Methods and Practices." In *The SAGE Handbook of Grounded Theory*, edited by Antony Bryant and Kathy Charmaz, 1–28. Thousand Oaks, CA: Sage.

Castells, Manuel. 1996. *The Rise of the Network Society: The Information Age.* Cambridge, MA: Oxford.

Corbin, Janet. 2009. "Taking an Analytic Journey." In *Developing Grounded Theory: The Second Generation*, edited by Janice M. Morse, Phyllis Noerager Stern, Juliet Corbin, Barbara Bowers, Adele E. Clarke, and Kathy Charmaz, 35–53. Walnut Creek, CA: Left Coast Press.

Corbin, Janet, and Anselm Strauss. 2008. *Basics of Qualitative Research: Techniques and Procedures for Developing Grounded Theory*, third ed. Thousand Oaks, CA: Sage.

De Bruijn, Hans, and Ernst ten Heuvelhof. 2008. *Management in Networks: On Multi-actor Decision Making*. London: Routledge.

Dyke, Chuck. 2006. "Primer on Thinking Dynamically about the Human Ecological Condition." In *How Nature Speaks: The Dynamics of the Human Ecological Condition*, edited by Yrjo Haila and Chuck Dyke, 279–301. Durham, NC: Duke University Press.

Glaser, Barney, and Anselm Strauss. 1967. *The Discovery of Grounded Theory*. Chicago: Aldine.

Hunter, Monica, Robert Agranoff, Michael McGuire, Jill Greenbaum, Janice Morrison, Maria Cohen, and Jing Liu. 2008. *Metro High School: An Emerging STEM Community*. Columbus: PAST Foundation/Battelle Center for Science and Mathematics Education Policy.

Keast, Robyn, and Keith Hampson. 2007. "Building Constructive Innovation Networks: Role of Relationship Management." *Journal of Construction Engineering and Management* 133(5): 364–373.

Kettl, Donald F. 2006. "Managing Boundaries in American Administration: The Collaboration Imperative." *Public Administration Review* 66(s1): 10–19.

Kettl, Donald. 2009. *The Next Government of the United States: Why our Institutions Fail Us and How to Fix Them*. New York: W.W. Norton Company, Inc.

Kickert, Walter J.M. and Joop F.M. Koppenjan. 1997. "Public Management and Network Management: An Overview." In *Managing Complex Networks*, edited by Walter J.M. Kickert, Erik-Hans Klijn, and Joop F.M. Koppenjan, 35–61. London: Sage.

McGuire, Michael 2002. "Managing Networks: Propositions on What Managers Do and Why They Do It." *Public Administration Review* 62(5): 426–433.

McGuire, Michael, and Robert Agranoff. 2010. "Networking in the Shadow of Bureaucracy." In *The Oxford Handbook of American Bureaucracy*, edited by Robert Durant, 372–395. Oxford: Oxford University Press.

———. 2011. "The Limitations of Public Management Networks." *Public Administration* 89(2): 265–284.

McGuire, Michael, and Chris Silvia. 2009. "Does Leadership in Networks Matter? Examining the Effect of Leadership Behaviors on Managers' Perceptions of Network Effectiveness." *Public Performance and Management Review* 33(2): 179–206.

Miles, Matthew B., and A. Michael Huberman. 1994. *Qualitative Data Analysis*, second ed. Thousand Oaks, CA: Sage.

Page, Stephen. 2008. "Managing for Results across Agencies: Building Collaboration Capacity in the Human Services." In *Big Ideas in Collaborative Management*, edited by Lisa Blomgren Bingham and Rosemary O'Leary, 138–161. Armonk, NY: M.E. Sharpe.

Rethemeyer, R. Karl, and Deneen Hatmaker. 2008. "Network Management Reconsidered: An Inquiry into Management of Network Structures in Public Service

Sector Provision." *Journal of Public Administration Research and Theory* 18(4): 617–646

Saz-Carranza, Angel. 2012. *Uniting Diverse Organizations: Managing Goal-oriented Advocacy Networks*. London: Routledge.

Saz-Carraza, Angel, and Sonia M. Ospina. 2011. "The Behavioral Dimension of Governing Inter-organizational Goal Directed Networks: Managing the Unity/ Diversity Tension." *Journal of Public Administration Research and Theory* 21(2): 327–365.

Silvia, Chris. 2011. "Collaborative Governance Concepts for Successful Network Leadership." *State and Local Government Review* 43(1): 66–71.

Silvia, Chris, and Michael McGuire. 2010. "Leading Public Sector Networks: An Empirical Examination of Integrative Leadership Behaviors." *The Leadership Quarterly* 21(2): 264–277.

Teddlie, Charles, and Abbas Tashakkori. 2009. *Foundations of Mixed Methods Research: Integrating Quantitative and Qualitative Approaches in the Social and Behavioral Sciences*. Thousand Oaks, CA: Sage.

10 What Can Governance Network Theory Learn from Complexity Theory? Mirroring Two Perspectives on Complexity

Joop Koppenjan and Erik-Hans Klijn

INTRODUCTION: INTERVENING WITH PROJECTS IN COMPLEX GOVERNANCE SYSTEMS

Governance network theory (GNT) addresses complexity. It provides a conceptual framework to analyze problem solving and policymaking in complex network settings. These settings are characterized by at least three forms of complexity:

1. Cognitive complexity: the presence of wicked problems that are technologically demanding and also imply various values and dynamics and therefore are hard to solve (Rittel and Webber 1973; Koppenjan and Klijn 2004);
2. Strategic complexity: the involvement of various interdependent actors that each have their own perceptions and strategies; and
3. Institutional complexity: a fragmented institutional context due to the presence of various organizational structures and institutional rules.

GNT suggests forms of network management or (meta-)governance to deal with these complexities. At the same time, it is clear that the recommendations about how to deal with complexity are limited. Although GNT is about dealing with complexity, it is also limited by complexity, with respect to both its explanatory power and its prescriptive potentials.

Complexity theory (CT) originally emerged in biology and natural sciences but gradually has found its way into the social sciences and public administration (Byrne 1998; Teisman et al. 2009; Gerrits 2012). Given its in-depth approach to complexities and complex systems, it addresses complexity in a new way and provides an interesting and promising new perspective on the complexities involved in governance networks.

In this contribution, we examine the potentials of CT for addressing complexity and see whether it provides a different analysis of complexity than GNT. More specifically, we investigate in what respect CT concepts and explanations may be fruitful for the further development of GNT.

We do so by applying both theories to the same case, following the famous example of the U.S. political scientist Graham Allison, who analyzed the 1962 Cuban missile crisis using three perspectives (Allison 1971). The case to be studied is the integral area development of the Heart of South, an urban regeneration project in Rotterdam, the Netherlands. In 2007, the municipality of Rotterdam initiated this project, aiming to redevelop the shopping and business center on the south bank into a mature center of Rotterdam-South, thus revitalizing the whole neighborhood and stimulating economic and employment activity. This case is suitable for comparing GNT and CT because it involves a complex network or system of interdependent actors that, in realizing the project, have to deal with various interconnected physical, technological, and social problems.

In the next section, we present the two theories. Then, in section 3, the Heart of South project is introduced. In sections 4 and 5, the case is analyzed from the perspective of the two theories, respectively. In section 6, these analyses are compared with regard to the way both theories conceptualize complexity, explain governance processes, and derive governance implications. Section 7 presents the implications of these findings for the further theoretical development of GNT.

TWO PERSPECTIVES ON COMPLEXITY

In this section, we compare governance network theory and complexity theory. We do so by discussing how each addresses complexity in governance network processes in terms of the conceptualization of decision making and its context, the evaluation criteria used, the explanations offered, and the management strategies recommended or identified. In doing so, we unavoidably make simplifications. There are of course many strands of network theory and complexity theory (Mitleton-Kelly 2003; Gerrits 2012). Acknowledging this variation and without pretending to cover the full variety within GNT and CT, we think both approaches are consistent enough to justify an attempt to grasp the core assumptions and concepts representative of each of them to make a meaningful comparison. The two perspectives are synthesized in Table 10.1.

Governance Networks Theory: Strategic Games in Fragmented Institutional Settings

The concept of governance networks is central to GNT. Governance networks are more or less stable patterns of social relationships (interactions, cognitions, and rules) between mutually dependent public, semi-public, and private actors that arise and build up around complex policy issues or policy programs (Agranoff and McGuire 2003; Mandell 2001; Scharpf 1978; Rhodes 1997; Kickert et al. 1997).

Table 10.1   Two Perspectives on Projects and Decision Making

	Network Perspective	Complexity Perspective
Decision making	Game between various actors with different perceptions and strategies, highly dynamic	Complex nonlinear dynamics as result of the individual behavior of agents and feedback mechanisms. System evolves from one stable situation to another after disturbance (punctuated equilibrium)
Context	Network as pattern of relations between actors and sets of (informal) rules, and more remote arenas in other networks that influence decisions in the network	Context is a performance landscape that changes continuously under the dynamics of the system itself and its co-evolution with other systems
Evaluation criteria	Good decisions are those that satisfy a wider range of stakeholders and do not impose costs on actors outside the network who are not represented in the decision-making process	System's vitality, the possibility of the system surviving changing circumstances, and producing outcomes that are beneficial for the agents
Explanation	Success is dependent on situations in the process (acknowledgement of interdependencies, bridging social and cognitive barriers), management (active network management), and institutional factors (joint rules, good connections)	Because of nonlinear dynamics and emergent characteristics, it is difficult to point at factors that cause good outcomes. Explanations arise from the interactions of the agents and the patterns and feedback mechanisms that arise out of these
Management	Deliberate attempts to facilitate the interactions of actors, enhance content reflection, and design process rules for interactions. Management is crucial for achieving good outcomes	Adaptive management, emphasis on using changes and opportunities that result from dynamics and "surfing" along with the system to reach outcomes

Decision Making

GNT sees interaction as a strategic game between various actors (Rhodes 1997). During these games, the actors attempt to influence the content and progress of the process (Scharpf 1978; Sabatier and Jenkins-Smith 1993). This results not only in conflicts and stagnations, but also in breakthroughs, compromises, negotiated package deals, and innovative, enriched project definitions. Governance network processes are therefore complex and dynamic. This complexity stems from the variety and variability of perceptions and strategies in interaction processes and also from the fact that these interactions take place at different places—arenas (Rein and Schön 1992; Koppenjan and Klijn 2004).

Context

The decision-making context consists of the patterns of relations between sets of actors and the rules and resource divisions that structure their interactions; in other words, the network. Actors form and recreate that structure in their interactions (Giddens 1984). When they abide by the (informal) rules of the network, they sustain them. At the same time, they also re-interpret the rules, gradually changing them (Koppenjan and Klijn 2004). Decision making in specific arenas may cut across various networks. Representatives of various networks will be guided by different and perhaps even conflicting sets of rules. This adds to institutional fragmentation and complexity.

Evaluation

If actors have different goals and perceptions (and thus evaluate outcomes differently) or when goals and perceptions change over time, ex ante goals cannot be used as a yardstick to assess success and failure (Sullivan and Skelcher 2002). GNT speaks of success when actors succeed in arriving at win-win solutions, transaction costs remain limited, and the costs of the outcomes are not transferred to external actors who are not involved in the decision making (Teisman 2000; Koppenjan and Klijn 2004).

Explanations

GNT suggests explanations at various levels. At the process level, explanations are found in actors acknowledging their interdependencies and transforming their go-alone strategies into collaborative strategies. Also, the extent to which actors succeed in coordinating interactions that occur in various arenas is an important explanation for their success. At network level, the presence or absence of institutional factors such as relations, joint rules, and trust may enhance or hinder joint action (Provan, Huang, and Milward et al. 2009; Klijn, Edelenbos, and Steijn 2010). At the management level, the presence of conscious efforts to facilitate and mediate interaction between various parties in games and networks is a powerful explanation for governance network success or failure (Klijn, Steijn, and Edelenbos 2010).

Management

GNT suggests two categories of management strategies or metagovernance: process management or institutional design (Gage and Mandell 1990; Agranoff and McGuire 2003; Meier and O'Toole 2001; Koppenjan and Klijn 2004; Sørensen and Torfing 2007). *Process management* attempts to facilitate interactions between actors in policy games. If management strategies are aimed at altering the institutional characteristics of the network (like changing actor positions, entry rules, or other more drastic ways to intervene in the network structure), they can be labeled *institutional design strategies.*

Complexity Theory Perspective: Complex Adaptive Systems

CT looks at the interactions and dynamics of complex systems. Complex systems are "comprised of numerous interacting identities (parts), each of which is behaving in its local context according to some rule(s), law(s) or force(s)" (Maguire and McKelvey 1999, 26). Complexity theory emphasizes that, when the individual parts of complex systems (the agents) respond to their own local conditions, they cause the system as a whole to display emergent patterns, even if there is no deliberate coordination or communication between the parts (Maguire and McKelvey 1999; Teisman et al. 2009). In other words, and as many complexity theories stress, systems are self-organizing and display emergent properties.

Decision Making

Complexity theory emphasizes that decision making has a nonlinear character (Gerrits 2012). This results from the unexpected behavior of the involved agents and the unforeseen consequences of the agents' interaction. If we view the decision-making process as an interaction system, we can see that the emergent properties and the relatively autonomous character of the agents cause systems to have unpredictable and complex dynamics. Seemingly stable equilibriums can be suddenly disrupted by unexpected events. One of the reasons for this is that these equilibriums are often sustained by complex feedback mechanisms. Positive (reinforcing) feedback drives change, whereas negative (balancing and moderating) feedback maintains stability (Stacey 1995). These feedback mechanisms can be very complex in themselves and can result in a system stagnating (i.e., a locked-in situation), even though a diverse set of interactions is taking place within it; but they can also drive rapid change and high turbulence. In this process from stability to chaos, new structures are formed. Thus systems remain stable until, as result of (increasing) pressure, a certain threshold is passed, and then they move to a new equilibrium. In CT theory, this is called *punctuated equilibrium* (Baumgartner and Jones 2009; Gerrits 2012).

Context

From a complexity theory perspective, decision making is not isolated but connects to a wider environment, and systems development stems from co-evolution with other systems (Kauffman 1993). The concept co-evolution can be described as "the evolution of one domain or entity [that] is partially dependent on the evolution of other related domains or entities or that one domain or entity changes in the context of the other(s)" (Mitleton-Kelly 2003, 7). "Entities" is a general term and can refer to individuals, teams, or organizations.

In social systems, such as decision-making systems, co-evolution results from a combination of the strategic actions of agents and collectives of agents. Strategies are seen not as one-sided responses to a changing environment or another actor, but as constant adaptive moves related to the context, affecting both the initiator of the action and all others influenced by it (Mitleton-Kelly 2003). Actually, agents in a system find themselves in a "landscape" like a biological organism that is constantly changing as a result of changes in the system and changes in other systems (Gerrits 2012). Rhodes (2008) calls this the performance landscape. Changes in the performance landscape may mean that a system that used to perform adequately no longer does. Co-evolution involves adaptations of performance to changes in the performance landscape.

Evaluation

In complexity theory, there are no clear success criteria. From a complexity and evolutionary perspective, one would probably emphasize the vitality or resilience of systems (Teisman et al. 2009). Good outcomes may be outcomes that are beneficial for the components of the system (the agents).

Explanation

Explanation from a complexity perspective is not that easy in the sense that concepts such as nonlinear dynamics, emergent properties, and co-evolution negate the possibility of simple causal relationships. Explanations are sought in the interplay of the agents and their behavior, the resulting (emergent) outcomes, and how the interactions within the system are influenced by interactions in other systems. CT warns that effects will not result directly from governmental intervention. CT requires analysis of the patterns of interactions, the resulting punctuated equilibriums, and the feedback mechanisms that produce those outcomes (Baumgartner and Jones 2009; Teisman et al. 2009).

Management

Managing complex systems is not easy given the dynamics, unexpected co-evolution, and self-organizing character of systems. Some authors even consider systems unmanageable (Flood 1999). Insofar as management is conceived possible, it will require "smart interventions" or adaptive management. Interventions should be adaptive to the evolution of systems and use the opportunities that those dynamics create. Managing complex systems is like "riding the fitness landscape" (Pascale 1999). This image of the manager resembles the notion of a policy entrepreneur in Kingdon's streams model (Kingdon 1984). A policy entrepreneur is someone who attempts to connect the different streams (problems, solutions, and choice opportunities).

These characterizations of GNT and CT are used to analyze the case study in sections 4 and 5. In the next section, the case is introduced.

DECISION MAKING IN THE HEART OF SOUTH PROJECT: A THREE ROUNDS INTERACTION

The most problematic district in Rotterdam is situated on the south bank of the city. The average level of education is low, unemployment and crime rates are high, and the district has a high concentration of migrants and of social problems. It is also an area vacated by higher income and status groups when they make a career. In fact, the south bank is a city of its own, with a total of 200,000 inhabitants (Rotterdam Municipality 2010). In this section, we present the most important events that evolved around the attempts of the municipality of Rotterdam to revitalize the center of Rotterdam-South by initiating the so-called Heart of South project.

Data were collected by analysis of official documents and thirteen interviews with the main stakeholders. Also, we participated in a series of peer meetings with the project leader (about eight in the period 2010–2011) in which we discussed strategic issues. In the period between 2007 and 2011, three rounds of events can be distinguished in the way the project evolved (Teisman 2000).

Round 1. February 2007 to November 2008: Toward an Integral Perspective

In February 2007, the executive board of mayor and aldermen of the municipality of Rotterdam issues the white paper *Stadsvisie 2030* (Urban Vision 2030), in which it communicates its strategic vision on the future development of the city of Rotterdam. In particular, the economic development and the livability of the city are stressed. In the white paper, thirteen prioritized projects are designated. One of the more important projects on the list is the Heart of South project. The redevelopment of the Ahoy conference and exhibition center halls, the shopping mall and public transport hub Zuidplein, and the residential and shopping district Pleinweg, are considered essential for the social and economic recovery of the area. Within the Project Management Office of the municipality of Rotterdam, responsible for the preparation and realization of large physical planning projects in the city, a project organization is charged with the preparation of the Heart of South project. Within this project organization, various types of expertise from within the municipal organization are brought together. This project organization is headed by a project manager.

In December 2007, a consultation round is organized. In this consultation round, stakeholders (representative of residents, welfare organizations, cultural organizations, shopkeepers, and business) emphasize that, besides investment in the physical infrastructure and economic development, attention must be paid to the social and cultural development of the area.

In November 2008, the white paper *Koers en Inzet* (Direction and Means) presents the results of the consultation round and sketches the outlines of the implementation program for Heart of South. It includes, besides the original physical measures, the social and cultural project called the Social Heart program. Next, formal political decision making by the Rotterdam municipal executive board (consisting of the mayor and aldermen) and the municipal council (in which elected political parties represent the inhabitants of the city of Rotterdam) is required to move to the next step of the planning process.

Round 2. November 2008 to January 2010: A New Political Reality

The white paper *Koers en Inzet* turns out not to be the decisive document because the municipal board does not take a decision on it. The global economic crisis of 2008 confronts the board with the need to cut budgets. As a result, the list of prioritized projects to be realized in Rotterdam is reconsidered. Some are cancelled, others postponed. With regard to Heart of South, it is decided to abandon the integral perspective. The most important parts of the project will be continued, but as separate projects. Within the project organization, opportunities are explored to preserve the integral approach. The board accepts this and instructs that the integral implementation program should be drafted in such a way as to fit both the municipality's overall project program and its new financial reality.

On 12 January 2010, the implementation plan is accepted by the board. The plan includes the idea of developing the project as a public–private partnership (PPP), thus mobilizing financial contributions from market parties.

Round 3. February 2010 to September 2011: Toward Tendering . . . or Not?

In March 2010, the municipality announces its intention to start a public tendering procedure for the development, construction, operation, and maintenance of the Heart of South area. A concession period of 20 years is foreseen. After a market consultation, planning teams and workgroups elaborate and finalize the tendering document. In January 2011, the business case is finalized and agreed upon. Next, the municipal management team agrees with the proposals and the road is clear for political decision making by the board and the council.

The board is asked to ratify the investment proposal on February 1. Given the precarious budgetary situation of the municipality, the board wants to first decide on the long-term investment plan and set priorities among the various projects that are up for decision making, before deciding upon the Heart of South. It proves impossible to take a decision on March 15 because new information on municipal budget deficit comes available. A new date is set: May 17. However, at a board meeting on May 16, a conflict arises on the need to cut the municipal budget, and an alderman resigns.

As a result of the inability to take a political decision, the project organization has to postpone the tendering process. The project organization, which is upscaled and ready to make the next move, also has to pull in and wait. Intensive interactions between the project group and the municipal council eventually lead to the council accepting the conditions and the idea of a tendering process in September 2011. The next round, searching for a private partner, can start.

THE GOVERNANCE NETWORK PERSPECTIVE: THE QUEST FOR WIN-WIN OUTCOMES

In this section, the case is analyzed in more depth from the governance network perspective. This perspective focuses on the question of the extent to which processes of framing and interacting result in consent on a joint project content, how the institutional characteristics of the Heart of South network enhances or hinders this, and the extent to which this process was facilitated and mediated by network management.

In the *first round,* decision making on the Heart of South project evolves in three arenas. First, in the political-administrative arena of the municipality, the economic and social problems of the Rotterdam-South area are discussed, as a result of which the municipal public service is commissioned to come up with a solution. Consequently, a second arena evolves. In this arena, the Heart of South project organization defines a project in terms of physical infrastructural and economic measures that have to be taken. Because of the injunction to use an integrative perspective, a third arena comes into play: the arena in which the public service interacts with representatives of stakeholders in the planning area. These actors have a different frame for the problems that have to be tackled; they emphasize a sociocultural perspective. A win-win situation is realized by simply adding the sociocultural ambitions to the existing project definition.

During the *second round*, interactions evolve in two arenas: the political-administrative arena and the project organization arena. In the first arena, a frame shift has taken place: from the need to tackle social and economic problems toward concerns about the financial consequences for the municipality. In light of this new frame, the outcome of the former interaction round is considered overambitious and the decision is taken to scale the project down. Next, within the project organization arena, attempts are made to preserve the definition of the project as an integral endeavor, which requires looking for resources elsewhere. The arrival of a new project manager with experience in the private sector assists in elaborating the idea of bringing in the market. The project organization's network management efforts are focused on negotiating a win-win outcome with the organization's political superiors (Alderman Karakus from physical planning, the municipal executive board, and the municipal council).

In the *third round*, interactions in at least five arenas seem to be of relevance. Besides the activities developed in the project organization arena, a new arena is created by starting the market consultations. In a third arena, the line organization—the management in the project management office—and the project organization fight over how the requirements of a PPP should be aligned with standard bureaucratic procedures. A fourth arena that becomes important is that of bureaucratic politics, in which—as a consequence of the growing awareness of financial risks and the burden of projects for the municipality—long-term investment planning is being developed in an arena where various project organizations within the municipality are competing for support for their projects. The fifth arena is the arena of political-administrative decision making at the top of the municipal organization in which the decision is being made on the investment plan and on the selection and content of the projects. Each of the project organizations increasingly engages in lobbying this arena.

Although the project organization tries to organize the political decision-making process to obtain formal consent to start the project, within the political-administrative arena the problem is framed as one in which the priorities of the municipality should be decided upon in a rational way. For this, the *Long-Term Investment Plan* provides the framework. As a result, the Heart of South project has to wait its turn. The project organization finds it increasingly difficult to link up all interactions within the various arenas and to manage these various network relationships. Attempts fail at coordinating the relationship between the arena and the market parties and the formal decision making in the political-administrative arena. Managing these relationships is simply beyond the span of control of the project manager. In addition, one may ask to what extent the relationship with stakeholders in the Heart of South area is maintained. The impression exists that this arena has been out of the picture for quite some while.

Within the political-administrative arena, the future of the various large physical planning projects initiated by the Rotterdam municipal Project

Management Office is debated. The Hearth of South project eventually survives because a cost-benefit analysis shows that it will create a lot of jobs in some of the most problematic neighborhoods of Rotterdam.

THE COMPLEXITY THEORY PERSPECTIVE: LOOKING FOR A NEW EQUILIBRIUM

From a complexity perspective, the decision making around Heart of South, viewed as an interaction system, has a different interpretation. In this interpretation, the analysis focuses on the increasing feedback dynamics of the interaction within the interaction system and its co-evolution with other systems, and on the system's reaction thereto. These dynamics change the performance landscape under which the system and the agents in the system operate and put pressure on the existing punctuated equilibrium—here understood as the stability of the coalition of actors that supports a specific project content (Baumgartner and Jones 2009).

In the *first round*, the decision-making process more or less proceeds according to the regular rules and expectations that guide project development in Rotterdam. Although a new equilibrium has to be achieved by incorporating the social program in the plans, this is no great change. In other projects (such as the Pact of South), an integral perspective has already been adopted, and the plans that result from this can easily be incorporated in the Heart of South project. The decision-making system itself experiences hardly any external pressure and can easily adapt to the limited internal pressure towards a more integrative approach to the project. This is done by a minor adjustment to the project content and the set of stakeholders. Co-evolution with other systems is limited to developments in the Pact of South project.

In the *second round*, this changes when external pressure from other systems grows. Because of the financial crisis and the city's declining income, there is growing pressure on decision making, and the project increasingly co-evolves with other systems. Decision making still takes place however, mainly within the decision-making system of the project. The new equilibrium that is achieved (the PPP format generating a private budget to realize the project goals) can be seen as a system survival reaction by the agents in the system to that external pressure. The managerial actions are strongly adaptive in the sense that they try to integrate the new demands of the performance landscape (financial cutbacks) and connect them to the system's survival (with the new PPP proposal, decision making can proceed).

It is only in the *third round* that the decision-making system is strongly disturbed and could be termed as chaotic and out of equilibrium. In this round, there is a sharp increase in the co-evolution of the decision-making system of the Heart of South project with other projects in the city (seen as separate interaction systems) and with the wider political system.

The financial stress creates a situation in which all physical planning projects and their decision-making systems suddenly become connected to one another. This also results in increasingly chaotic and unpredictable behavior and unexpected outcomes, because the consequences of strategic actions in each of the interaction systems have consequences for other systems. Agents in the various interaction systems, which now can also be viewed as subsystems, try to secure their projects. This leads to strategic actions and turbulence. This complexity makes the future of the Heart of South project uncertain, but the preparation of the tendering process has to go on. The project is so tightly interconnected with the environment that any attempt at management is almost an illusion. Interactions within the process are so complex that any decision and outcome is possible. The decision of the city council to accept the Heart of South project as one of the limited number of projects that will actually be realized ended this round by reaching a new equilibrium.

COMPARING THE TWO ANALYSES

In this section, we discuss three differences between the two perspectives that we deem important: how the perspectives address complexity, the explanations they offer, and their approach to management.

Looking at Complexity

In GNT, complexity is caused to a large extent by the multitude of various actors in a fragmented institutional setting, causing collaboration problems. CT shows more fragmentation, as the analysis focuses on the relation between the decision-making system and other (sub)systems. Whereas in GNT economic pressure is seen as an external factor influencing arenas in the network, complexity theory tends to see it as a co-evolving system. Thus, both complexity theory and the network perspective see complexity as unavoidable, an essential characteristic of administrative life.

Nevertheless, the two theories define complexity differently. In GNT, complexity is largely caused by actors and institutions. It can be dealt with by involving actors in interaction processes. In that way, a negotiated environment can be created. Institutional fragmentation might be dealt with by institutional design, although GNT is not overoptimistic about the effectiveness and viability of this strategy. CT sees other sources of complexity: emerging characteristics of systems that result in unexpected and unpredicted nonlinear outcomes and modifications of performance landscapes that go beyond the role of actor behavior and institutional change as addressed by GNT. CT theory also analyzes the way technical and natural systems (for instance ecosystems) co-evolve with social systems (Gerrits 2012).

The added value of CT can be found in the way it conceptualizes complexity. In particular, concepts like feedback, emergence, nonlinearity, punctuated equilibrium, performance landscapes, and co-evolution seem to have added value in analyzing and understanding complexities in governance networks, compared to GNT.

Looking at Explanations

The different perspectives on complexity also lead to different interpretations of events. For instance, in the third round of the Heart of South case, complexity increases considerably. GNT understands the events in this round as a growing inability of management to cope. CT simply understands that round as a phase of growing complexity within the interaction system and of non-linear dynamics as a result of the growing connectedness of (sub)systems. In that sense, CT certainly further downplays the role of (central) steering and management in complex systems.

Whereas the political hesitation in the third round to make a project decision is seen by the network perspective as the result of a lack of connecting activity and capability, from a complexity theory perspective the analysis focuses on the specific logic that governs these actors, being part of a different (sub)system. The CT perspective stresses that politicians are reacting to growing uncertainty on the one hand and the risks they face of damaging their reputation (and the negative media exposure that would generate) on the other hand.

Looking at Governance

Within CT, the role of management strategies in the analysis of complexity is downplayed. What then does CT have to offer network theorists and practitioners who are interested in the governance implication of complexity? First of all, CT helps us to realize that the manageability of complexity is far less than we may already assume. Second, CT may help us to rethink our approach to management. CT provides us with some clues about how to deal with complexity, beyond the network management strategies developed so far. CT seems to suggest four additional approaches to management: adaptive management, reducing positive feedback to enhance existing equilibriums, strengthening negative feedback to enhance existing equilibriums, and enhancing positive feedback to distort an equilibrium.

Adaptive Management
This implies that management tries to "surf along" with the dynamics of the system and its performance landscape by adapting strategies aimed at the content of proposals and at the design of interactions processes and rules. This is actually how the managerial actions in especially round 2 of the case

study can be understood. It seems likely that this strategy is most successful in systems that are not too dynamic.

Reducing Positive Feedback

Positive feedback refers to interactions that aim to build up tensions that will result in the distortion of the existing equilibrium of a system. In the case study, we interpreted the existing equilibrium as the stability of the coalition that supports the project. In the third round of the case study, systems were connected and highly dynamic. The project manager tried to keep his project separate from the discussion on the municipality's long-term investment planning, thus reducing the interconnectivity of his project to the wider system, and reducing disturbing influences.

Strengthening Negative Feedback

Negative feedback is aimed at mobilizing interactions that support the existing equilibrium. After the project manager failed to disconnect the Heart of South project from other systems and their dynamics, he focused on mobilizing negative feedback by enhancing support for his project.

Enhancing Positive Feedback

The opposite strategy to strengthening negative feedback creates disturbance by enhancing positive feedback. This is mainly of interest in a situation in which the aim is to open up relatively closed networks and to change the decisions made there. This strategy may include the strengthening of ideas, actors, rules of the game, and couplings among (sub)systems that further change.

CONCLUSION: LEARNING FROM COMPLEXITY THEORY

The comparison of GNT and CT has helped us to get a clearer view on the specific contributions of each of these perspectives on problem solving and policymaking in complex network settings. GNT is strong in its conceptualization of interactions, the impact of institutional factors, and management strategies. GNT is less equipped to deal with complexities that stem from interactions with the physical and technological components of systems, or feedback mechanisms within or among systems and their environment. Also, it has a strong managerial perspective. The strength of CT is its attention to a wider set of dependencies that affect systems, to the adaptive nature of systems, and to the way systems move from one punctuated equilibrium to another. The weaknesses of CT are its relatively abstract nature and the lack of attention to management.

Our application of the two theories to a concrete case brought many similarities to light. Within CT, agency is recognized as the core driver of complexity in social systems. Applying abstract concepts like co-evolution, feedback, and punctuated equilibrium brings CT theory much closer to familiar concepts and explanations provided by GNT than expected beforehand.

An obvious difference between the two perspectives is their appreciation of the role of (meta-)governance. CT does not share GNT's implicit assumption that managerial action will help to deal with complexity. Although the limits of government steering are recognized in the network literature, the managerial turn that GNT took in the last ten years has obscured this point. CT downplays these expectations.

As far as the question as to what the theories might contribute to the governance of complexity in the Heart of South case is concerned, GNT shows that the ever-increasing number of actors and arenas during the process reduced its governability to a point that genuine network governance strategies became futile—the eventual success seems to have been sheer luck. CT might have helped to sensitize actors to complexities that stem from external feedbacks from turbulent fitness landscapes and might have suggested new network management strategies aimed at anticipating and coping with this type of feedback.

With regard to further theory development, the two perspectives may reinforce each other. GNT might help complexity theorists to further conceptualize the role of agency and governance in complex (social) systems. CT might help governance network theorists to deepen *and* broaden their understanding of the phenomenon of complexity, and to rethink their ideas on network governance. The latter may lead to a mere extension of the repertoires of governance management strategies, but perhaps requires a more radical revision of the idea of governance.

REFERENCES

Agranoff, R., and M. McGuire. 2003. *Collaborative Public Management: New Strategies for Local Governments.* Washington DC: Georgetown University Press.

Allison, G. T. 1971. *Essence of Decision.* Boston: Little, Brown and Company.

Baumgartner, F. R., and B. Jones. 2009. *Agendas and Instability in American Politics*, second ed. Chicago: University of Chicago Press.

Byrne, D. S. 1998. *Complexity Theory and the Social Sciences: An Introduction.* London: Routledge.

Flood, R. L. 1999. *Rethinking the Fifth Discipline: Learning within the Unknowable.* London: Routledge.

Gage, R. W., and M. P. Mandell, eds. 1990. *Strategies for Managing Intergovernmental Policies and Networks.* New York/London: Praeger.

Gerrits, L. 2012. *Punching Clouds: An Introduction to the Complexity of Public Decision-Making.* Litchfield Park AZ: Emergent Publications.

Giddens, A. 1984. *The Constitution of Society: Outline of the Theory of Structuration.* London: Macmillan.

Kauffman, S. 1993. *The Origins of Order: Self-Organization and Selection in Evolution.* Oxford: Oxford University Press.

Kickert, W. J. M., E. H. Klijn, and J. F. M. Koppenjan, eds. 1997. *Managing Complex Networks: Strategies for the Public Sector*. London: Sage.

Kingdon, J. W. 1984. *Agendas, Alternatives and Public Policies*. Boston/Toronto: Little, Brown and Company.

Klijn, E. H., J. Edelenbos, and B. Steijn. 2010. "Trust in governance networks: Its implications on outcomes." *Administration and Society* 42 (2):193–221.

Klijn, E. H., B. Steijn, and J. Edelenbos. 2010. "The impact of network management on outcomes in governance networks." *Public Administration* 88 (4):1063–82.

Koppenjan, J. F. M., and E. H. Klijn. 2004. *Managing Uncertainties in Networks: A Network Perspective to Problem Solving and Decision Making*. London: Routledge.

Maguire, S., and B. McKelvey. 1999. "Complexity and Management: Moving from Fad to Firm Foundations." *Emergence* 1 (2):19–61.

Mandell, M. P., ed. 2001. *Getting Results through Collaboration: Networks and Network Structures for Public Policy and Management*. Westport CT: Quorum Books.

Meier, K. J., and L. J. O'Toole. 2001. "Managerial Strategies and Behavior in Networks: A Model with Evidence from U.S. Public Education." *Journal of Public Administration and Theory* 11 (3):271–94.

Mitleton-Kelly, E. 2003. *Ten Principles of Complexity and Enabling Infrastructures. Complex Systems and Evolutionary Perspectives of Organisations: The Application of Complexity Theory to Organisations*. Amsterdam: Elsevier.

Pascale, R. T. 1999. "Surfing the Edge of Chaos." *Sloan Management Review* Spring: 83–94.

Provan, K. G., K. Huang, and B. H. Milward. 2009. "The Evolution of Structural Embeddedness and Organizational Social Outcomes in a Centrally Governed Health and Human Service Network." *Journal of Public Administration Research and Theory* 19:873–93.

Rein, M., and D. A. Schön. 1992. "Reframing Policy Discourse." In *The Argumentative Turn in Policy Analysis and Planning*, edited by F. Fischer and J. Forester, 145–66. Durham NC: Duke University Press.

Rhodes, M. L. 2008. "Complexity and Emergence in Public Management: The Case of Urban Regeneration in Ireland." *Public Management Review* 10 (3):361–80.

Rhodes, R. A. W. 1997. *Understanding Governance*. Buckingham: Open University Press.

Rittel, H., and M. Webber. 1973. "Dilemmas in a General Theory of Planning." *Policy Sciences* 4 (2):155–69.

Rotterdam Municipality. 2010. *Ambition Document Heart of South*. Rotterdam: Project Management Buro. http://www.deelraadinfo.nl/dsresource?objectid=627 57&type=org (in Dutch).

Sabatier, P. A., and H. C. Jenkins-Smith. 1993. *Policy Change and Learning. An Advocacy Coalition Perspective*. Boulder CO: Westview Press.

Scharpf, F. W. 1978. "Interorganizational Policy Studies: Issues, Concepts and Perspectives." In *Interorganizational Policy Making: Limits to Coordination and Central Control*, edited by K. I. Hanf and F. W. Scharpf, 345–70. London: Sage.

Sørensen, E., and J. Torfing. 2007. *Theories of Democratic Network Governance*. Hampshire/New York: Palgrave Macmillan.

Stacey, R. 1995. "The Science of Complexity: An Alternative Perspective for Strategic Change Processes." *Strategic Management Journal* 16: 477–95.

Sullivan, H., and C. Skelcher. 2002. *Working Across Boundaries: Collaboration in Public Services*. Basingstoke: Palgrave Macmillan.

Teisman, G.R. 2000. "Models for Research into Decision-Making Processes: On Phases, Streams and Decision-Making Rounds." *Public Administration* 78:937–56.

Teisman, G., A. van Buuren, and L. Gerrits, eds. 2009. *Managing Complex Governance Systems*. Oxford: Routledge.

11 Network Performance
Toward a Dynamic Multidimensional Model

Denita Cepiku

INTRODUCTION

This chapter is a theory-building endeavor aimed at developing an interpretative model of network performance by systematizing and enhancing the existing literature and by analyzing a longitudinal case study. The case study used in this chapter—a network active in the fight against malaria in the northern Ethiopian region of Tigray—has been chosen as it is particularly appropriate for the aims of this research as both the problem it tackles and the characteristics of the network established to deal with it are very complex. Furthermore, the analysis covers a five-year time frame, permitting the investigation of the network in a dynamic rather than static way. The network includes a diversified pool of actors (public, private and nonprofit, operating globally and locally, located in Europe and Africa). The partners included the Italian Ministry of Health, the World Health Organization (WHO), Novartis-Italia, the Tigray Health Bureau (THB), the community health workers (CHWs), the San Gallicano Dermatological Institute, and the Italian Hospital of Makallè[1].

The chapter contributes to improving our understanding on how to evaluate networks for their performance, especially when these are community-based and composed of both public and private actors. The research questions addressed are the following: 1) Which are the most relevant performance dimensions as perceived by the different constituencies of a network? 2) Which are the determinants that influence network performance? and 3) How do these factors influence network performance?

NETWORK PERFORMANCE: LITERATURE REVIEW AND MAIN GAPS

It is widely accepted that it is appropriate to analyze networks at multiple levels and several authors have adopted this position since the article from Provan and Milward (2001) proposing a conceptual framework for community-based public sector networks. This chapter departs from this seminal article and enriches the conceptual framework by integrating the determinants of performance (partly tackled by Kenis and Provan 2009 but also Provan and Milward 1995 and Provan and Sebastian 1998) and by proposing some causal links between these determinants and the different levels of performance and between network management and performance (Klijn, Steijn, and Edelenbos 2010). Furthermore, we use the literature review to propose a list of possible performance assessment criteria (Mandell 1990; Meier and O'Toole 2001; Provan and Milward 2001; McGuire and Agranoff 2007; Meneguzzo and Cepiku 2004; Cepiku and Meneguzzo 2004; 2008; Isett et al. 2011; Klijn, Steijn, and Edelenbos 2010).

Performance Assessment of Networks Based on the Literature

The literature has identified different levels of network performance considering that the performance (including effectiveness) of networks can neither be measured as the sole achievement of the goal of one of the actors nor exclusively as the goal of the network itself. While the former is not representative of the network, it is not possible to a priori identify the latter. For Kickert, Klijn, and Koppenjan (1997), using the classical criteria of goal attainment is a fallacy because, in networks, goals are not given but sought (the so-called goal-enrichment process). McGuire and Silvia (2009) argue that effectiveness can still be measured by the extent to which a network achieves its goals, as determined by the community, the clients, and the manager.

Provan and Milward (2001) consider network performance in terms of the outcomes produced for the benefit of each partner, the outcomes achieved for the community at large, and network-level outcomes. Performance management in networks is said to be relevant in several regards: to motivate the partners in continuing their commitment and to inform them on the convenience of the network as compared with other organizational forms. Network participants work to achieve their individual organization's goals as well as a shared, collective goal (McGuire and Agranoff 2007, 21).

The model proposed in this chapter builds on these ideas and, by adopting a dynamic view, distinguishes between intermediate and final results.

Systematizing the evaluation criteria emerging from the literature review further refines the theoretical model.

Network management strategies can be assessed by measuring: conflict resolution; the extent to which the process has encountered stagnations or deadlocks; the productive use and reconciliation of differences in perspectives; and the frequency of interactions between actors (Klijn, Steijn, and Edelenbos 2010). Administrative efficiency, inclusiveness of decision making, stability and flexibility of rules and of the organizational form, and satisfaction of the participants with network governance are other criteria useful for assessing the quality of interaction.

The assessment of the *institutional design* of the network involves both the structural characteristics of the network and issues of power / authority (Mandell and Keast 2008).

The network *outcomes at the environmental level* involve the assessment of the overall benefits for the community that goes beyond client-increased well-being (i.e., the direct benefits to the users of the service or the beneficiaries of the policy) and considers the costs to the community, the social capital created, and public perceptions that problems are being solved (Provan and Milward 2001).

The network *outcomes at the single-partner level* refer to the satisfaction of each network member with both the management of the network and the support for results coming from the network (Crosby and Bryson 2010, 226; Kenis and Lemaire 2012, 642).

Endogenous and Exogenous Determinants of Network Performance

The literature distinguishes between exogenous and endogenous determinants of network performance. Exogenous elements include those characteristics over which network managers or participants have little or no control. Endogenous factors, on the contrary, can be instrumentally managed by the network itself.

In terms of *exogenous determinants*, Provan and Milward (1995) and Provan and Sebastian (1998) include the network context among the determinants of network performance, including system stability, resource munificence and cohesion, and support and participation from the community. The network context is a relevant determinant of both the quality of interaction inside the network and the final outcome produced for the partners and the community. In their "exogenous theory of public network performance", Kenis and Provan (2009) identify some exogenous factors that influence the performance of a network: the form of the network (shared governance, lead organization or network administrative form), the type of inception (voluntary vs. mandated), and the developmental stage of the network (different performance is expected from newly emergent networks as compared to mature networks). Other exogenous elements include an existing goal consensus, competing institutional logics and the complementarity of partners, their number and geographical location, trust and previous collaboration history, external legitimation (support from public opinion, community, and other stakeholders), the purpose of the network, the nature of tasks and severity of the problem, environmental shocks, and the number and kind of constituencies, among others. The presence and relative relevance of these elements change from case to case and from one policy sector to another.

The *endogenous factors* influencing network performance include elements such as the network management process and the leadership style. Networks have been assessed based on traditional measures while ignoring the importance of process variables and their impact on outcomes in networks (Voets et al. 2008). Considering these factors is in line with the managerial perspective that stresses the role of governing mechanisms as the assumed primary determinants of success and failure (McGuire and Agranoff 2007, 23; Rodriguez et al. 2007). Provan and Milward (2001) exemplify effectiveness criteria including a mix of process issues (e.g., agency survival, network growth, membership interaction, service coordination) and outcome issues (e.g., range of services, cost-effectiveness of services, impact on clients). Also Klijn, Steijn, and Edelenbos (2010) make a clear distinction between process and content outcomes and put the emphasis on the need to assess not only network performance but also the quality of interaction (i.e., network management). Crosby and Bryson (2010, 219–23) include several elements of integrative processes and practices such as a wise design and the use of forums, formals agreements supporting accountability, deliberate and emergent planning, conflict management, and trust-building activities.

Literature Gaps

Several gaps in the literature on network performance can be identified. The current literature on network performance has developed in separated streams: 1) an exogenous versus endogenous view, 2) process-oriented versus structural approaches, 3) whole networks versus single organizations as units of analysis (especially comparing the private with the public sector literature), and 4) a static rather than a dynamic view of the network.

Oversimplification and confusion are noticed when comparing models of network performance coming out from the literature. For instance, the same categories of determinants (e.g., the network's structure) sometimes appear among exogenous factors and sometimes among endogenous ones.

While apparently simple in theory, the distinction between determinants and intermediate and final results of cooperation is empirically problematic. For instance, good planning and contact frequency is an intermediate result of cooperation but could also be seen as an element of network design and hence as a determinant of network success. The same goes for the distinction between exogenous factors and external resources: for example, initial goal consensus and complementarity between the partners is an exogenous element although network management and results produced in time, influence it.

In practice, the difference between exogenous and endogenous elements is linked to the timeframe of interaction, with the former pertaining to the phase up to the point where the network is up and running and the latter pertaining to interactions between the network participants and the wider environment after the inception of the network.

The prevalence, in the literature, of static network performance models that do not take due account of the dynamic nature of the links between the different components is a serious impediment to overcoming these gaps.

Some authors have called for longitudinal analyses to improve the understanding of how networks perform over time. The case study analyzed in this chapter addresses this need and gives some additional insights that are incorporated to the theoretical model.

A DYNAMIC MULTIDIMENSIONAL MODEL OF NETWORK PERFORMANCE

To overcome the gaps in the literature review we propose an empirically grounded theory-based model illustrated in Figure 11.1.

This model of network performance contributes to the existing literature in several regards. First, it provides a dynamic distinction between several categories of determinants that goes beyond the two oversimplified and not straightforward categories—exogenous and endogenous—that we find in the literature. The distinction varies with the characteristics of the network, most importantly the type of inception (voluntary or mandated)[2]. Moreover, the exogenous-endogenous view does not allow identifying some determinants that, although external to network management, can be influenced by it. Therefore, only some of the determinants are completely beyond the management's control, while others—which we call internal and external resources—can be influenced by the network management, although partially and only with a delayed effect after the network has produced some results.

Second, we argue that the institutional design of the network (shared governance, lead organization or network administrative form) (Kenis and Provan 2009) cannot be a-priori listed among the exogenous factors. Only if the network is mandated and the organizational form has been determined

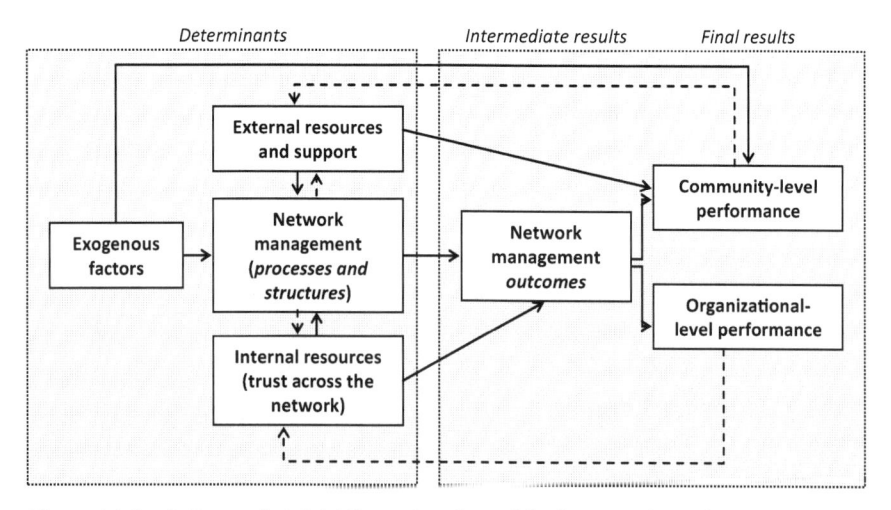

Figure 11.1   A Dynamic Multidimensional Model of Network Performance

top down or by law is this exogenous element. This holds also for other parts of network management[3]. Therefore, the main exogenous determinant in our model is the type of inception.

Third, in our model we distinguish between the process and structural characteristics of network management (considered among the determinants) and the network management outcomes in terms of the quality of interaction (considered to be intermediate results of the network). The final results of the network are considered both in terms of outcomes produced for the benefit of each partner and outcomes achieved for the community at large. In other words, we keep the three levels—organization, network, and community—identified by Provan and Milward (2001), but we distinguish between the intermediate (quality of interaction) and final (community- and organization-level) outcomes that are not placed at the same level[4].

Fourth, the dynamic view of network performance provided here supports the argument that the relation between the determinants and the intermediate and final results is bidirectional instead of one way. For instance, the initial levels of trust may influence the network structure and management processes but, as the network develops, effective network coordination and steering should contribute to lower conflict and further enhance trust between partners (or the reverse). Also small gains in the early stages of network development may produce incremental increases in external trust. The same goes for external resources such as political support and civic capacity that affect network performance but are in turn influenced by the network activities and results (Page 2010).

Figure 11.1 presents this revised theoretical model that is meant to overcome the above named gaps in the literature. The Tigray case that follows highlights the model.

THE TIGRAY ANTI-MALARIA NETWORK

The analysis now turns to the case study of the Tigray antimalaria network.

Malaria is one of the main global health issues leading to approximately 225 million malaria cases and 781,000 deaths each year, although it is preventable and treatable[5]. Two decades ago, Novartis and Chinese partners transformed an herbal remedy, used for centuries in Chinese medicine, into an effective modern medicine that earned approvals from regulatory agencies in both developed and developing countries. In 2001, Novartis signed a ten-year Memorandum of Understanding with the WHO to make Coartem—a combination of artemether (an artemisinin derivative) and lumefantrine—available without profit to malaria-endemic countries.

Despite the availability of drugs, access to antimalarial medicines was still an issue for many patients. The Tigray network was therefore launched in 2005 and it was intended to be a solution to a roster of outside critics[6].

With a limited investment of less than $570,000, the network served 130,000 people in their villages, also using a community coproduction approach. The project was funded by Novartis Farma SPA Italy ($400,000) and by the Italian Ministry of Health ($125,000), through the WHO. The WHO also contributed $13,895 and the Tigray regional government budget included many of the additional costs[7].

Novartis provided the supply of Coartem treatments for the target population and financial contributions covering the expenses for the rapid diagnostic tests (RDTs), the network management activities, the postgraduate and short-term training, and some instrumental goods.

The project had intervention and control arms in two comparable districts selected for the study and used two different methods of deploying the drug: in the Alamata intervention district, Coartem was administered to the population by CHWs as well as by health workers in health facilities, following early diagnoses of malaria based on RDTs. In Raya Azebo, the control district, standard malaria case management continued with Coartem being prescribed at health facilities but not at the community level (cf. WHO 2009, 11, Table 4).

In the intervention district, the CHWs treated approximately 58% of all suspected and confirmed cases of malaria, while 32.3% were treated in health centers and hospitals and 10.1% in clinics and health posts. This not only increased access to Coartem, but also allowed the treatment of other diseases to be improved. The 33 CHWs involved in the project were a subset of the hundreds of community volunteers who were treating patients close to home before the national treatment policy changed to Coartem. The project built on the established system and further reinforced it.

The network produced varied results (clinical, managerial, economic, and social), at different levels and for several constituencies, including the wider community and each partner[8].

APPLICATION OF THE REVISED MODEL

The dynamics of the Tigray antimalaria network allow identifying the main determinants and dimensions of performance and to preliminary investigating the links between them. Each of the elements of the revised theoretical model can be seen in the case study, as illustrated by Figure 11.2.

A detailed analysis of these elements now follows.

Network Performance Determinants

As mentioned, the network was created to deal with a very complex problem and critical public opinion. Throughout the years, it had to manage the expectations across a broad and diverse range of constituencies (patients, the press, government health agencies, activist groups) as well as stakeholders

Determinants		Intermediate results	Final results
Exogenous factors - Voluntary network - Mature network - High initial goal consensus and complementarity - Partners located in Europe and Africa - Global health extremely complex problem - Many constituencies **External resources** - Critical public opinion - Limited human and financial resources **Internal resources** - Good levels of trust between the partners (previous collaborative relations) **Network management characteristics (processes and structure)** - Clear partners' roles - Committed and legitimate leadership - Good fit between shared-governance structure and a two-tiered scientific and managerial leadership		**Network management outcomes** - Good planning and good contact frequency - Network management costs kept low thanks to information and communication technologies - Partners' motivation nurtured through conferences and journalists' field visits - Participatory decision-making (PMT and community involvement) - Strategies for building trust, legitimacy and support from critical constituencies - Stable network structure but turnover of some representatives - Innovative network management approach to be transferred to other districts and to be employed in fighting other diseases - Goal enrichment: Coartem was used as an entry point for making the whole healthcare system work better - High flexibility conferred to the network by the private partner - Satisfaction of participants with network governance	**Community-level performance** - Increased access to effective treatment - Malaria-related deaths reduced by 40%, compared to the control district - The malaria patient load at health facilities decreased by a quarter - Community satisfaction - Cost savings (US$ 1,41 per patient) on disease management with use of rapid diagnostic tests - Lower use of CHWs by women - Strengthened role of volunteers and improved social capital, promoting community participation in malaria control **Organization-level performance** - <u>Tigray Health Bureau</u>: enhanced managerial and clinical capacity; improved skills of volunteers; international visibility - <u>Novartis</u>: improved reputation and image; improved employee motivation and internal climate; strengthened stakeholder relations - <u>Public actors (WHO, Italian MoH, THB)</u>: enhanced effectiveness of intervention programs; international visibility - <u>All</u>: Better risk management thanks to the presence of the WHO and of the Italian hospitals in loco

Figure 11.2 Performance Determinants, Dimensions, and Dynamics of the Tigray Network

internal to each of the partner organizations. On the other hand, the strong spirit of community involvement and participation, which pervades all aspects of the life of the people of Tigray helped to achieve high levels of final performance (i.e., the 40% reduction in malaria deaths in the intervention district compared with the control district (WHO 2009). The CHWs were indispensable and could not be replaced by health extension workers, with their workload, vast catchment areas, and multiple responsibilities. The long-term commitment of CHWs, who are native to the area, to the services provided was exceptional. In many parts of the world, the dropout rate of volunteers is often high.

These elements represent, in our model, the external resources on which the network can count and were positively influenced during the implementation of the project by the early results it produced.

The internal resources, namely trust between the partners, were high at the start of the project thanks to previous formal and informal collaborative relations between the partners (the previous WHO-Novartis-Chinese partnership for developing and adopting Coartem, the relations between the Italian hospitals and the Tigray authorities, and the collaboration of THB and WHO/RBM in implementing previous community-based malaria control programs). It facilitated interaction and trust was further strengthened following both the network management characteristics (shared-governance form and leadership) and the intermediate and final organizational level results.

Finally, the exogenous factors exerted a mixed effect; these included the voluntary nature of the network and the high initial goal consensus as well as the different nature of network partners and the complexity of the problem among others.

A feedback effect from the final results to external legitimacy was observed: the project was acknowledged by several corporate social responsibility awards as an innovative model of public-private partnership in fighting malaria, and achieved significant international visibility. Its activities and results attracted significant media coverage.

The institutional design of the Tigray antimalaria network resembles a "shared governance" form (Provan and Kenis 2007). Since the beginning, the partners decided to constitute an interinstitutional project monitoring team (PMT) that pursued the aim to "cooperate and to take rapid decisions on behalf of the signatory parties and to monitor the development of the project, also on the basis of regular reports from Tigray"[9]. The establishment of a technical-administrative group that met monthly in teleconferences was instrumental for establishing common ground, accommodating the interests of all partners, and ensuring a thorough follow up of the project.

Differently from more centralized forms, a "shared governance" network has all the network partners participating in the decision-making process, but may prove inefficient with frequent meetings and difficulty in reaching consensus. Fundamental in overcoming this critical aspect was the coordination of the PMT by Novartis that assumed the role of network manager: this consisted in moderating meetings and ensuring that monthly teleconferences were organized, minutes kept, agendas and action points drafted, and follow-up activities as well as the quality of the dialogue monitored constantly. An important role was that of confronting the parties with the perceptions and interests of the "outside world": Italian, US, and Chinese journalists' field visits helped both to keep the partners' attention and commitment high and to improve the relationship with the media on social responsibility items. Furthermore, Novartis contributed to enhancing the flexibility of the project. Monthly teleconferences and quarterly reports delivered by the THB were the main interaction and internal communication tools. Gantt diagrams were used during the project and the partners were aware of the importance of reaction times.

The WHO, imbuing the network with a high external legitimacy, assumed the scientific and technical leadership. It is uncommon for global PPPs to give a guiding role to the WHO and place the ownership of the recipient countries central. These were key characteristics of the Tigray network. Legitimacy and reciprocal trust allowed any conflict to be kept to a minimum during the project and enabled continued collaboration.

The agreement formalized many aspects of network management and stated that the decisions of the PMT will be taken by consensus. The risk of perceiving domination by one of the organizations that might have produced a lack of commitment by the partners was handled very effectively. Efforts were made toward enhancing the ownership of the THB. All data generated from the project were considered the property of the THB, which also had the final decision on the authorship of publications. This unambiguous division of roles and responsibilities and the convergence of partners' aims gave the network a clear direction, made it an efficient way of interaction, and integrated short-term success with long-term viability.

Intermediate Outcomes: The Quality of Interaction

All the partners reported high satisfaction with the network management and institutional structure and were constantly committed to the network's management. Key factors included the clear definition and formalization of roles, good planning, and good contact frequency (mainly through teleconferences). Costs were kept low thanks to the use of information and communication technologies. Without doubt, the highly effective network management processes and structures allowed excellent results to be achieved with a limited amount of human and financial resources. As observed by the WHO (2009): "The project would ideally have been conducted by a minimum of two full-time, dedicated professionals, for project management and coordination, while no single full-time expert was involved".

Most interestingly, combining a shared-governance form with distributed leadership was fundamental in overcoming some tensions, identified by the literature as common in networks.

For instance, the internal versus external legitimacy tensions were effectively solved. Novartis was essential in providing the system of communication and interaction, increasing the satisfaction of the partners with the network management and, thus, strengthening internal legitimacy. The value of everyone's contribution was recognized, ensuring that everyone received credit for joint action. Nonetheless, the message was that the network, instead of single organizations, was the key actor behind the results achieved and this, along with the fundamental presence of the WHO, enhanced the external legitimacy of the network.

Another tension intrinsic to networks is the trade-off between efficiency and inclusiveness: the PMT allowed the full participation of all the network members in the decision-making process, while the network manager dedicated significant efforts to drafting agendas and action plans and setting up a monitoring system of the network management, thus improving the speed of action and efficiency.

Community-Level Performance

The primary objective of the network was the reduction of malaria mortality in the region, but an important goal enrichment process took place and the project produced several additional results.

Community groups involved in the final project assessment were pleased that malaria diagnosis and treatment could be provided near their homes, as transport expenses, time spent seeking treatment, and disease severity dramatically diminished. The participants, noting that the CHWs were subsistence farmers, welcomed their commitment, because the CHWs provided diagnosis and treatment not only during morning and evening sessions but whenever malaria cases occurred, thus sacrificing their own working time. The CHWs were seen to provide their service with respect and courtesy. The community found that CHWs provided timely diagnosis and treatment, by checking clinical symptoms against the results of the RDTs, whereas there were long queues at health facilities and sometimes no treatment was given even after queuing for a whole day (WHO 2009).

The use of RDTs enabled appropriate case management and cost reductions. The project demonstrated that RDTs, which can be performed in about 15 minutes from fingerstick blood samples by technicians who have received only minimal training, could be integrated into the practice of CHWs. The use of these tests, as opposed to clinical diagnosis, saved as much as $1.41 per patient examined. CHWs were able to exclude 90% of non-*Plasmodium falciparum* cases and treat only confirmed *P. falciparum* cases with Coartem.

The project improved health service use in a resource-constrained rural setting by lowering the malaria case burden for health facilities. In the intervention district, there was a lower malaria patient load at health facilities (54.774) as compared to the control district (101.535).

The activities were not only limited to producing these results, but also to making them sustainable over time by building capabilities and ownership of the local structures and by involving the community in the implementation and evaluation activities of the project. The project improved the skills of CHWs, teaching them how to use simple RDTs, how to administer Coartem safely, and how to report regularly to staff in the general health services. The project was an entry point for other community/home based health services in the country. While the volunteers are farmers that local health structures recruit from time to time in healthcare activities, the project enforced the CHW structure by defining and regularizing the procedures of the reimbursement they were entitled to for leaving their farm activity and enhancing their capacities for communicating with the health posts.

The project also contributed to building the capacity of malaria managers in public healthcare structures through short- and long-term postgraduate training courses. Also the accountability of the THB was enforced as each decision was discussed with and reported to the PMT.

Partner-Level Performance

Producing value for each of the partners was also important because the Tigray antimalaria network was voluntary and any partner could decide to withdraw from it.

Novartis enhanced its corporate reputation and gave its employees a sense of pride for working in a company that drives such initiatives with a huge public health impact. Going beyond drug supply and financial support allowed Novartis to establish active cooperation with high profile institutional partners and to exert greater control over its external environment. It also gained insight on how single drug development projects are translated into general health policies.

The other partners were also able to better accomplish their institutional missions, strongly related to the health levels and quality of life of the Tigrean population. In addition to the primary clinical impact, the regional health authority benefited from improved social capital in the territory as the project strengthened the tradition of community participation in malaria control. The skills of the staff and of volunteer CHWs were also improved and could be useful in addressing other health problems. The THB staff achieved an additional benefit in completing scientific publications on malaria that are key for their career advancement.

The WHO and the Italian partners enhanced the effectiveness of their intervention programs thanks to the unique input from volunteers (trusted by the communities) and a prominent pharmaceutical company (business skills and mindset).

A final point emerging from the case study refers to the constituents. We found a model based on three actors (principals that fund and monitor the results, and agents and clients that benefit from the results) particularly inadequate for understanding the networks dynamics. These categories were not exclusive in our case—but this arguably holds for networks in general—because three out of the five partners were both funders and agents. The THB was not only an agent, responsible for the in-field project implementation, but also a principal because it provided some of the resources and monitored the results of the project. Further research is therefore needed to develop a multiple constituencies approach to networks.

CONCLUSIONS AND DIRECTIONS FOR FURTHER RESEARCH

The chapter's aim was to develop an interpretative and dynamic theoretical model identifying the main network performance determinants and dimensions. Through an extensive literature review and the analysis of

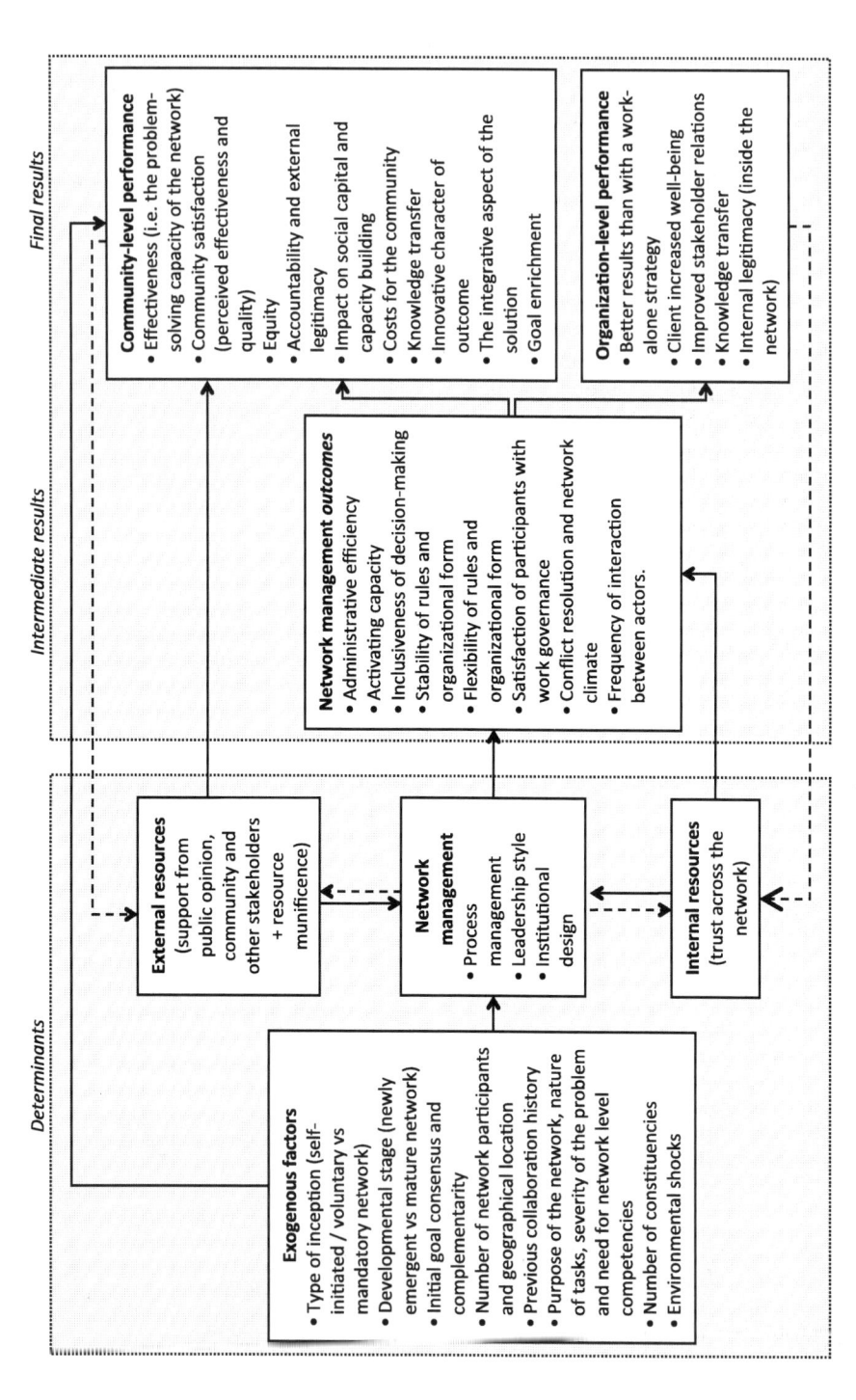

Figure 11.3   A Review of Possible Network Performance Assessment Criteria

a longitudinal case study, we illustrated the following categories of determinants of network performance:

- Exogenous elements;
- External resources;
- Internal resources; and
- Network management characteristics.

These factors provide a more nuanced and clear description of the determinants than those found in the literature. They determine the performances of a network that include:

- Intermediate results; i.e., network management outcomes;
- Final results for each partner organization; and
- Final results for the community.

The model was completed with possible assessment criteria (Figure 11.3) for each of these elements.

Most importantly, the longitudinal case study helped to highlight the links that operate between determinants and between these and the main levels of performance. For instance, for their nature (external rather than internal), it is reasonable to expect that exogenous factors will more intensively influence the community-level performance of the network, while the internal resources, on which the network can count, will have a greater impact on intermediate performance in terms of the quality of interaction. The return effects are also relevant: community results will produce a stronger effect on the external support to the network, while the organizational-level performance will affect the internal resources on which the network can count.

The direction, time lapse, and their relative intensity can be the object of future research, based on multiple case studies or quantitative analysis.

ACKNOWLEDGEMENT

The research received funding from the Italian Ministry of Education, Research and University (High National Interest Scientific Research Project-PRIN 2008: "Governing, managing and developing networks of public administrations and public/private partnerships in labour and knowledge-intensive sectors") and from Novartis. I would like to thank Angela Bianchi and Caterina Capaccioli (Novartis), Gianfranco Costanzo (Italian Ministry of Health, Department for Innovation), and Hailemariam Lemma Reda (Tigray Health Bureau) for their valuable insights and comments during the research. I am also grateful to Prof. Myrna Mandell and the two anonymous reviewers for their comments.

NOTES

1. The case study analysis included as sources of information a review of the official documentation such as the memorandum of understanding, the Gantt chart of the project and other planning documents, as well as the intermediate and final reports. Full access to the detailed minutes of monthly teleconferences from 2004 to 2009 was allowed and open interviews with the main partners of the project were carried out. Complete details of interviews undertaken can be secured from the author.

2. The model is based on the assumption that the network is voluntary. In the presence of other kinds of inceptions, some of the determinants may move from partial management control to no management control.

3. For instance, for some local government networks in Italy (the so-called unioni di comuni), the law establishes that the leadership is held in rotation by the mayors, which makes the leadership form, at least in part, an exogenous factor.

4. It is worth noting that the term performance is used here in a neutral way to include both good and bad results of the network. For instance, at the community level of network performance, costs or negative effects on the community are also considered.

5. Cf. WHO Fact Sheet No.94: Malaria. 2010; WHO World Malaria Report. 2010; WHO: 10 facts on malaria. 2009; Roll Back Malaria Partnership. Malaria in Africa. 2011.

6. Cf. for instance the Wall Street Journal and Médecins Sans Frontières cited in Spar and Delacey 2008: 8.

7. Such as departmental staff salaries, the purchase of insecticide, operational costs for insecticide spraying and other recurrent costs, including drugs used by CHWs other than AL.

8. The network, and thus the following Figure 2 that gives account of its results, do not include the control district.

9. In the formal agreement, this was called the Project Monitoring Team, the name reflecting the limited envisaged tasks. Since the early stages of the project, though, the partners became aware that the network coordination activities were far more complex, considering, among others, the geographical distance of the partners and the aims of the project.

   Cf. Agreement, signed on July 13, 2004, between the Italian Ministry of Health, the State of Tigray Health Bureau, MoH Ethiopia, the WHO-Roll Back Malaria Programme, Novartis Farma s.p.a. (Italy), the Italian Hospital of Quiha'—Tigray and the department of Preventive Medicine in Migration, Tourism and Tropical Dermatology of the hospital San Gallicano of Rome in the field of public health.

REFERENCES

Agranoff, Robert. 2003. *Leveraging Networks: A Guide for Public Managers Working Across Organizations*. IBM Endowment for the Business of Government.

Cepiku, Denita, and Marco Meneguzzo. 2004. "Public Sector Networks: What Can We Learn from Different Approaches?" In *Challenges of Public Management Reforms. Theoretical Perspectives and Recommendations*, edited by S. P. Osborne, G. Jenei, K. McLaughlin, and K. Mike, 103–33. Hungary: Budapest University.

Crosby, Barbara C., and John M. Bryson. 2010. "Integrative Leadership and the Creation and Maintenance of Cross-Sector Collaborations." *The Leadership Quarterly* 21 (2): 211–30.

Isett, Kimberley R., Ines A. Mergel, Kelly LeRoux, Pamela A. Mischen, and R. Karl Rethemeyer. 2011. "Networks in Public Administration Scholarship: Understanding Where We Are and Where We Need to Go." *JPART* 21 (I): 157-i17.

Kenis, Patrick, and Keith G. Provan. 2009. "Towards an Exogenous Theory of Public Network Performance." *Public Administration* 87 (3): 440–56.

Kickert, Walter J. M., Erik-Hans Klijn, and Joop F.M. Koppenjan. 1997. *Managing Complex Networks, Strategies for the Public Sector.* London: Sage.

Klijn, Erik-Hans, Bram Steijn, and Jurian Edelenbos. 2010. "The Impact Of Network Management Strategies on the Outcomes in Governance Networks." *Public Administration* 88 (4): 1063–82.

Mandell, Myrna P. 1990. "Network Management: Strategic Behavior in the Public Sector." In *Strategies for Managing Intergovernmental Policies and Networks,* edited by R. W. Gage and M. P. Mandell. New York: Praeger.

Mandell, Myrna P., and Robyn Keast. 2008. "Evaluating the Effectiveness of Interorganizational Relations Through Networks." *Public Management Review* 10 (6): 715–31.

Meier, Kenneth J., and Laurence J. O'Toole. 2001. "Managerial Strategies and Behavior in Networks: A Model with Evidence from U.S. Public Education." *Journal of Public Administration Research and Theory* 11 (3):271–93.

McGuire, Michael, and Robert Agranoff. 2007. *Answering the Big Questions, Asking the Bigger Questions: Expanding the Public Network Management Empirical Research Agenda.* Paper presented at the ninth Public Management Research Conference, Tucson, Arizona, October 25–27.

McGuire, Michael, and Chris Silvia. 2009. *How God? The Impact of Leadership on Network Effectiveness.* Paper for the Public Management Research Association Conference, Columbus, Ohio, October.

Meneguzzo, Marco, and Denita Cepiku, eds. 2008. *Network Pubblici: Strategia, Struttura e Governance.* Milano: McGraw-Hill.

Page, Stephen. 2010. "Integrative Leadership for Collaborative Governance: Civic Engagement in Seattle." *The Leadership Quarterly* 21 (2) 246–63.

Provan, Keith G., and Brinton H. Milward. 2001. "Do Networks Really Work? A Framework for Evaluating Public Sector Organizational Networks." *Public Administration Review* 61 (4): 414–23.

———. 1995. "A Preliminary Theory of Network Effectiveness: A Comparative Study of Four Community Mental Health Systems." *Administrative Science Quarterly* 40: 1–33.

Provan, Keith G., and Juliann G. Sebastian. 1998. "Networks within Networks: Service Link Overlap Organizational Cliques, and Network Effectiveness." *Academy of Management Journal* 41: 453–63.

Rodríguez, Charo, Ann Langley, François Béland, and Jean-Louis Denis. 2007. "Governance, Power and Mandated Collaboration in an Interorganizational Network." *Administration and Society* 39 (2):150ff.

Voets, Joris, Wouter Van Dooren, and Filip De Rynck. 2008. "A Framework for Assessing the Performance of Policy Networks." *Public Management Review* 10 (6): 773–90.

WHO. 2009. *Deployment at Community Level of Arthemeter-Lumefantrine with Rapid Diagnostic Tests at Community Level, Raya Valley, Tigray, Ethiopia.* World Health Organisation Global Malaria Programme, June.

Part IV
Implications and Conclusion

12 Bridging the Theoretical Gap and Uncovering the Missing Holes

Robert Agranoff

INTRODUCTION

This volume aspires to contribute to the theoretical base of public networks and in the long run to the theory of networks. As Abraham Kaplan (1964, 295–296) maintains, "A theory is a symbolic construction . . . guiding the enterprise of discovering new and more powerful generalizations". In approaching this task this volume incorporates both qualitative and quantitative research cultures, bridging research questions, data analysis modes, and methods of inference (Goertz and Mahoney 2012). With an attempt to bridge both research approaches, we bring this volume to a close by: 1) presenting the issues that the papers in this volume have advanced; 2) identifying one set of the unanswered issues in network theory, that of their limitations; 3) raising the even broader question of the status/role of the public sphere nongovernmental organizations (NGOs) and public agencies as they operate in the age of the network; and, 4) identification of a series of issues in network theorizing that remain. These include: a) the confusion between "a network" and "to network", b) the huge, "public value" question in network performance, c) the distinctiveness of networks in the public arena, d) operational management issues within these structures, and e) the future of networks with open-source information using electronic formats. There is clearly more that needs to be done.

WHAT THESE PAPERS HAVE ADVANCED

In addition to broad and deep explanations of what networks do in the public sphere, their theoretical underpinnings have been advanced that range from interorganizational relations studies to public policy implementation analyses and service delivery modes. A picture has been conveyed that networks need to be understood in all of their complexity: multiformed, multifaceted, adaptive systems that draw on mixes of governance and structural properties, undergirding a theoretical ferment that is framed from three main fronts—structuring for interorganizational connections, policy/network governance, and collaborative service delivery. To these the dimension of complexity theory can be injected as a means of accounting for those physical and technological components of systems. Complexity would include managerial perspectives, that is, allowing for the possibility of but raising governance network theory as complex interaction processes. Combining the dimensions of network approaches—resource dependency, multi-actor, policy, and management—to enhance theoretical power adds important diagnostic criteria; particularly multilevel analysis, and the potential of a practice-based self-assessment tool, while at the same time enabling the progression of deeper, unitary considerations of network phenomenon. Also, different meanings of network are identified by three major conceptual frameworks, leading to a three-fold paradigm: interaction of actors at different levels (structural), crossing spheres and organizations (institutional), and the state as a meta-network (functional). An important untapped analytical potential of network analysis identified here is that of the role of governance networks in democratizing various forms of policy-making. In this respect, it is suggested that network analysis can bring out the democratic value of these entities as they enhance political dialogue. Networks can challenge established power structures.

Network theory includes that which operates within their structures. Using one empirical case, network management looks deeply into how managers activate potential partners; mobilize resources, knowledge, and operations; frame problems, issues, and potential courses of action; and synthesize the agreements into multiorganization programs and feedback. These are, however, protracted interactive processes that challenge the ability of networks comprising different organizations to accomplish results. Therefore, care in process must be taken to reach the synergistic outcomes that networks seek. The contribution of working through multiagency engagement challenges participants to overcome the considerable barriers of collective inertia. However, they can be enhanced by concentrating on goals, trust, culture-building, and leadership development. A theory of networks needs to include, as will be developed, more concern for the dynamics of managing within. Of particular importance, as is pointed out in a number of chapters in this book, are various dynamics of deliberative action.

Looking within also contributes to understanding the all-important dimension of network performance. In this respect network management can influence results, according to the complex adaptive systems paper in this collection. As such, it is essential to understand that process and structural characteristics of networks do contribute to outcomes. These outcomes appear to be related to the benefit of each partner and for the broader community. A more analytical review of performance suggests that managing for results by use of managerial tools and knowledge-building as modes of structured performing are critical to network performance. Each of these approaches in this journey into network theory needs to transcend both thick qualitative description/analysis and quantitative studies of network properties, network resource munificence, and network properties. To advance beyond current stages of analysis and build more powerful network theory research must transcend system dynamics and network logic using more of the current approaches employed in policy and management analysis, such as system dynamics, agent-based modeling, social network analysis, and qualitative comparative analysis.

There is considerably more theory to be built. As the analysis of collaborative inertia within networks suggests, analysis needs to begin with the downside of network analysis, that incorporates more than standard issues such as protracted processing costs and knowledge/resource/power limitations. In addition to network benefits, there are additional costs and barriers to performance that need to be part of network analysis (McGuire and Agranoff 2011).

EXTENDING THE TRAJECTORY

Network theory regarding the interactions of publicly engaged organizations is being advanced by notable increments. While not necessarily a coherent *corpus* of work, its significance is witnessed by the increasing number of articles and books published on this subject. However difficult it might appear to build a so-called grand theory of public networks, given the disparity of definitions and approaches (Börzel 1998; Isett et al. 2011), the amount of theorizing is a welcome sign of a healthy endeavor (Berry and Brower 2005; O'Toole 1997). Extending theory builds on the numerous articles cited throughout this volume, but there is more to be done.

One way to begin is to look at how networks change over time. Often looked at with the assumption that networks are static entities they are clearly not the same entities through their formulation and operation and expiration stages. This is made clear from the application of complexity theory and managerial operations depicted in this volume. Additionally, methodological tools have been developed (Wasserman and Faust 1994; Contractor, Wasserman, and Faust 2006) that can be used to apply to these critical dynamics. Like the networks in this book that involve harbor development, STEM education, local democracy, and social development, understanding their operation over time is essential.

Another dimension is to recognize that networks are not the only vehicles of collaborative management (Ansell and Gash 2008). In a recently published volume, Agranoff (2012, 37–39) identified approximately twenty-seven different means of linking organizations operating in the public sphere (e.g., contracting, interagency agreements, shared staff). Sometimes casually and inappropriately lumped into the analytic category "networks", they are not. They do, however, equally serve to manage interorganizational connections. They operate, as Vandeventer and Mandell (2007, 20–22) indicate, to foster linkages short of a network because some problems that require action across boundaries are easily solvable, or differences cannot be resolved, or involved key issues that are avoided, or key actors will not come to the table. They identify at least a dozen such reasons why a network should not be formed. Most important, of course, is why take on such protracted multicultural undertakings when the transaction costs can be so high? It is often assumed that networks happen "as if by magic", overlooking the often substantial cost of relationship building and maintenance as well as dispersed decision making, as pointed out by several chapters in this book.

Another less recognized concern that is normally overlooked is that operating in a network does not always work. They have real limitations. McGuire and Agranoff (2011) have addressed this head on, concluding that while networks can bring the various parties together, overcome agency turf and resource limitations, they run into operational, performance, or legal barriers that prevent agreement and/or the next action/implementation step. Even solutions agreed to in principle face obstacles in converting them to policy energy, dealing with internal agency ineffectiveness, experiencing process blockages, or mission drift, and/or others. One clear example is that in many cases network participants lack authority to make final decisions. In this regard O'Toole (1997, 445) observes with regard to network operatives, " . . . they do not have the formal wherewithal to compel compliance with such cooperative undertakings". In this regard it was concluded (McGuire and Agranoff 2011, 250) that:

> Network studies have to come to grips with the process of accommodation and adjustment by acknowledging the weak scope of network authority: networks are, in essence, limited in their ability to make things happen. We must know more about the heretofore unstudied barriers to action, such as how and when agreements become implemented, the power imbalances during the implementation process, and the efficacy of alternatives to networks.

Several papers in this volume address problems of process difficulties and obstacles to performance, providing new insights and ways forward as well as pointing to the body of work yet to be tackled. A further concern is that of the relationship of public networks with government agencies.

NETWORKS AND BUREAUCRATIC AGENCIES

In discussing the paradox of civil society, Michael Walzer warns that the "antipolitical tendencies that commonly accompany the celebration of civil society" are overstated; the "network of associations incorporates, but it cannot dispense with, the agencies of state power" (1998, 138). He continues that "[c]itizenship is one of the many roles that members play, but the state itself is unlike all other associations. It both frames civil society and occupies space within it, fixing the boundary conditions and the basic rules of associational activity, compelling association members to think about the common good" (138). While not always regarded in this way, networks have not displaced or eclipsed the power or centrality of government agencies.

Perhaps neither networks nor governments dominate in reality. Although there is a lot of talk about the state "hollowing out" through contracts, partnerships, networks, etc. (Goldsmith and Eggers 2004; Milward, Provan, and Else 1993; Milward and Provan 2003), the ability of these government agency interlocutors to influence the public agency domain appears real but limited in scope: "accommodations are made, decisions are influenced, strategies are altered, resources are directed, intensive groups exert undue influence, and public responsibility is indirectly shared" (Agranoff 2007, 219). Importantly, McGuire and Agranoff (2010) conclude that networks normally find themselves working *with* governments as the latter maintains key legal and fiscal controls/functions. Networks seem to function in and around governments' legal, fiscal, and operational functions (see also Salamon 1995, 2002). Also, statutory authority to engage in networks almost never "authorize agencies to collaborate in networks with others" (Bingham 2008, 258). Moreover, there are also the previously mentioned alternatives to networks, e.g., contracts, grants, loans, and so on which promote links between governments and between levels of government and NGOs. Finally, it is important to recognize that not all agency administrators are caught up in networking or collaborative activity. Indeed, with the exception of agency boundary spanners, many public agency administrators spend as little as 15 to 20 percent of their time in all types of cross-agency work, including involvement in networks (Agranoff and McGuire 2003).

A research agenda is needed on the role of government agencies in networks and in network formation and operation. To start, networks have to be evaluated within their real world contexts. They—and the for-profit and nonprofit actors comprising them—are limited in role, capacity, and authority compared to their public agency partners. Public agency roles and resources typically include legal mandates to take action to address the problem(s) targeted by networks. This now includes agency staffing capacity, those extensive financial resources that governments control, the legitimacy government participation brings to networks, and the managerial responsibilities that public agencies assume in their mandate to action. Networks often lack direct control over formal ties, such as grants, contracts, and service agreements that bind the other parties together. The only powers that networks as entities normally have are those delegated by governments, those exerted by their partners (including government agencies), and some of their own limited inherent powers (e.g., the ability of partners to withhold expertise that government lacks). Finally, networks as entities rarely implement agreements or programs derived by partners, which is normally by the network's participating organizations.

These limitations suggest an additional subagenda for theoretical research. McGuire and Agranoff (2010, 391) maintain that the agenda move away from the presumption that a network-governed form of hollow state exists, with all that this entails. There is a tendency in the literature to assume that: 1) networks are becoming the exclusive service delivery mechanism of choice by public managers, 2) networks are a relatively new phenomenon, and 3) hierarchical and bureaucratic mechanisms are being supplanted by networks. These do not appear to be useful premises on which to craft new theories and practices.

Prior research has bypassed the role of government and has focused on determining the antecedents to or determinants of collaboration, the motivating factors that compel agencies to join multi-actor networks, how collaborative structures emerge and how they evolve over time, and how barriers encountered by networks were overcome (Koliba, Meek, and Zia 2010; Silvia and McGuire 2010; Keast, 2011). "How-to" publications heralding the emergence of networks have also become commonplace (e.g. Goldsmith and Eggers 2004). This apparent love affair with networks, with few exceptions, rarely address fundamental issues of the place of networks in a constitutional system of authority, and their essential role in interacting with several governments. Clearly the role of the public agency, with its continuing legal, fiscal, and program oversight role is an important arena of research.

NETWORKS, GOVERNMENT AGENCIES, AND THE ORGANIZATIONS THAT COMPRISE THEM

There clearly has been less attention on the impacts of networks on the organizations—public, nonprofit, and private—themselves as they continue to operate within their own structures along with networks. This opens up a whole new arena of research. Some areas of impact may well need to be left to more standard organization theory research. However, three issues appear difficult to separate from the theoretical construction of networks: organizational conductivity, organizations working in the network as they plan and implement, and networks as an important subset of public services implementation in their potential for interoperability/reciprocal programming.

To demonstrate organizational theory change as related to networks, the emergent roles of government agencies are illustrated, although these principles may well apply to all organizations operating in the public sphere while operating in networks. It appears that bureaucratic organizations in networks are being reconstructed along three important lines. First, they have become increasingly conductive, that is they are increasingly organized for work "outside" of the agency as well as inside it. Saint-Onge and Armstrong (2004, 213) define such agencies as those geared externally, creating partnerships, alliances, coalitions, and cross-organizational teams by enhancing the quality and flow of knowledge geared to the agency's strategy. Second, as a result, organizations now do more than passively play some role in network decision and operation but work proactively and interactively with their associates. As programs are implemented and services are delivered organization administrators and specialists work alongside government and NGO agents to facilitate the flow from legislation to rules/regulations/standards/performance expectations to operations within delivery nonprofit and for-profit agencies. Third, organization representatives now work within networks of agencies at the service delivery level, taking early and regular roles in service network promotion and operation. To government organizations the stakes of passivity or inactivity are too high; today's representatives need to be in the network, not above it (Agranoff 2011; forthcoming).

These types of interactions lead bureaucrats and their partners to become more *proactive* by engaging in network building among the varied participants in public-generated programming. As bureaucratic officials become more involved in this type of building and operating in networks, they find that their home organizations are changing to meet the challenges of networking. Thus, bureaucratic and organizational boundaries among network partners are more open and flexible and boundary spanning becomes a core rather than a supportive effort. The demands of the public agency to become more deeply engaged in network behavior appear to be opening and loosening bureaucratic structures.

INTEROPERABILITY

An increasingly important managerial dimension of organizational change brought on by involvement in networks is a function of the fact that most network agreements/programs/policies are carried out by two or more involved organizations. As mentioned, rarely is the network structure the operating agent. This aspect of collaborated network management has been captured as *interoperability* (Jenkins 2006, 321), which can be defined as reciprocal communication and accommodation to reach interactive operating policy and programming. As Chapter 3 in this volume on deliberative action indicates, interoperable management involves the concerted actions taken by different agencies working on the same issues or programs. There is a need for more studies of public networks that uncover the protracted processes of achieving interoperability, which in turn will more deeply define collaborative management by network. The process needs to be broken down into various cross-agency operational steps.

Interoperability must be understood as the most intense form of collaborative management by network. It refers to public programming when a series of governmental, nonprofit, and for-profit agencies are expected or are attempting to work together, whereby their policies and procedures need to be made to work interactively toward similar and/or common aims that combine policy and administration. Agencies obviously need to be integrated at an operating level. It is in this sense that interoperability signifies some level of interactive working policy and management that challenges organizations in networks.

Interoperable management thus refers to regularized programming involving two or more entities for which operating policies and processes have been interactively articulated and are executed to some considerable degree by multiple organizations. This process has been defined by the US Government Accountability Office not as an end itself but as a means to achieve the ability to respond when coordinated actions of a reciprocal nature are required. It is based on communicated and agreed-upon goals, planning, operational information, role differentiation, and an operating system that supports communication (GAO 2004).

REMAINING ISSUES AND CONCERNS

What Constitutes a Public Network?

This is not a small analytical matter since the research community has used virtually any and all analytical concepts to delineate networks in public management. For example, this has led any number of analysts to equate "contact" variables on a survey to represent network behavior. As Rhodes (2003, 21) suggests, "network" is an everyday term used by consumers and managers (and perhaps politicians) to describe the web of relationships in which they are embedded, giving rise to different meanings that need to be captured. Very early in the game of theorizing, Alter and Hage (1993, 46) defined *boundary spanners* as those who engage in the tasks of coordination and task integration, networking as organization actors engage in acts of creating/maintaining a cluster of organizations for exchange/action/ production, and *networks* as structures that permit interorganizational interactions of exchange, concerted action or joint production. Moreover, Kilduff and Tsai (2003, 91) distinguish between *serendipitous* networks or haphazardous, decentralized, loosely coupled connections that are and based on shared ties and *goal-directed* networks that exhibit "purposive and adaptive movement toward an envisioned end state" (92).

Clearly the kind of public networks examined in this volume are goal-directed, using boundary spanners to use networking while moving organizational boundaries by organizing in networks. This minimal test would seem to exclude situations where organizations merely experience occasional ties, dyadic interactions, diffuse boundaries, shared ties only, and occasional contacts, or the absence of shared goals, all of which also appear as networks in the research community, in effect inflating and/or misusing the concept of network. Delimiting theoretical scope becomes important for the maturation of theory and thus public management network analysis requires the drawing of parameters around use of the term "network". In short, it means focus on the construction of meanings given by government managers and their interlocutors as they work within organized entities that involve parts of organizations nonhierarchically (O'Toole 1997). This includes the broader issue of "democratic network governance", that is, cross-sectoral and based in civil society involvement where issues of deliberation, citizen responsibility, as well as questions of equity, accountability, and democratic legitimacy to serve public purposes are at stake (Mandell 2008; Skelcher 2005; Sørensen and Torfing 2007). There are also the management and policy development structures of exchange that normally use the term "network", structures involving multiple nodes—agencies and organizations—with multiple linkages, ordinarily working on cross-boundary collaborative activities to agree on a course of action and/or to carry out agreements made by these multiple organizations (Klijn and Koppenjan 2000; McGuire 2002). They constitute one form of collaborative activity for facilitating and operating multiorganizational arrangements to solve problems that cannot be solved, or solved easily, by using single organizations (Agranoff and McGuire 2003, 4).

The "How Good" Question

There has been increasing attention paid to performance issues in public networks (e.g., Koliba, Campbell, and Zia 2011; Koliba this volume; Cepiku this volume; Mandell and Keast 2009). Perhaps *the* big question is whether networks do make some difference that single organizations cannot. In a path-breaking work on interagency collaboration, Bardach (1998) invoked Mark Moore's (1995) idea that the work of managers in the public sphere is aimed at enhancing public value, that is increasing efficiency, effectiveness, or fairness, or perhaps responding to a new political aspiration. Bardach asks if public value is the aim whether any two or more social entities that work together create public value that organizations working alone do not. "My hypothesis is that substantial public value is being lost to insufficient collaboration in the public sector" (11). This question has become even more important in the ensuing years as "public value thinking and action includes the capacity to analyze and understand interconnections, interdependencies, and interactions between complex issues and across multiple boundaries" (Bennington and Moore 2011, 15).

Agranoff and McGuire (2001, 318–321) applied Bardach's collaborative management issue to networks as one of their "big questions" in network research. It was suggested that networks were required to meet the increasing complexity and diversity (Kooiman 1993) in an information age (Lipnak and Stamps 1994) where power is dispersed, not centralized, and the demand for unifying tasks is increasing. Moreover, the public sector is increasingly called upon to take on the most difficult of multisource problems that require joint steering of multi-faceted courses of action where networked program structures may be the best choice available (Provan and Milward 1991, 1995; Agranoff 1991; Ferlie and Pettigrew 2006; Keast, Brown, and Mandell 2007). Finally, it was advanced that when wide agreement is necessary and action needs to be jointly steered, network-derived actions may be the most consistent with multigovernment and multiorganizational action. It may be the best policy test (Lindblom 1959).

The reason for these advantages is because networks may be better suited than the hierarchical structures of bureaucratic organizations that mass-produce standardized services but can be too inflexible to fast-developing and changing problems. John Bennington (2011, 40) concludes that:

> Networks have greater potential than either hierarchies or markets to function as complex adaptive systems, with capabilities for coordination between many different actors and organizations, and the organizational flexibility to respond to continuous change.

Bennington also maintains that public value extends beyond market/economic considerations to include social and cultural value-building, social capital, social cohesion, social relationships, social meaning and cultural identity, individual and community well-being, and political value. Networks can add to the public realm by stimulating and supporting democratic dialogue, active public participation, and civic engagement (45).

More research on how and why networks emerge will help to expand value understanding of program approaches and results. The complex and hard-to-reach issue of how good is the network approach may someday be part of these analytics. One possible way to start is to test the assumptions of when networks should not be formed (e.g., problems are simple, can be solved dyadically/triadically) and when they should be formed (e.g., solutions point to multiple resources and agencies) to see if this empirically holds true (see Vandeventer and Mandell 2007). It would not only be a start but would test the flexible adaptation to complexity dimension identified by Bennington that is generally assumed. Indeed, if public networks are occupying niches once held by bureaucracies it is important to build theory that explains key aspects of their efficacy. Such "testing" calls for the application of forms of evaluation and assessment that extend well beyond the small number studies currently preferred toward meta-analyses of cases, particularly those that cross sectoral and industry boundaries (Isett et al. 2011; Berry et al. 2004).

New Tools of Network Management

An interesting set of within network managerial premises are emerging that appear to distinguish it from that of standard hierarchical management.

First, there may well be a new management POSDCORB that in part distinctively sets off network management, as empirically demonstrated by McGuire and Agranoff in this volume: activation, mobilization, framing, and synthesizing. The concept of interoperability, or reciprocal communication and operation, was introduced earlier as a network management approach. Leadership in networks is an often identified arena of management, where studies on studies have been piled up for some time. They range from Bennis and Biederman's (1997) fifteen tips on how to move great groups toward creative collaboration to more empirical studies like the Koppenjan and Klijn (2004) analysis of how network managers cope with uncertainty. A number of chapters in this book also deal with the issue of leadership in networks, including the chapter by Keast and Mandell that introduces the concept of a process catalyst as a theoretical framework for leadership in collaborative networks.

Organizing within networks has also been an emergent concern since the early work of Provan and Milward (1991, 1995) on lead organizations in networks, along with the work of Provan and Kenis (2008) on lead or distinct network based administrative entities. Networks as organized structures normally are comprised of the organizational resources brought to the network by partnering organizations. Often this includes hierarchical position, technical staff expertise, and dedicated network staff (McGuire 2009). It is known that differentials exist in the ability of organizations to influence networks by the power and influence brought into operations (Gray 1989; Schapp and van Twist 1997) which is blended with or can be modified by the social production of network participants while dealing with new ideas or reaching deliberative solutions (Stone et al. 1999).

Organizing raises the question of the existence of structural forms or hierarchical equivalents in networks. Agranoff's (2007, 83) study of 14 networks identified their structures as collaborarchies, "self-organizing entities that are normally enabled or chartered, have distinct nonhierarchical authority structures, employ regularized cross-agency communication systems, and have distinct internal power structures along with set internal arrangements." Subsequent research (Agranoff 2012, 138–144) concluded that these same networks were structured with many organized roles, including network champions, agency administrator steering partners, signatory but less involved copartners, governing structure members (core group, executive committee, council), standing committee members, technical and problem-based work group participants, other technical staff from agencies and organizations, and network staff (see also Holbeche 2005; Mandell 2001; Rethemeyer and Hatmaker 2008). Work on network structure is clearly just beginning, and combined with work on theory-building in regard to nonhierarchical organizing, should enhance core or internal network knowledge.

Closely related to organizing and operating within is that of control in networks. Identified by Kenis and Provan (2006, 228), control involves "the use of mechanisms by actors to monitor the actions and activities of organizational networks to enhance the likelihood that the network-level goals can be attained". They suggest that control cannot be easily imported from knowledge on the control of organizations. "For both government policy makers and funders (both government and foundations) it is imperative to understand better why networks succeed or fail and what the impact of control is for overall network performance. From organizational literature we have learned that, in general, there is a relationship between control and performance" (229).

Open Source Technology and Networks

The Koliba paper on performance in this volume, approaching aligning network performance with system dynamics, calls for capturing network theory-building with computer simulation modeling with such techniques as system dynamics, agent-based modeling, social network analysis, and qualitative comparative analysis, as new data-mining programs are allowing large volumes of verbal and numerical data to be analyzed for patterns. They will no doubt not only enhance network performance, but will also extend knowledge in several different arenas. Other emergent techniques including argumentative mapping applied alone or coupled with Public Participative or Collaborative GIS programming (Dragicevic and Balram 2004) also offer new sets of insights into the ways in which network members cluster around spatially related problems as well as the cleavages between network members (Mahmood, Horita, and Keast 2012).

More may yet be possible. In an interesting new volume on networked science, that is online interaction, Michael Nielson (2012) suggests that continued interaction can expand collaborative volume in some areas of inquiry, achieving what he calls conversational critical mass. This can be accomplished by modularizing collaboration by splitting up tasks into smaller subtasks that can be attacked independently. It will also encourage small contributions, reduce barriers to entry, and broaden the range of expertise. Thereby a rich and well-structured information commons can emerge, building work incrementally as well as collaboratively.

Regarding networks, open source information has the potential to add to the deliberative power of interacting parties, directing attention from information that participants already know to that which they need to approach problems, serving the important function of "collective insight" (Nielson, 2012, 66). To the extent that networks operate in open cultures of sharing "where as much information is moved out of people's heads . . . and onto the network" (Nielson, 2012, 183), the search for meaning may well undergird network processes.

Are Public Networks Distinct?

Inasmuch as governments as legitimate and authoritative bodies constitute one of the most frequent, if not the most frequent, participants in networks, a look at this distinction would also appear to be in order. As this volume makes clear, in both policy and management networks government agencies are part of the public entities that we call networks. They exist at all levels of government and do not necessarily supplant traditional public functions but become important elements of a community of public operations. Governance networks differ from corporatist models in many ways. The primary differences lie in the fact that a variety of interests, sometimes differing, are brought to the collaborative structure and that government is not petitioned by a set of closed interests for reward, protection, or dispute settlement but the various interests are said to investigate, design, and sometimes agree on direction *with* government (Rhodes and Marsh 1992; Rhodes 1997; McGuire and Agranoff 2010; Klijn and Koppenjan 2000; Börzel 1998).

CONCLUSION

The path to the development of a dedicated public sector network research program and theory has been long. However, it can now be argued that a distinctive program of public sector network research and theorizing exists, with a set of core ideas or principles that are not directly borrowed or tacked on from interorganizational relations or other foci. These leading/ core ideas have emerged from ongoing efforts to differentiate public sector networks from other competing and/or similar programs. They are further defined and propelled forward through healthy discussion and debate which serves to distill new hypotheses for examination. As well as new hypotheses, a progressive research program also remains alert to new approaches that alert researchers to new types of phenomena: Together these elements push the boundary of exploration and discovery.

Like networks themselves, network theory development relies heavily on a facilitating context that enables new thinking and practice to flourish and grow. This book provides a step in this process. It is hoped that others in the field will be able to build on the theoretical foundations that have been laid down by the authors in this volume. If this book provides a basis to encourage new thinking and thinkers that go beyond the scope of this book, then it will have served its purpose.

REFERENCES

Agranoff, R. Forthcoming. "Reconstructing Bureaucracy for Service Innovation in the Governance Era." In *Public Innovation Through Collaboration and Design*, edited by Chris Ansell and Jacob Torfung. London: Routledge.

———. 2012 *Collaborating to Manage: A Primer for the Public Sector*. Washington, DC: Georgetown University Press.

———. 2011. "Collaborative Public Agencies in the Network Era." In *The State of Public Administration: Issues, Challenges, and Opportunities*, edited by Donald C. Menzel and Harvey L. White. Armonk, NY: M. E. Sharpe.

_____. 2007. *Managing Within Networks: Adding Value to Public Organizations.* Washington, DC: Georgetown University Press.

_____. 1991. "Human Services Integration: Past and Present Challenges in Public Administration." *Public Administration Review* 51 (5): 426–36.

Agranoff, R., and M. McGuire. 2003. *Collaborative Public Management: New Strategies for Local Governments.* Washington, DC: Georgetown University Press.

_____. 2001. "Big Questions in Public Network Management Research." *Journal of Public Administration Research and Theory* 11 (3): 295–326.

Alter, C., and J. Hage. 1993. *Organizations Working Together.* Newbury Park, CA: Sage.

Ansell, C., and A. Gash. 2008. "Collaborative Governance in Theory and Practice." *Journal of Public Administrative Research and Theory* 18 (4): 543–72.

Bardach, E. 1998. *Getting Agencies to Work Together.* Washington, DC: Brookings Institution Press.

Bennington, J. 2011. "From Private Choice to Public Value." In *Public Value: Theory and Practice,* edited by J. Bennington and M. H. Moore. Houndmills, Basingstoke: Palgrave MacMillan.

Bennington, J., and M. H. Moore. 2011. "Public Value in Complex and Changing Times." In *Public Value: Theory and Practice,* edited by J. Bennington and M. H. Moore. Houndmills, Basingstoke: Palgrave Macmillan.

Bennis, W., and P. W. Biederman. 1997. *Organizing Genius. The Secrets of Creative Collaboration.* Cambridge, MA: Perseus.

Berry, F. S., and R. S. Brower. 2005. "Intergovernmental and Intersectoral Management." *Public Performance and Management Review* 29 (1): 7–17.

Berry, F. S., R. Brower, S. OK Choi, W. Goa, H. Jang, M. Kwon, and J. Word. 2004. "Three Traditions of Network Research: What the Public Management Research Agenda Can Learn from Other Research Communities." *Public Administration Review* 64 (5):539–52.

Bingham, L. B. 2008. "Legal Frameworks for Collaboration in Governance and Public Management." In *Big Ideas in Collaborative Public Management,* edited by L. B. Bingham and R. O'Leary. Armonk, NY: M. E. Sharpe.

Börzel, T. A. 1998. "Organizing Babylon—On the Different Conceptions of Policy Networks." *Public Administration* 76 (2): 253–73.

Contractor, N. S., S. Wasserman, and K. Faust. 2006. "Testing Multitheoretical, Multilevel Hypotheses About Organizational Networks." *Academy of Management Review* 31 (3): 681–703.

Dragicevic, S., and Balram, S. 2004. "A Web GIS Collaborative Framework to Structure and Manage Distributed Planning Processes." *Journal of Geographical Systems* 6 (2): 133–53.

Ferlie, E., and A. Pettigrew. 1996. "Managing Through Networks: Some Issues and Implications for the NHS." *British Journal of Management* 7 (March): 81–99.

GAO (US Government Accountability Office). 2004. *Homeland Security: Federal Leadership and Intergovernmental Cooperation Required to Achieve First Responder Interoperable Communications.* Report GAO-04-470. Washington, DC: US Government Printing Office.

Goertz, G. and J. Mahoney. 2012. *A Tale of Two Cultures: Qualitative and Quantitative Research in the Social Sciences.* Princeton: Princeton University Press.

Goldsmith, S., and W. D. Eggers. 2004. *Governing by Network.* Washington, DC: Brookings.

Gray, B., 1989. *Collaborating: Finding Common Ground for Multiparty Problems.* San Francisco: Jossey-Bass.

Holbeche, L. 2005. *The High Performance Organization.* Amsterdam: Elsevier.

Isett, K. R., I. A. Mergel, K. LeRoux, K. Mischer, and K. Rethemeyer. 2011. "Networks in Public Administration Scholarship." *Journal of Public Administration Research and Theory* 21 (1): 167–73.

Jenkins, W. O. 2006. "Collaboration over Adaptation: The Case for Interoperable Communications in Homeland Security." *Public Administration Review* 66 (3): 319–22.

Kaplan, A. 1964. *The Conduct of Inquiry: Methodology for Behavioral Science.* San Francisco: Chandler.

Keast, Robyn L. 2011. "Joined-up Governance in Australia: How the Past Can Inform the Future." *International Journal of Public Administration* 34 (4):221–31.

Keast, Robyn, Kerry Brown, and Myrna P. Mandell. 2007. "Getting the Right Mix: Unpacking Integration Meanings and Strategies." *International Public Management Journal* 6 (3): 363–71.

Kenis, P., and K. G. Provan. 2006. "The Control of Public Networks." *International Public Management Journal* 9 (2): 227–47.

Kilduff, M., and W. Tsai. 2003. *Social Networks and Organizations.* Thousand Oaks, CA: Sage.

Klijn, E.-H., and J. F. M. Koppenjan. 2000. "Public Management and Policy Networks: Foundations of a Network Approach to Governance." *Public Management* 2 (2): 135–58.

Koliba, C., E. Campbell, and A. Zia. 2011. "Performance Management Systems of Congestion Management Networks: Evidence from Four Cases." *Public Performance and Management Review* 34 (4): 520–48.

Koliba, C., J. Meek, and A. Zia. 2010. *Governance Networks: Public Administration Policy in the Midst of Complexity.* New York: Taylor and Francis.

Kooiman, J. 1993. *Modern Governance: New Government-Society Interactions.* London: Sage.

Koppenjan, J. F. M., and E. H. Klijn. 2004. *Managing Uncertainties in Networks.* London: Routledge.

Lindblom, Charles E. 1959. "The Science of Muddling Through." *Public Administration Review* 19 (1): 79–88.

Lipnack, J., and J. Stamps. 1994. *The Age of the Network.* New York: John Wiley and Sons.

Mahmood, M. N., Horita, M., and Keast, R. 2012. "Using Argumentative Mapping and Qualitative Probabilistic Network in Resettlement Planning Process: A Case Study of Padma Multi-purpose Bridge Project." *Proceedings of 2012 International Conference on Construction & Real Estate Management,* October 1–2, Kansas City, MO.

Mandell, M. P. 2001. "The Impact of Network Structures on Community-Building Efforts: The Los Angeles Round Table for Children Community Studies." In *Getting Results Through Collaboration: Networks and Network Structures for Public Policy and Management,* edited by M. P. Mandell. Westport, CT: Quorum Books.

Mandell, M. P. 2008. "New Ways of Working: Civic Engagement Through Networks." In *Civic Engagement in a Network Society,* edited by K. Yang and E. Bergrud. Charlotte: Information Age.

Mandell, M.P. and R. Keast. 2009. "A New Look at Leadership in Collaborative Networks: Process Catalysts." In J.A. Raffel, P. Leisnik, and A.E. Middlebrooks eds., *Public Sector Leadership: International Challenges and Perspectives*. Cheltenham, UK: Edward Elgar.

McGuire, M. 2009. "The New Professionalism and Collaborative Activity in Local Emergency Management." In *The Collaborative Public Manager*, edited by L. Bingham and R. O'Leary. Washington, DC: Georgetown University Press.

———. 2002. "Managing Networks: Propositions on What Managers Do and Why They Do It." *Public Administration Review* 62 (5): 426–33.

McGuire, M., and R. Agranoff. 2011. "The Limitations of Public Management Networks." *Public Administration* 89 (2): 265–84.

———. 2010. "Networking in the Shadow of Bureaucracy." In *Oxford Handbook of American Bureaucracy*, edited by R. F. Durant. New York: Oxford University Press.

Milward, H. B., and K. G. Provan. 2003. "Managing the Hollow State: Collaboration and Contracting." *Public Management Review* 5 (1): 1–18.

Milward, H. B., K. G. Provan, and B. A. Else. 1993. "What Does the 'Hollow State' Look Like?" In *Public Management: The State of the Art,* edited by B. Bozeman. San Francisco: Jossey-Bass.

Moore, M. H. 1995. *Creating Public Value: Strategic Management in Government.* Cambridge, MA: Harvard University Press.

Nielson, M. 2012. *Reinventing Discovery: The New Era of Networked Service.* Princeton: Princeton University Press.

O'Toole, L. J. 1997. "Treating Networks Seriously: Practical and Research-Based Agendas in Public Administration." *Public Administration Review* 57 (1): 45–52.

Provan, K. G., and P. Kenis. 2008. "Modes of Network Governance: Structure, Management and Effectiveness." *Journal of Public Administration Research and Theory* 18 (2): 229–52.

Provan, K. G., and Milward, H. B. 1991. "Institutional-Level Norms and Organizational Involvement in a Service-Implementation Network." *Journal of Public Administration Research and Theory* 1 (4): 391–417.

———. 1995. "A Preliminary Theory of Interorganizational Effectiveness: A Comparative Study of Four Community Mental Health Systems." *Administrative Service Quarterly* 40 (1):1–33.

Rethemeyer, R. K., and D. M. Hatmaker. 2008. "Network Management Reconsidered: An Inquiry into Management of Network Structures in Public Sector Service Provision." *Journal of Public Administration Research and Theory* 18 (4): 617–646.

Rhodes, R. A. W. 2003. "Putting People Back into Networks." In *Governing Networks,* edited by A. Salminen, 9–23. Amsterdam: IOS Press.

———. 1997. *Understanding Governance: Policy Networks, Governance, Reflexivity and Accountability.* Buckingham, UK: Open University Press.

Rhodes, R. A. W., and D. Marsh. 1992. "New Directions in the Study of Policy Networks." *European Journal of Political Research* 21 (2): 181–205.

Saint-Onge, H., and C. Armstrong. 2004. *The Conductive Organization.* Amsterdam: Elsevier.

Salamon, L. M. 2002. "The New Governance and the Tools of Public Action." In *The Tools of Government,* edited by L. M. Salamon. New York: Oxford.

_____. 1995. *Partners in Public Service.* Baltimore, MD: Johns Hopkins University Press.

Schapp, L., and M. J. W. van Twist. 1997. "The Dynamics of Closedness in Networks." In *Managing Complex Networks,* edited by W. J. M. Kickert, E.-H. Klijn, and J. F. M. Koppenjan. London: Sage.

Silvia, C., and M. McGuire. 2010. "Leading Public Sector Networks: An Empirical Examination of Integrative Leadership Behavior." *The Leadership Quarterly* 21 (2): 264–77.

Skelcher, C. 2005. "Jurisdictional Integrity, Polycentrism, and the Design of Democratic Governance." *Governance* 18 (1):89–110.

Sørensen, E., and J. Torfing, eds. 2007. *Theories of Democratic Network Governance.* Basingstoke, UK: Palgrave-Macmillan.

Stone, C. N., K. Doherty, C. Jones, and T. Ross. 1999. "Schools and Disadvantaged Neighborhoods: The Community Development Challenge." In *Urban Problems and Community Development,* edited by Ronald F. Ferguson and William T. Dickens. Washington, DC: Brookings Institution Press.

Vandeventer, P., and M. Mandell. 2007. *Networks that Work.* Los Angeles, CA: Community Partners.

Walzer, M. 1998. "The Ideal of Civil Society: The Path to Social Reconstruction." In *Community Works: The Revival of Civil Society in America,* edited by E. J. Dionne, Jr. Washington, DC: Brookings Institution Press.

Wasserman, S., and K. Faust. 1994. *Social Network Analysis.* New York. Cambridge University Press.

Contributors

Denita Cepiku: Denita Cepiku is an aggregate professor in public management at the University of Rome "Tor Vergata". Her main research interests are in the areas of network management, coproduction, comparative public management reform, and strategic planning. She is a board member of the International Research Society for Public Management (IRSPM) and chair of the European Academy of Management (EURAM) strategic interest group on public management.

Chris Huxham: Chris Huxham is emeritus professor at the University of Strathclyde Business School. Her long-standing research career, which earned her several awards, focused on the management of collaboration. She has written many journal publications and books and is coauthor with Siv Vangen of *Managing to Collaborate: The Theory and Practice of Collaborative Advantage* (2005, Routledge, London).

Erik Hans Klijn: Erik Hans Klijn is a professor at the Department of Public Administration at Erasmus University Rotterdam. His research and teaching activities focus on complex decision making, network management, public private and branding, and the impact of media on complex decision making. He has published extensively in international journals and is an author with Joop Koppenjan of the book *Managing Uncertainties in Networks* (2004, Routledge) and with Jasper Eshuis of the book *Branding in Governance and Public Management* (Routledge, 2012).

Christopher Koliba: Christopher Koliba is a professor in the community development and applied economics department at the University of Vermont, where he also serves as the director of the master of public administration program. He received his Ph.D. and M.P.A. from the Maxwell School of Citizenship and Public Affairs at Syracuse University. His research and teaching interests include network governance, complexity science, organizational learning and change, systems analysis, and action research. He has ongoing research programs relating to watershed governance, transportation planning, food systems, and energy distribution networks. He is the author of numerous articles and lead author of the 2010 book: *Governance Network in Public Administration and Public Policy* (CRC Press).

Joop Koppenjan: Joop Koppenjan is a professor of public administration at the Erasmus University Rotterdam. He studies network governance, public private partnerships, and public service delivery. Areas of application are infrastructure-based sectors such as transport, and water and energy, and social sectors such as education, care, and safety. This research often has a comparative focus, either between policy areas or between countries. Recently he published *The New Public Governance in Public Service Delivery* (The Hague: Eleven, 2012).

Michael McGuire: Michael McGuire is professor of public and environmental affairs at Indiana University, International Scholar at Kyung Hee University, and managing editor of *Public Administration Review*. He has expertise in public management networks, collaboration, and intergovernmental relations, focusing on how public managers operate, facilitate, and lead collaborative networks of organizations. He has published more than 50 articles, chapters, reports, and reviews, as well as a coauthored (with Robert Agranoff) an award-winning book, *Collaborative Public Management: New Strategies for Local Governments*. He is a Fellow of the National Academy of Public Administration.

Deborah Rice: Deborah Rice is a postdoctoral researcher at the University of Oldenburg. In her dissertation research at the VU University Amsterdam, she studied agency processes in Dutch, Danish, and British job centers from a multilevel perspective. Deborah's main research interests lie in the areas of public-sector governance, social policy, and social theory.

Eva Sørensen: Eva Sørensen is a professor in public administration and democracy at the Department of Society and Globalization at Roskilde University in Denmark. Her main research interests are the implications of institutional change for the role perceptions of politicians, public administrators, and citizens, and the role of governance networks in enhancing effective, democratic, and innovative public governance. She is currently the director of a large research project on collaborative innovation in the public sector and has written extensively about these and related topics. Among her latest publications is *Interactive Governance: Advancing the Paradigm*, (Oxford University Press, 2012).

Siv Vangen: Siv Vangen is senior lecturer in management and head of the Department of Public Leadership and Social Enterprise at The Open University Business School. Her long-standing research agenda focuses on the management of collaboration. She has written many journal publications and won several awards. She is coauthor with Chris Huxham of *Managing to Collaborate: The Theory and Practice of Collaborative Advantage* (2005, Routledge, London).

Joris Voets: Joris Voets is assistant professor in public management at the Department of Management, Innovation and Entrepreneurship, Faculty of Economics and Business Administration, University of Ghent (Belgium). He was senior representative at the Public Management Institute at Leuven University (Belgium) and program coordinator of the Policy Research Centre on Government Organization in Flanders (SBOV). His research, teaching, and consultancy is focused mainly on governance, management, and performance of collaboration between public organizations.

Index